THE LOST BEACH BOY

THE LOST BEACH BOY

Jon Stebbins with David Marks

Virgin BOOKS

First published in Great Britain in 2007 by
Virgin Books Ltd
Thames Wharf Studios
Rainville Road
London
W6 9HA

A catalogue record for this book is available from
the British Library.

ISBN 978 1 8522 7391 0

The paper used in this book is a natural, recyclable product
made from wood grown in sustainable forests. The
manufacturing process conforms to the regulations of the
country of origin.

Typeset by TW Typesetting, Plymouth, Devon

Printed and bound in Great Britain by
Mackays of Chatham Ltd, Chatham Kent

CONTENTS

Jon Stebbins:

*For Iris and Sophie – some have gone,
and some remain . . .*

David Marks:

For Carrie

A special thanks to
Phil Cooper from
David and Jon.

A FOREWORD BY JEFFREY FOSKETT

Although Dick Dale is crowned 'King of the Surf Guitar', it was Brian Wilson and The Beach Boys who really brought the sound to the public forefront. I think that one of the most overlooked roles in any band is that of rhythm guitar player. If The Beatles didn't have John Lennon's driving rhythm on all of their rock and roll hits, the songs would have paled. The same is true for The Beach Boys. If David Marks didn't chunk away at the 'Toes on the Nose' rhythm guitar, their sound would have suffered greatly. I know that both David and Carl Wilson were excellent rhythm players. I have performed with both, and it's strange how, in later years, David became a much more prolific lead guitar player while Carl excelled in his timely rhythm. The specific 'sound' that was on the early Beach Boys records was one that has been utilised rarely in the music industry, probably because it was so closely associated with The Beach Boys. It contained lots of subtle Hammond spring reverb, but not enough to drown out the individual chords being hammered away. Also the chord formations or inversions were unique at the time. It was still early rock and roll, so not unlike The Beatles, Carl and David knew the chords that were on 'jazz' records or Chuck Berry and Fats Domino records. Those guys were born out of the big band and jazz era and consequently their chordal patterns, inversions and formations on their early rock and roll records were based in that foundation. The Beach Boys married those with the 'chunky reverb rhythm' and *voila* – vocal surf music was born.

Jeff Foskett is a renowned guitarist and vocalist who currently performs in the Brian Wilson Band. Through the years Jeff has also performed as a touring member of The Beach Boys, Papa Doo Run Run, and as an acclaimed solo artist.

A FOREWORD BY DARIAN SAHANAJA

I became aware of Dave and the Marksmen back in the mid-eighties, during my initial obsession with the American garage movement of the sixties. I had discovered the original *Nuggets* LP and was beginning to collect vinyl of the genre when I first heard 'I Wanna Cry', the soundtrack for Dave's wacky Hawthorne home movies that were in circulation at the time. That thunderous wall of twelve-string electric guitar stomped down against my chest like no other before. Huge tom fills and thumping bass had my nerves trembling. And then that vocal, that melody was so evocative, so haunting ... The record absolutely slayed me.

Then it dawned on me that this was music by a Beach Boy. Huh? Yeah, that surf-punk-looking guy whose image I knew so well from The Beach Boys' early album sleeves. The one who certainly was not Al Jardine. It was a tangent, for sure, but somehow it all started to make sense. The attitude I felt from those Marksmen recordings seemed to match the image captured in those photos. I want to say that he came off looking like a different type of rebel than even Denny Wilson's rebel. Someone wanting to break out of the typical surf aesthetic and do something grittier. And in Marksmen recordings like 'I Wanna Cry' and 'I Could Make You Mine', I believe David Marks succeeded in doing so.

Darian Sahanaja is a highly talented musician whose keyboards, vibes and vocals are a fixture in the Brian Wilson Band. Darian is also a founding member of the pioneering group The Wondermints, and has toured with Ann and Nancy Wilson's Heart.

A FOREWORD BY BILLY HINSCHE

David and I literally met on stage during my lengthy run with The Beach Boys, when he would show up for the occasional 'special guest' appearance, but I never really got to know him until fairly recently when he generously offered to perform at the El Rey theatre in LA for a Carl Wilson Foundation event in 2001. We are now friends for life.

I thought I was a pretty good guitar player until I worked alongside him in a series of different bands over the past few years. In short, he puts me to shame, and I have said this both privately and publicly. You see, David has a very personal and long-standing relationship with his guitar and a real hunger to play that is rare in my experience. He's the kind of serious guitar player that I can only aspire to be. The rich textures and complex chords he conjures up in his original material are those of a true master and are absolutely mesmerising yet often a mystery to me. His voice is still strong and he is a great singer. But it's his guitar-playing abilities that set him apart.

Most people don't know that not only is David capable of playing in his edgy signature 'surf' style (that he created and developed), but he is also adept at handling the most challenging self-taught Bach fugues and suites replete with layered counterpoint, and other classical instrumental pieces that he trained for during his tenure at the Boston Conservatory in the early seventies. There is a lot more to David than has met the public ear to date, and his best work is yet to come.

Billy Hinsche performed with The Beach Boys for over twenty years through their peak period as a concert attraction. During that time Billy's voice, keyboards and guitar were staples of The Beach Boys' sound in concert and on record. He was also a founding member of Dino, Desi & Billy, one of the mid-sixties' most popular teen acts. Billy is currently on the Board of Directors for the Carl Wilson Foundation, a charitable organisation dedicated to his late brother-in-law.

A FOREWORD BY DENNIS DIKEN

You are holding in your hands a book that I've been waiting to read all my life. Now the world – and that includes yours truly – will get the opportunity to learn more about David Marks and relish previously unheard ancient history of the fabulous Beach Boys. Hooray!

I was hooked on The Beach Boys for life when I first heard 'Surfin' USA' and 'Shut Down' in early '63. But I didn't see a photo of the group until I got 'Fun, Fun, Fun', with its boss picture sleeve for my seventh birthday in February '64. Later that year, I began studying their LP covers at the local A&P supermarket and Two Guys department store and I discovered that there was one guy pictured on the first four albums who was not on that 45 cover.

As time passed by I pieced together the Marks bio from various sources. He grew up close to the Wilson family near Hawthorne, California, played guitar and sang on the seminal Beach Boys recordings and either quit or was kicked out of the fold just as the band was getting off the ground. But I never stopped wondering why the only Beach Boy other than Denny who had the cool, bushy blond surfer look took a hike. I'd even sought out his work with The Moon, the criminally overlooked band he recorded with in the late sixties. I felt that a large chunk of important Beach Boys lore somehow got deep-sixed somewhere down the line.

Sometime in the nineties I heard David rejoined the group and I caught him performing with the boys on the TV programme *Baywatch*. My curiosity was rekindled. And then he was gone again.

Then in September 2004 I finally met the man and his wife Carrie at JFK International as we were waiting to fly to London. My man Jeff Foskett called me to play drums on a gig across the pond with David and Billy Hinsche. When we landed and stood in line to go through customs we were knackered, having crossed the Atlantic on an overnight flight. Still, I couldn't help myself. I badgered David (politely, mind you) about Beach Boys sessions that I'd wondered about all my life. And he answered every question . . . and then some. I couldn't believe the memories David was sharing with me. One time over lunch he casually looked at his wrist and showed me the scar he still carries from when Denny lunged towards him with a pocket knife to initiate the shocked lad in a blood-brother ritual he'd seen on TV. At age nine.

Well, you get the picture. He was *there*, man! And he is here, thankfully, to tell his story. Between these covers is the real deal that any fan of The Beach Boys and pop history will dig. The wait is over. Tach it up!

Dennis Diken is the drummer and co-founder of the celebrated pop/rock band The Smithereens. Dennis and The Smithereens have released a string of acclaimed LPs and singles over the past two and a half decades. Dennis is also a noted author and music historian whose writings and opinions are well respected throughout the industry.

1. LOST IN A DREAM

David peered at Brian through the small, wood-framed window. With his hands cupped to shield his curious eyes from the glare, he tried his best to see what was going on in there. He was sure it must be something important, but at ten years old, David had no idea it would change the lives of everyone he knew. He was just fascinated by Brian and he wanted to get a closer look. David gently laid his red Schwinn bicycle down on the Wilsons' front lawn and quietly peeked through their screen door. There was no sign of Brian's parents or brothers, so he let himself in. He entered silently and passed through another doorway immediately on his left. Making sure his Converse trainers moved without a squeak, he slowly tiptoed down two wooden steps, through a short hallway, and there he hid in the shadows, watching. Inside the Wilsons' music room stood seventeen-year-old Brian Wilson, alone and focused. Lanky and bright, with piercingly sensitive eyes, Brian was known around the neighbourhood as a fine athlete. He was a good boy with a slightly irreverent sense of humour. And he loved music.

Brian was a hero and a role model to his youthful neighbour David Marks. He knew he shouldn't be spying on him but he could not take his eyes off what he was seeing. Brian looked so serious – like he was in church, like he was praying. He held the cover of a record. David had seen it in the Wilsons' home before. It was by Brian's favourite singing group, The Four Freshmen. David thought they looked really old to be freshmen. From the shadows, he could clearly see the label as Brian slid it out of the paper sleeve. The silver writing on it said 'Capitol'. And when Brian slapped the disc on his folks' nifty hi-fi record player, he did something very strange. Instead of playing the record through, Brian kept picking up the needle and putting it back down. To David, it looked like he was going crazy. He did it over and over. Two or three notes would play, then Brian picked the needle back up and put it down, two or three notes again and back up, and down again, the same three notes. Over and over, Brian lifted and dropped the needle ... and then he paused and stared intensely at nothing.

Brian eventually turned to the family piano and fingered three specific notes. They sounded like the same ones that were playing on the record. And then Brian sang them. It wasn't exactly a hum, or any words, but something in between like musical vowels and consonants: oooh, ahhh, mmm. And Brian sang them in such a high voice – like a girl. It almost made David giggle but he fought the impulse and remained perfectly silent. Then he heard Brian sing more. It was beautiful. David had heard Brian sing with his parents and brothers before but never quite like this. What he was singing today sounded like hymns, choirs, prayers – it reminded David of church. Then Brian went back to the turntable. He resumed his routine. Up and down went the needle. The old freshmen sang three different notes before Brian stopped them again. He lifted and put down the needle over and over, at least ten times, then returned to the piano. David had a hard time understanding why someone who could throw a football as far as Brian would spend a sunny July afternoon doing this. It was a beautiful mystery and he wanted to know more.

Say what you want about David Marks, but there's no question he has a unique perspective on Brian Wilson and The Beach Boys. Close enough and curious enough to see it all, but removed from the subjective pressures of the family connection, David's view is clear. Dave was a part of The Beach Boys long before they were The Beach Boys. He knew Brian and his brothers before they were icons, before they were famous, before they were musicians. It may be hard to imagine, but to David Marks, Brian Wilson is still the guy who taught him how to throw a football. The rest just isn't as important to him.

The value of David's memory is priceless. He was there at the beginning. He was there every day. As the family who lived across the street, the Wilsons evolved from a seemingly average and sometimes troubled suburban Californian clan to the first family of American popular music, and David was right there, watching. Not only did he witness the acts of a culture-changing drama, he became one of the players himself. The momentum of history absorbed him and gave him a role. And still David Marks remained independent of the machine, unfazed by the politics and, against all odds, he survived the resulting vortex. Today, David is the only ex-Beach Boy who travels freely between the battling, lawsuit-consumed factions that remain. He has no stake in it. He poses no threat. He sometimes plays guitar with current Beach Boys Mike Love and Bruce Johnston, he plays an occasional gig with ex-Beach Boy Alan Jardine and his sons, and he's still friends with the musical genius who started it all, Brian Wilson. David is unique because his bridges to the past remain intact. They've never been rebuilt or remodelled, never retrofitted or updated. David's bridges to Beach Boys history are the originals, no revision necessary. Heck, he's barely used them – until now.

To a degree, David was nearly expunged from The Beach Boys story because he refused to look back. He was buried by myth and minimised by his own disconnection and indifference to legacy. Regularly described as someone who 'briefly' filled in for Beach Boys co-founder Al Jardine, David never really fought the label. But if you really think about it, the label is absurd. Describing his role as 'brief' disregards the fact that he was there at the most crucial time of The Beach Boys' genesis. He arrived in the Wilsons' world in 1956, began playing music with them in 1958, and rode with them from national nobodies to the very peak of their initial wave. In adulthood, he became an often drunk and disconnected cynic who outwardly showed little regard for The Beach Boys' status as icons. Most interviews conducted with David in the seventies, eighties and nineties reflect a generally uncaring attitude and a loose regard for the details. But things have changed. This is the evolution of David Marks. He threw it all away only to realise later that he was part of something special, something unique.

In 1963, at a very impulsive fifteen years of age, David told Beach Boys manager and father Murry Wilson to take his job and shove it. As a result, he lost his foothold as one of the original Beach Boys – not to mention millions of dollars. It was relatively easy for the already roaring hit machine to spit David out without losing momentum. And Dave did little himself to remind people that what he gave The Beach Boys before he walked away actually counted for something. He let others define him, and as a result he was used, taken advantage of, and basically tossed aside. But still, he harbours no trace of bitterness or self-loathing. In fact, in my three decades as a musician, rock historian and journalist, I've never met anyone in show business who is less hung up on fame than David Marks. He gives the appearance that it all slides off him with no real effect. He's been doing it for years; he's had a lot of practice. He just keeps smiling that big, wide smile, the ear-to-ear grin that used to make teenage girls swoon in the early sixties. It's the same smile that's on all the early Beach Boys LP covers. Whether holding a surfboard or a guitar, or leaning on a Corvette, the bright David Marks smile is permanently there.

It's an easygoing 'Boy, have I got it made' kind of a smile. But face it – and David has – it's been a pretty tough road. Out of The Beach Boys as a young teen, his solo career didn't pan out, his other bands didn't sell and broke up, he lost

contracts, lost contacts, lost gigs, lost money, lost his way . . .
No recognition, no Gold Records on his wall, no Lifetime
Grammy, no Rock and Roll Hall of Fame. Instead he's
experienced major drug and alcohol problems, multiple ar-
rests, been jailed numerous times, had failed relationships,
faced the challenge of single parenthood and, to top it all off,
been diagnosed with a death sentence at barely fifty years of
age. And that's just a sampling of his troubles. Despite it all,
David Marks still wears the same smile. He may have peaked
at fifteen, but he still managed to grow. He could have easily
ended up on endless TV shows, complaining about how his
parents let him down and about how Murry Wilson screwed
him. Or he certainly could have gone out dangling on the end
of a rope or wrapped up in a coroner's van, like so many
tragic child stars who burn out early. But David Marks didn't
ever burn out completely. The flame flickered in the wind, but
it never died. David got high, he got crazy, and he got
depressed and confused. And he got lost, way lost. But as a
musician, he just got better.

David Marks is the best pure musician The Beach Boys
produced. Flat out, he's the best. He plays his instrument at a
higher technical level than anyone from that band ever did or
ever will. Take it from Beach Boys family member and
forty-year music business veteran Billy Hinsche: 'David is a
phenomenal musician. He's far beyond what most people
would ever imagine.' Multi-platinum songwriter and prolific
record producer Daniel Moore agrees: 'David is a great
player. He can play anything from Chuck Berry to blues, jazz,
even classical. His style is fluid and as quick as they come.'
But that's part of the square peg syndrome that has clouded
David's place in Beach Boys history. The Beach Boys are
considered rock's all-time greatest vocal group, and David
isn't really a singer. He's a fantastic guitarist who can sing.
The other Beach Boys were the opposite. They were fantastic
singers who could play. When The Beach Boys were hiring
studio musicians to play on their own records, David was
working as a respected LA session guitarist. While The Beach
Boys were adding their voices to pre-recorded tracks laid

down by other musicians, David was playing his guitar in LA studios alongside session stalwarts like drummers Hal Blaine and Jim Keltner, guitarist Glen Campbell, and bassist Carl Radle. He also studied with classical masters like Vicente Gomez, and with Grammy-winning composers such as Alan Silvestri. Motown's Barry Gordy once called David the best guitarist in LA. He was tapped as Delaney & Bonnie's live guitarist, until a guy named Eric Clapton took his place. He's played sessions and gigs with a list of legends that includes Sam Cooke, Little Richard, Dick Dale, Jimmy Reed, Lou Rawls, Marvin Gaye, Sonny and Cher, Jimmie Haskell, Mel Carter, Leon Russell, Warren Zevon, Dr John, Delbert McClinton, T-Bone Burnett, and so many more. He even did solo session work for a fellow named Brian Wilson.

Away from The Beach Boys, David has written, recorded and played on four decades' worth of recordings, some released and some unreleased, some inconsistent and some brilliant. And I'll remind you that, between the ages of thirteen and fifteen, he participated in the creation and massive success of America's greatest rock band. He played guitar on seven of their biggest hit songs, and on their first four classic LPs. His signature Fender Stratocaster sound is present on many of the rock era's most beloved recordings, including 'Surfin' Safari', 'Surfer Girl', 'Surfin' USA', 'Shut Down', 'In My Room', 'Little Deuce Coupe', 'Catch A Wave', '409', 'Hawaii', 'Lonely Sea' . . . The list goes on. He played and sang on The Beach Boys' first string of national sold-out tours and television appearances. And he rode their initial wave to international prominence – all before he was old enough to have a driving licence. But instead of a wall full of platinum records and a hallowed place in the annals of rock, David Marks has only his family, his guitars, and his memories.

Many well-meaning Beach Boys fans have no clue that David Marks possesses a deep talent. He's regularly described as a flash in the pan, a lucky neighbour and a quick footnote in rock history. He's thought of as an early-sixties curiosity and a distant smiling face on an old album cover. I used to be one of those people until I started paying closer attention to the real David Marks. When you peel away the layers and look beyond the surface, when you examine the facts, and learn the story, when you really *listen* to the music, there is a different conclusion that gradually becomes evident. David Marks is a distinct part of the reason The Beach Boys are among the greatest acts in popular music history. He's one of the many essential elements that blended into a one-of-a-kind musical happening. When The Beach Boys, with young David on guitar, began recording their initial string of Capitol Records singles, their nationwide explosion happened. In my opinion, that it all came together at precisely this moment was no accident. David Marks is part of why it happened. And he may be among the last to admit it.

David Lee Marks may have been handed the short end of the rock and roll stick but he'll be the first to tell you why. 'I was young and stupid,' he says, and in such a comfortable, confident way that these words could only come from the mouth of someone who is both mature and wise. 'I was my own worst enemy, I was cocky, and I thought I could make it alone.' He then asks, 'How many fifteen-year-olds would make a smart decision under those circumstances? I was famous and spoiled, and fate took advantage of me.'

Fate may have been named Murry Wilson, or Alan Jardine, or the Wilson family, or just the hard knocks of showbiz. But David Marks puts his own name at the very top of any blame list because he now understands what he's been trying to ignore for over forty years. Despite all of his efforts to avoid the inevitable, David Marks will always be a Beach Boy . . . and that's a good thing.

2. THE PENNSYLVANIA TWIST

S ome may find it hard to believe. It's especially hard to fathom given the iconic image of the 1962 Beach Boys at the ocean's door. But those five, healthy, tanned Southern Californians clutching that nine-foot-long surfboard and jubilantly wading into the surf's edge were not all California natives. In fact, David Marks was born in Erie, Pennsylvania, of all places. And he wasn't alone. Ironically, there was a second future Beach Boy who lived right nearby. Ohio native Al Jardine wasn't in the aforementioned surfboard shots, but he did factor into the formative stages of The Beach Boys. The thought of a Beach Boy's first beach experience being on the icy shores of the Great Lakes is somewhat amusing. Make that two of the original Beach Boys, and it's closer to disturbing. Both David and Alan came out to California the same year, 1955, although the older Jardine was already thirteen when he came west. David was only seven. By the time David turned thirteen years old, he'd be in the middle of his initial run with The Beach Boys and looking as Californian as they come.

David Lee Marks was born on 22 August 1948, of Jewish-Italian heritage. David's mother, Josephine Ann Carlo, was a petite and pretty girl whose family owned a gas station in New Castle, Pennsylvania. Those who had witnessed Josephine's birth knew she had entered the world wearing the 'veil'. This rare occurrence is when, at the moment of birth, both the child's head and face are virtually blanketed with part of the amnion, one of the membranes enveloping the foetus. In some cultures the veil phenomenon is considered a highly revered sign of a child's spiritual uniqueness. To her Italian immigrant family the symbol of 'the veil' was immediately recognised, and Jo Ann's potential for empathic or clairvoyant ability was no secret among her relatives. But just because Jo Ann's family knew, it didn't necessarily mean they nurtured her gift. There was an underlying wariness of her ways, and as a result her childhood was sometimes difficult. She felt contained and misunderstood. As her life played out, the psychic sensitivity that had been stifled in Pennsylvania found room to grow in California. There, Jo Ann's metaphysical explorations and clairvoyant tendencies became a part of her daily existence, and in turn these elements of her persona influenced those around her, including Brian Wilson.

David's father, Elmer Lee Marks, was built thick and heavy, like an industrial freezer. He had been a celebrated New Castle prep football star. Elmer was offered a scholarship to Notre Dame University based on his hard-nosed style on the gridiron. He opted instead to enlist in the navy during World War II, and served on a destroyer escort in the Pacific campaign. After his navy enlistment was up, Elmer worked as a mechanic in Jo Ann's parents' gas station, and it was there that he first met his future bride. Elmer was a straightforward, likeable fellow, with hands like vice-grips and thinning hair. As a boy, David was somewhat intimidated by the physical and verbally direct presence of his father. Though Elmer was quite close to his only child, it was the constantly doting Jo Ann who became David's most engaged and influential parent.

With a family to support, Dave's father left the Carlo family gas station to work at an axle factory on the outskirts of New

Castle. There he performed maintenance and repairs on massive hydraulic and pneumatic equipment. 'He had gimped-out and mutilated fingers from working on drills, and axles, and heavy machinery, all day,' says David. The family income was supplemented by Jo Ann's job as a retail clerk at the Winter Company, which specialised in men's clothing. Jo Ann often brought home adult-style suits and overcoats that were made in a child's size for David. 'He was the best dressed boy in New Castle while I worked there,' says Jo Ann. At first, the Marks lived in a run-down duplex on Croton Avenue that lacked decent heat. Soon they bought a bare-bones two-bedroom prefab box among rows of government housing on Warren Avenue. But David spent much of his time in the comfort of his grandparents' large two-storey home at 835 Morton Street.

From age three to six, David was dropped off every morning at his Grandma Carlo's and spent the day with her until Jo Ann retrieved him in the late afternoon. Dave's grandma raised Pekinese puppies in her basement, and David helped her feed and care for them. 'They were nasty little dogs that used to bite everybody,' says David. 'When you went down in the basement it was like an alligator pit with those little dogs snapping away.' David remembers his grandmother serving him coffee and toast on many icy mornings, never realising until much later that coffee was a beverage best kept away from young children. David's grandpa, too, had some interesting delicacies for young David to sample. 'He'd feed me pickled eels and give me wine to wash it down with. I guess in Europe this would have been socially acceptable.'

Jo Ann had one older brother and two younger sisters. The youngest, named Andrea, was much closer in age to David than she was to Jo Ann. 'My mom's youngest sister was only four years older than me and she treated me like an older sibling would. When I spent mornings and afternoons with my grandmother, my Aunt Andrea was always there torturing me,' remembers David. 'We ended up being very close but when I was little she always wanted to kill me and pull my eyes out.' Aunt Andrea explains why: 'We fought like cat and dog because David was a brat.' Getting beaten up by a girl every day didn't faze David. 'From an early age, through my whole life, I've been dominated by strong females,' he says. 'My mom is a really strong woman too.' David's effusively silly personality may have been cultivated by the constant female attention he received. Young David's built-in feminine audience was always reacting to his goofy antics, good and bad, so his penchant for 'acting up' grew less restrained as he got older.

Music was something that first caught David's attention coming through the small speaker on his grandmother's white plastic kitchen radio. With seemingly boundless energy, David would dash and dance about the house to the twangy sounds of early-fifties country music. Steel guitars and fiddles echoed through the old tiled kitchen and filled the entire house. But it was David's initial encounters with 'live' music that froze his routine of constant motion. In the presence of real musicians David firmly focused on the melody and rhythm at hand. There in his grandparents' living room was the sight and sound of David's Grandpa Carlo plucking magic notes on his fancily sculpted Italian mandolin. He was joined in impromptu musical performances by two young relatives from the old country: 'Uncle Benny', the singer, and 'Uncle Johnny', who strummed an impressive deep red Gibson hollow-body guitar. Benny and Johnny were well matched physically, both being dark and lean with classic Italian structure including large noble noses, a feature David admits to having inherited from his mom's family. In fact, he may have inherited more than a larger-than-average schnozz from his Italian forebears. Benny and Johnny were the ones who gave David his first awareness of music-business fame. Young David was awe-struck as the two men performed an array of romantic ballads and American songbook standards with great energy and surprising skill. 'When he was about five years old, he started showing interest in the guitar when his uncles would come over and play music,' says Jo Ann. 'They'd sit there in the evening playing their mandolins and guitars, and David was really excited by that. David would get down on the floor and try to hold the instruments and get some kind of sound out of them. That guitar was bigger than he was but he was really determined to play it.'

As David watched in wonder, Benny and Johnny suddenly became New Castle celebrities when they made a successful appearance on Ted Mack's nationally televised *Amateur Hour* television show. On the Saturday night of the big show at 8.30 p.m., David and his family gathered around their small TV with great anticipation. First they watched Elmer attempt to clear the TV's chronically poor reception. He scrambled the rabbit ears and whacked the television top until Benny and Johnny finally took to the NBC stage. There they flawlessly serenaded America just as they had serenaded David in his grandparents' home. For a brief few weeks the duo was the toast of New Castle. They engaged in a constant red wine-soaked celebration, dancing their nights away with a string of local beauties and revelling in their instant fame. It all ended abruptly when Johnny ploughed his new Buick into a large tree and broke both of his legs. Then, without warning, the pair disappeared from New Castle and retreated back to Italy. David never saw them again. Still, Benny and Johnny's Ted Mack TV performance certainly had an impact on little Dave. That memorable event in 1953 was undoubtedly the show business highlight in the lives of the Marks-Carlo clan, at least for the time being.

Something about the vibrations in Pennsylvania just weren't good enough for Jo Ann Marks. She was sure she wouldn't be staying there for ever. 'My mom wanted to see movie stars and get away from the snow and thunderstorms,' says David. Jo Ann puts it differently: 'I knew that California held something special for my life. I knew that from the time I was a little girl. I just knew there was something waiting to happen out there that was bigger than my family or me.' Perhaps Jo Ann's ability to see more than what was directly in front of her gave her the confidence to convince Elmer that the West Coast held their family's future. The fact that Elmer's parents had already moved to the Golden State two years earlier only eased her mission.

In the summer of 1955 David's parents packed up their new turquoise and white four-door Mercury Monterey and headed west. Some things would undoubtedly be missed. Dave left behind a few favourite schoolmates at Rose Avenue grammar school and he'd certainly miss his cherished daily visits with his Grandma Carlo. And there were other family members too, some of whom he'd developed a closeness with that would remain vivid in his memories beyond his time in Pennsylvania. There would be a few return visits in the years ahead, but once Elmer's Mercury rumbled away in the thick morning mist, New Castle, Pennsylvania, would be regarded as a brief and distant segment of Dave's life. It was the great California dream they were speeding towards that would ultimately define David's story.

Elmer's father's first name was also David, but everyone called him 'Pappy'. Even when he was a fairly young man, that's the tag he went by. In the early part of the decade, Pappy Marks and his wife Stella had moved to San Leandro, California, not far from San Francisco. Within a short time, they transitioned south to LA. It was there, in the blinding Los Angeles sunshine, along palm-lined boulevards, that David Marks and his parents joined them, motoring into their new life with nothing but Jo Ann's inkling that California held their destiny. They temporarily took up residence in a cheap pink motel right down the street from the entrance to Metro Goldwyn Mayer studios in Culver City. Dave recalls, 'My dad's parents lived in a trailer park right next to the backlot of MGM where they had all the sets for the old westerns. So we moved to a place near them.' It didn't take long for Jo Ann to spot her first movie star. While driving over to Pappy and Stella's trailer one afternoon she saw leading man Van Johnson tooling along La Cienaga Boulevard in his flashy red sports car. The dream was on.

Within a couple of months, Elmer was working at Douglas Aircraft and sporting the same job description he'd had at the New Castle axle factory, albeit on a larger scale. The Markses rented a nondescript house near the Los Angeles International Airport on 101st Street in Inglewood. They barely had time to settle in before fate intervened and they were forced to move again. The massive 405 freeway was under construction and its projected path barrelled right through their new neighbour-hood. The Markses' rental house was sitting among the blocks of homes suddenly designated for removal. This unforeseen predicament nudged Elmer and Jo Ann into searching near the Douglas plant for a small home to buy. Next stop: Destiny.

In the summer of 1956, Los Angeles was a place that held unending potential and plenty of dead ends as well. The difference between LA and New Castle was like fire and ice. For Jo Ann and David, it was a quick and easy adjustment. The saturating sunshine seemed to only make each of them more of what they already were. Jo Ann became more curious about the metaphysical, and her fantastically sensitive percep-tion flourished in the socially liberal environs of Southern California. David became more of a hyperactive ham. Con-stantly 'on', always the entertainer, Hollywood seemed a natural habitat. He perpetually flitted about like a pint-sized Jerry Lewis with no Dean Martin to temper his behaviour. That July, as Elvis Presley, Fats Domino, The Platters and Gene Vincent dominated the LA radio airwaves, David Marks began to take notice. Rock and roll's blazing energy perfectly matched the constant warmth he felt outdoors in his new surroundings. It also stoked the test-the-limits attitude he was beginning to demonstrate to those around him.

Suburban Southern California must be what the word 'sprawling' was invented to describe. In the 1950s, block after block of middle-class homes spread in all directions, multiply-ing like millions of stucco clones. What were the odds that the Marks family would end up exactly where they did? Long. But against those odds they purchased a modest, comfortable three-bedroom abode at 11901 Almertens Place. It was situated directly on the Inglewood side of Kornblum Avenue, the dividing line between the city of Hawthorne and the city of Inglewood. On the Hawthorne side of Kornblum was an older and equally modest home at 3701 West 119th Street. Almertens and 119th morphed from one to the other as they met at Kornblum. A city apart, but right across the street, was the neighbour family to end all neighbour families. Dave's first encounter with them would be as unforgettable as his last.

3. AND NOW ... FROM HAWTHORNE (AND INGLEWOOD), CALIFORNIA

As he dutifully helps his folks unload the Mercury, David pays no attention to the laughter generating from across the street. Then a wadded-up foil food wrapper seems to come out of nowhere, plunking David on his right leg. A second wrapper whizzes by, landing near his feet, and a third bounces off his shoulder and rolls away. Dave is astounded to look up and see two older boys winging small pieces of trash at him from across Kornblum Avenue. Slightly embarrassed to be a target, he takes a good look at the source of his garbage shower. One of the boys is wiry and tough-looking, with a crew cut, a chipped front tooth, and what appears to be a healing black eye. The other kid has a friendly round face with big, bright red cheeks. The round one is giggling uncontrollably as the skinnier boy busies himself finding more things to throw. Finally realising that they have gained David's undivided attention, the pair begin to chant at him in unison:

'Hawthorne rules! Inglewood sucks! Hawthorne rules! Inglewood sucks!' The two kids doing all the yelling are brothers named Dennis and Carl Wilson.

The brothers soon became David's second family. 'The three of us would pretty much run wild in the neighbourhood,' says Marks. Dennis and Carl had an older brother too. 'Brian was already a teenager and didn't hang around with us much except when he needed recruits to play touch football in the Wilsons' yard,' remembers Dave.

But Dennis and Carl were always around. 'Dennis was my mentor and role model. I wanted to do whatever Dennis did, which was usually something destructive.' David watched in awe as Demolition Dennis crafted homemade weapons – hatchets, spears, slingshots and, on occasion, even an effective bomb. One day a Dennis concoction of CO_2 cartridge, match heads, powder from firecrackers and fuse stuffed into a length of metal pipe created a surprisingly effective cannon. 'It blew a hole in a brick wall twenty feet away,' remembers David. 'And they say *Brian* is a genius.'

'Dennis and I were really like brothers even though I was closer in age to Carl. Whenever Dennis felt like going out to cause trouble he'd come over and get me,' remembers David. There was something similar in Dennis and David's make-up. Neither could sit still. Neither was interested in conforming to the world around them. Instead, they challenged it together. They became actual blood brothers when Dennis pulled out a blade one day and sliced open David's hand and then his own to blend their life force. 'Being friends with Dennis Wilson was like having your own Indian guide entertaining you,' says David. 'He had a knack for showing people unforgettable experiences.' On one hot afternoon, Dennis tossed David's lit Bunsen burner into some dry brush behind David's house, and several trucks from the local fire department ended up being roused to battle the blaze. Vandalism and petty theft were part of the regular neighbourhood routine. David, Dennis and their pal Greg Jones would steal sweets from the 'Little Store' down the block that was owned by a couple named Gil and Marge Lindner. Dennis also cut down trees at the nearby elementary school for sheer entertainment value, and his partner in crime, David, was completely entertained. In the immediate aftermath of their delinquent activities the pair would hide in the dark aqueduct that ran behind Dave's house. Carl tried his best to keep up with Dennis and David's never-ending quest for trouble. But Carl was burdened with the limitations of being the heavier, slower Wilson.

'Carl was a fat kid,' says David, getting right to the point. Sometimes he'd fall and be left behind in the dust during peak periods of mischievous fun. 'He'd start crying, which made Dennis laugh even harder,' says David. But when tubby little Carl had cried enough, they'd always trudge back and retrieve him.

And to his credit Dennis, even at age twelve, protected both Carl and David from any Hawthorne bullies who wandered into their ever-expanding territory. 'Dennis loved to fight and he never cared who they were or how big they were ... He was king of the neighbourhood and nobody messed with him,' says David. But regularly being in the presence of Dennis 'the Menace' cut both ways. Like when he showed up at David's door shedding real tears, breathlessly telling him that Brian had burned to death when the Wilsons' water heater suddenly exploded. To further sell this to gullible David he produced a mason jar full of ashes and moaned convincingly that this was all that was left of his big brother. David's eyes widened and his jaw dropped as he peered at the container of ashes cradled in Dennis's hands. 'He laughed his ass off at me for believing him,' recalls David.

It turned out that Brian's survival was a good thing for David, whose interest in music was growing. Trumpet lessons in the fourth grade were a beginning. 'My grandmother bought me a trumpet so I had to take lessons because I didn't want to hurt her feelings,' remembers David. Actually the trumpet seemed a natural choice, because big band leader and trumpet icon Harry James was an early idol for both David and his father. Elmer had a stack of big band 78s, which clued David in to the endless wonder of records. Soon David was acquiring his own vinyl 45s. He soaked up tracks by Chuck

Berry, Sam Cooke, The Olympics, Oscar Peterson, Jimmy Reed and Ray Charles. He absorbed the varied sounds of jazz, big band and blues. David went out of his way to learn exactly which people were the very best at making music. Little did he imagine that one of the best of all time lived right across the street.

'I used to sneak over to the Wilsons' house and peek into the music room and watch Brian practise,' says David. He witnessed a careful, painstaking process. Brian, alone and focused, was learning the intricacies of vocal arranging. The man who would arguably one day become history's ultimate pop vocal arranger had to start somewhere. 'I would watch Brian play a note or two off a record, then he'd pick the note out on the piano, sing it, and move on to the next part.' David enthuses, 'It was amazing to watch him train his ear like that. Sometimes I'd go inside and stand in the doorway, watching, listening. I'd be completely silent. I thought he was so into it that he had no idea I was there. I just wanted to be close to Brian because he loved the music so much. It was his way to escape into his own fantasy life. It was like his secret world.'

David also witnessed the effect music had on Brian's mother and father. Just like Brian, they both loved melody and harmony, and the main focus in the Wilson home was always music. Murry Wilson, the family patriarch, was a brash, physical type, not unlike Elmer in his outward tendencies. Dave describes Murry as being just like his dad – only *with* brains.

'Murry was very smart,' says David. 'For all the negative things that have been said about him, many of which are true, you have to understand that Murry was an extremely intelligent man.' The Wilsons' mum, Audree, was one of Dave's all-time favourite people. She playfully encouraged the devilish activities that he and Dennis enjoyed while still providing a sweet, nurturing influence.

'Every Sunday night, the Wilsons would have family singalongs, and I'd regularly join them,' remembers Dave. 'Murry would play the Hammond B3 organ, and Audree would play the upright piano, which stood next to the window where there was also a hi-fi record player. These get-togethers were a regular part of our lives years before The Beach Boys were ever conceived.' The boys would all sing, except for Dennis, who would only join in when Murry forced him to. When it became apparent that Brian had superior musical ability, his mother was delighted. David believes it wasn't quite the same with Murry. 'When Brian started showing his talents it took Audree's focus off of Murry and onto Brian. I think Murry always resented Brian for that,' says David.

Although Brian proved to be a huge influence on David as a musician, Brian's personal qualities may have affected David even more. Dave's wife, Carrie Marks, relates, 'David always told me that Brian had this really great leadership quality about him even before he started making music. All the neighbourhood kids looked up to Brian and tried to emulate him. This was when Brian was a teenager and he would recruit all the kids for football games. David said that it was because Brian showed an interest in music that all the little kids wanted to play music just like Brian. I find it interesting that David would point out that it was Brian's personality that made people want to play music like him and the actual music itself was secondary.' Carrie continues, 'I think that is a concept that often gets overlooked since everyone says, "Brian is a genius." Yeah, OK, we've heard that a million times, but look into how he displayed that "genius" *before* he had music as an outlet, and how his charisma and sense of humour also played an influencing role on many people's lives, whether The Beach Boys were a success or not. David is always quick to sing Brian's praises and to cite him as an influence in his music, but for David, what influenced him about Brian is probably not the same type of influence that most people are talking about when they list Brian as an influence. For David, the Brian he looks up to is the "Big Brother" across the street who taught him how to throw a football and not the troubled genius that wrote pocket symphonies.'

David Marks's musical path was initially inspired by a friend of his cousin Toni's, named John Maus. John was a local teenage musician who sang with his sister Judy during the intermissions of book club meetings that David's mother regularly attended. 'John and Judy' were minor celebrities in Southern California, having released several singles on the Dore label. One of their records, titled 'Hideout', was written by John and Judy's mother, Regina Maus, and was about a local nightclub. 'Hideout' became a Southern California radio hit in 1958. After flirting with regional success for a few years, John Maus got together with a friend named Scott Engle and their partnership evolved into an act named The Walker Brothers. As John 'Walker' of The Walker Brothers, John Maus gained international fame in the swinging sixties. In 1965, The Walkers churned out a string of major hit records with recordings like 'The Sun Ain't Gonna Shine Anymore' and 'Make It Easy On Yourself' – both considered pop classics today.

Few rock scholars have noted the connection between sixties pop idol John Walker and Southern Californian John Maus, the fellow who greatly influenced David Marks, and subsequently The Beach Boys. But they are one and the same. It was while tagging along to one of Jo Ann's book club functions at the Hermosa Biltmore Hotel in 1958 that David first got an eye and earful of John Maus and his electric guitar. Dave watched in awe as Maus performed. Just as he had been enamoured with Benny and Johnny back in New Castle, David was totally enraptured by Maus's playing. Within minutes of first catching sight of him, John Maus became David's newest hero. Tall, thin, blond and commanding in presence, the image and sound of Maus and his Fender Stratocaster changed everything in David's life. 'I knew I had to play guitar when I saw John that day,' says Marks, who was all of ten when his life's mission took hold. 'All I wanted was to be John Maus and play the guitar. From then on, I constantly bugged my parents for a guitar.' On Christmas Eve, 1958, David's folks came through. He unwrapped a brand-new Sears Silvertone acoustic guitar, and within days David was taking lessons from Maus.

Jo Ann Marks remembers, 'We bought David a guitar at Sears for twenty-eight dollars when he was ten years old. He was so happy; that guitar became his whole life. I used to come into his bedroom at night and he'd be asleep with the guitar in his bed next to him.' It was Dave's mother's friendship with Regina Maus that smoothed the way for John to give Dave his first guitar lessons. Even before he'd had his first lesson, David began tinkering with simple one-string melodies he made up in his head. He played one of them for Maus, who was impressed enough to suggest that David record it.

Dave recalls, 'John liked it and took me to see his friend Richie Podolor, who had a recording studio in Hollywood with his brother Don called American Recorders.' John, Judy and David went into American Recorders studio and cut an acetate recording of David's first original instrumental called 'China Sea'. Dave says, 'Richie Podolor engineered it and John played rhythm guitar. John let me use his Sunburst Strat and I picked out the melody. Judy Maus played the water glasses with a pencil. I thought it sounded great. I went home with my acetate dub and played it for Carl and Audree. I was crushed when Audree laughed at the sound of the water glasses on it.'

When historians write about The Beach Boys' earliest flirtations, as a group or individually, with recording studios, David Marks's name is somehow never mentioned. Instead, it's Brian's unsuccessful audition for the Original Sound label, or future Beach Boy Bruce Johnston's late-fifties entrée into sessionland, or most usually the Wilsons' and Al Jardine's connection to Hite and Dorinda Morgan at World Pacific Studios that get the ink. The Hite Morgan story should never be downplayed, nor its importance underestimated, because it resulted in The Beach Boys' first studio recordings as a group and their first release on the Candix label in 1961. But it should also be noted that David Marks recorded an original song in a professional studio in early 1959. Another notable point is that David recorded his tune with future music-business heavyweights John Walker and Richie Podolor working his session. To date, David Marks has never been credited as a pioneer or catalyst for The Beach Boys' recording ambitions. But ironically, it would be Don Podolor and American Recorders, where Dave cut his song 'China Sea', that would figure heavily in the biggest moment of The Beach Boys' career.

The Wilson home, which had been a virtually keyboard-only zone, would soon feel the winds of change. When a friend of Murry's came over with a guitar one night, Carl showed immediate interest. Before long, he'd talked his dad into buying him a Kay hollow-body electric guitar. David subsequently purchased a blond Carvin solid-body electric from John Maus. The table was set for David and Carl to find their 'electric' sound.

Dave remembers: 'Carl had started playing guitar too and heard about John Maus from me, and wanted to meet him. After I introduced them Carl also started taking lessons with John.' This is another case where written history has left David Marks in its shadows. While Maus is often given credit as Carl Wilson's first guitar teacher, it's usually pointed out as an afterthought that John also taught Dave Marks how to play too. Well, the actual fact is that Dave Marks brought Carl Wilson to John Maus. I asked John point-blank in May 2005: 'Who'd you teach first, Carl or David?' Without hesitation, Maus told me it was David. 'Dave told me about a kid he knew who played the guitar pretty well but couldn't play any lead,' says Maus. 'He brought Carl Wilson over to meet me and I began teaching him how to play some lead riffs. It's all unrelated stuff that, when put together, forms a kind of rock and roll vocabulary. I taught both Dave and Carl the same stuff and they took off on their own from there.'

Maus himself had been taught many of his six-string tricks from another local guitar player named Ritchie Valens. 'John was a good friend of Ritchie,' says David. 'He taught Carl and I the same things Ritchie had taught him, so in a sense Carl and I learned from Ritchie Valens.' Valens, who at that time was a rising Latino rocker, would achieve legendary rock and roll status with his hits 'Donna', and 'La Bamba', and also with his tragic death at age seventeen in a 1959 plane crash with Buddy Holly and the Big Bopper. 'Ritchie indirectly influenced a lot of what The Beach Boys ended up doing,' says David. It was Valens's 'Donna'-style guitar chord progression that fused with Brian's piano chords and became the style used on 'Surfer Girl' and 'In My Room'. An undeniable rhythm and blues ballad feel permeated many late-fifties radio classics, like 'Angel Baby' by Rosie and the Originals, The Five Satins' 'In The Still Of The Night' and Valens's 'Donna'. When Brian Wilson heard that David and Carl could nail that feel with their guitars, he used it to give The Beach Boys' early ballads a potent urban teen appeal.

During the summer of 1959, John Maus moved in and lived with the Marks family for a few months. This conveniently increased David and Carl's daily access to their guitar mentor. Aside from studying guitar, there was still time for the kind of things young boys do in the summer with time on their hands, like playing war games. 'In between playing our guitars, we'd have fights with BB guns and swords,' remembers David. One day, during a heated BB gun battle, Maus fired a shot at David that barely missed his eyeball. 'I could see the BB coming straight toward my eye. Luckily, it bounced off the bone in the corner of my eye socket. I knew I had to get John back for that so I circled around the garage, behind the house, and I snuck up behind him while he was lying in the grass in the army crawl position. I got off three good shots into his ass from point-blank before he jumped up screaming. Those were fun times.'

By the dawn of the 1960s, David put down his toys and became entirely devoted to playing his guitar. 'When I was a kid, there was a time when I played so much that when I'd try to go to bed at night my hands would ache so bad that I couldn't sleep. The only thing that would make them feel better is if I got up and played more,' says David. His obsession with the guitar altered his social habits as well. 'I started hanging out more with Carl than Dennis, who had moved on to causing trouble with girls,' says David. 'Over the next year or so, Carl and I played guitar every day after school.' The pair eventually quit taking lessons from Maus, and instead learned by just listening. 'We'd listen to records and pick our parts out by ear,' says David. 'It was the exact same way Brian had learned his harmonies. We would get together every day in my room and play records by Duane Eddy, Chuck Berry, Dick Dale, and The Ventures.' This hybrid of edgy Southern California surf style mixed with the classic Berry rock guitar vocabulary would eventually define the Wilson/Marks guitar sound.

Jo Ann Marks remembers, 'I'd come home from work and David and Carl would be sitting on the kitchen floor playing their guitars. It got to be an everyday routine, David and Carl sitting in the kitchen concentrating on their music. It was like a club with only two members; sometimes Dennis would hang around, but he didn't play an instrument yet.' As with the individual band members' early recording history, written accounts describing which elements initially combined to form The Beach Boys have usually not included David Marks's name. In my opinion, the daily guitar interactions between David Marks and Carl Wilson should be added to any descriptions of how The Beach Boys first gelled as an entity. The development of Dave and Carl's guitar sound and the interplay between them was crucial to the band's musical evolution.

Dave's mother Jo Ann was experiencing her own personal evolution as well. Her psychic abilities were finding ways to flourish in her new California setting. Knowledge of the occult and the deeply spiritual were commonplace in Jo Ann's new social sphere. Dave remembers, 'My mother got caught up in the beginnings of the California New Age Movement and metaphysics. She met a lady psychic named Reverend Francis Bond through my father's sister, my Aunt Dolly. She also became friends with another psychic, named J'nevelyn Terrell, who later became Brian Wilson's personal astrologer. My mom would go to meetings with these women and discuss metaphysics and the related books and literature. She'd come home and tell my dad and me about this stuff and we thought she was kind of wacky. But everyone around us was fascinated by it and she was more than willing to share her experiences.' Jo Ann's spiritual learning eventually found acceptance with Elmer and David and ultimately connected with neighbour Brian Wilson's own natural curiosity.

'Brian always showed a lot of interest in my mom's psychic abilities,' says David. 'It was something he wanted to know more about and my mom knew a lot.' One of the books that Jo Ann had in her home was *The Rosicrucian Cosmo-Conception* by Max Heindel. 'It explored the relationship between spirit and matter, science and Christianity, the different levels of consciousness, and the unseen forces at play in our existence,' explains David. When Brian found the book laying in the Markses' living room, he immediately wanted to know all about it. Brian was also very intrigued when he learned of Jo Ann's clairvoyant abilities. Jo Ann recalls, 'Brian was always asking me about vibrations and how I picked them up by holding an object or touching someone's hand. He used to come over all the time and ask me about that stuff. I can remember him riding in the back seat of our car and peppering me with questions about it. I think because Brian was a very sensitive boy he was highly curious and excited about these things. I told him his musical group, which wasn't even together yet, was going to be signed to Capitol Records. He liked that prediction, and of course it came true.'

It was sometime in 1960 that Brian Wilson began to pay serious attention to what David and Carl were doing together on their guitars. He started teaching them bits and pieces of songs he was already in the midst of composing on piano. 'I was often asked to go over to the Wilsons' house to play with the brothers,' remembers David. 'There was no commitment to even having a group, but we played together quite a bit. Brian really loved the contemporary feel our guitars brought to his songs.' Brian's earliest progressions would eventually turn into songs like 'Surfer Girl' and 'Cuckoo Clock'. Without knowing it, David was already helping to develop the guitar-based framework of The Beach Boys. 'One day me and Carl were in the Wilsons' music room playing that "Donna"-style strumming we'd learned from John Maus,' remembers David. 'Brian was on the other side of the room working out a melody on the piano. He got all excited about how that strumming related to his song and he called us over to the piano while he worked it out. It was the first song Brian ever wrote, which became "Surfer Girl". From then on, Brian started to take us a little more seriously and he began to teach us more chord progressions that later ended up on The Beach Boys' albums.'

But Brian wanted more. 'Brian tried to get me, Dennis and Carl to sing his harmony parts,' says David. 'But I wasn't a singer, Dennis hated to do it, and Carl's voice hadn't come into its own yet. Brian would get really frustrated with us and yell that we weren't good enough. When that happened, Dennis and me would just split.' As usual, Carl was left behind, which in this case helped him greatly. 'Brian would physically make Carl stay and sing with him,' David recalls. And it was Carl who soon learned to fulfil all of Brian's wishes consistently and perfectly. Dennis's contribution was one that wasn't requested by Brian but became just as important to his dreams of pop success. 'Dennis said he wouldn't sing with Brian,' Marks reveals. 'But he'd help him out by giving him words about surfing and cars so he could write songs that were "less goofy".'

While Brian often enlisted his closest Hawthorne friends like Bruce Griffin, Robin Hood and Keith Lent as co-vocalists, it was the Wilsons' cousin, Mike Love, who had long been Brian's favourite singing partner. 'Mike Love came from a black school in LA, Dorsey High,' says David. 'He was the only redheaded white guy in his class, and he was hip to all the black music. He had all the black lingo and the style down. He started singing songs with Brian by some of these black groups like The Coasters and The Olympics. I think it really influenced Brian because Mike was savvy to all this rhythm and blues music.' Mike's doo-wop and R&B influence gave Brian yet another flavour to taste. The two of them had been singing together for many years at family gatherings, and spontaneously whenever they were together. When they attended Angeles Mesa Presbyterian Church at weekends, the pair made a routine of walking home together singing Everly Brothers songs and honing their blend. Brian's improving range complemented Mike's distinct baritone abilities, but the pair's harmonic chemistry had room to improve. David remembers, 'One day Carl and I brought Brian, Mike and Dennis over to John Maus's mother's garage, where we had been rehearsing on guitars. When the five of us tried to sing something together, John's mom told us we sucked and made John kick us out of the garage.'

Dave's involvement with the Wilsons continued on a social level, whether they were clicking musically or not. One day Dennis talked David into sneaking into a funeral parlour with him to look at dead bodies. Dave was both fascinated and appalled. Dennis was just happy to give Dave a new experience. That was Dennis's speciality. They also spent countless sunny afternoons having fun at the beach. For hours, Dave and Dennis would ride cardboard down steep sand dunes in Playa del Rey. It was near the end of the LAX runways where they laughed the hours away, drinking beer, smoking cigarettes, and sand surfing. When they were too tired to continue they'd collapse in the sand and watch giant passenger jets floating closely over them. Sometimes they'd fantasise about being rock and roll stars, a dream as far from their reality as the horizon of the Pacific.

One day at the dunes, the fun ended abruptly when Dennis threw a beer can full of sand at David, splitting his lip all the way up to his nose and causing a torrent of blood to spurt from Dave's face. Dennis rushed David to the nearest emergency room in his mum's station wagon, apologising all the way. It took a pile of stitches to close the gash and a large scar remains on David's face to this day. Dave's wife Carrie Marks says, 'David really loved Dennis like a big brother and spent a good part of his life trying to be just like him ... and the other part recovering from it.' The facial scar is just one of many ways the wild child Dennis made a permanent impression on young David.

Carl gave David a number of unforgettable moments too, like the time he managed to do the impossible and get upside down on a go-cart. 'Everyone knew you weren't supposed to be able to flip a go-cart because they were so low and wide, and they had big fat wheels,' explains David. But unfortunately for Carl, his girth challenged the normal laws of gravity. While negotiating a tight corner at speed, the motorised apparatus – with a strapped-in Carl at the wheel – suddenly lost contact with the earth, lifted into the air, and rotated into an upside-down position. It quickly fell from the sky directly onto the head of its rotund operator. Fortunately for Carl some hay bales that acted as primitive racetrack barriers provided a softish landing. 'Since he didn't get hurt, Dennis and I couldn't help laughing our butts off at him, we were falling down and nearly crying, our sides were splitting,' says David. Carl just smiled meekly and brushed the hay out of his face.

While Brian kept up the search for strong voices, he never really imagined his biggest vocal asset lived under the same roof. 'Although Carl sang with Brian when he asked him to, it's not what Carl was really into,' says David. 'All Carl wanted to be was a good guitar player, but Brian kept making him sing.' Another singer Brian admired was his school buddy Alan Jardine. Al, whose family had moved from the east to California in 1955, attended Hawthorne High School, where he and Brian played varsity football together. The two football mates reconnected at El Camino Junior College, where both Al and Brian were taking classes. Al's passion was for acoustic folk music, both traditional and modern. Dave says, 'I don't know what Al and Brian had going on when they were in school together. From my observation, Al was into the Kingston Trio type of music.' Although Brian himself preferred a slightly more urban approach to music, he and Al did find common ground.

Brian felt especially comfortable working with Love and Jardine because they were approximately his age and they could really sing. Dennis, Carl and David were just little kids in comparison. But at least Carl listened to Brian. Carl later told *Tiger Beat* magazine: 'Mostly we sang Coasters songs and Four Freshmen arrangements as Brian was high on their style of vocalising.' While music was being made with different combinations of family, neighbours and school acquaintances intermingling, two interesting factions materialised around the Wilsons. There were the big guys – Brian, Mike and Al – who could sing like angels. And then there were the little guys – Carl and David – who played the devil out of their electric guitars. Carl was the bridge between both contingents while Dennis was immersed in his own girl-chasing, trouble-causing purgatory. He defied categorisation.

But it was Dennis who would inevitably provide Brian with what turned out to be his most valuable tool: a lasting cultural connection. When Brian, Carl, Mike and Al took a shot at recording a demo with Murry's friend Hite Morgan, things took a historical turn only when Dennis mentioned surfing. Murry Wilson told *Rolling Stone*, 'Dennis told them, "Write a song about surfing." He bugged them.' And they finally took his advice. It was the proposed surfing song that Morgan was most interested in recording. Brian and Mike took a little of Jan & Arnie's 'Jenny Lee', threw in some of their pet harmonies, combined it with Dennis's lyrical suggestion and the song 'Surfin'' was born. The primitive recording features a riff directly lifted from John Maus's 'Hideout', strummed by Carl on his unplugged Kay guitar, a stand-up bass plucked by Al, and a snare drum tapped by Brian's index finger. The instrumental foundation was closer to Al's Kingston Trio format than it was to Carl and Dave's Chuck Berry/Dick Dale template. Despite sonic limitations, the recording of 'Surfin'' in October 1961 proved to be an important moment in the history of rock and roll.

For David Marks, it was a hard moment to swallow. The late Beach Boys historian Timothy White wrote in his 1994 book, *The Nearest Faraway Place*: 'Because of his lessons with Carl and his friendship with Dennis, David had become part of the developmental sessions taking place in the Wilsons' home music room. No one had yet mentioned the fact of a "group" being formed, but when the boys came back from their meeting with the Morgans, energised by the need to cook up some surfing songs, David thought he might be included.' David explains the events from his perspective: 'Eventually there became talk of a recording studio. To my dismay, Al's mother had fronted Brian money for his and Al's band. Al was also instrumental in getting the session arranged with Hite and Dorinda Morgan, so they went ahead and recorded the song without me.'

Al recalls the moment he sold Brian on the idea of recording together. 'I said, "Brian, I know where to get all this equipment. Why don't we cut a record?" I was thinking in terms of folk music and not rock music. But Brian loved eclectic jazz music. Doo-wop was the one thing we all had in common. And that's how we formed that sound.'

For David, the sudden evolution of 'Surfin'' is still a painful memory. 'I was crushed that I hadn't been included because I had been playing and rehearsing the songs with the Wilsons,' he recalls. 'I just assumed I would be on the session. But I guess Brian didn't take me all that seriously because I was so young.'

In November 1961, the single 'Surfin'' was released on Candix Records. Its flipside was another folk-sounding tune called 'Luau' that was written by the Morgans' son Bruce. Al Jardine's contribution of stand-up bass and background vocals to the first Beach Boys single gave him a fundamental claim as an original band member, or a 'founder'. At the time no one knew the historical importance of that foothold, but decades later it would haunt David Marks's legacy and thwart his position in the written history of rock and roll.

Russ Regan, a record promoter for Candix, is the man who came up with the name Beach Boys. Brian and company had considered group names such as Carl and the Passions, The Cruisers, and The Pendletones at various points in their evolution. But it was Regan, who would later become an important advocate in Dave Marks's musical future, who thought of the name that stuck. When Regan's suggested moniker 'Beach Boys' was first slapped on a Candix 45 label, though, were The Beach Boys really a band with a firm line-up yet? Or were they a revolving group of personalities that clustered around Brian Wilson and his aura of leadership?

The long-established tale of Brian, Dennis, Carl, Mike and Al renting instruments while Murry and Audree vacationed in

Mexico on Labour Day weekend 1961 has been told and retold with conviction by nearly all parties involved. David has a vague recollection of being in and out of the Wilson home that day. 'I remember seeing the snare drum and thinking that was really cool,' says David. 'I hit it a couple of times until Brian told me to cool it, and then I ran outside and jumped on my bike and went tooling off. I had no sense that something unusual was happening.' The fact that instruments were there and that the guys were singing and playing seemed no different to him than many other days at the Wilson home. Al Jardine himself recently called the Labour Day weekend story into question by saying it was his mother's money that rented the instruments, and that the traditionally told version, in which the money was garnered from Murry and Audree Wilson, was basically untrue. Since Al opened the door of truth, let's take a look inside and see what else we find.

What are the true beginnings of The Beach Boys? Is it when Brian, Dennis and Carl began singing together? The three Wilson boys began blending three-part harmonies in the early to mid-1950s. In their room, or in the back seat of Murry's car, Brian, Dennis and Carl developed their vocal harmony as youngsters, and in a sense this was the basis for The Beach Boys' sound. Some might say The Beach Boys began when Brian and Mike, or Brian and Al, or Brian, Mike, Al and Carl, began singing together. In the 1950s, Mike Love joined the Wilsons at family gatherings for singalongs, and, separately, Mike joined Brian to work out doo-wop harmonies just for fun. In 1961, Brian began singing with Al Jardine and his friend Gary Winfrey, with whom Al had already formed a folk outfit called The Islanders. Brian eventually began teaching his Four Freshmen vocal arrangements to all combinations of brothers, cousins and friends. It's from these converging elements that most would agree The Beach Boys began.

In my opinion, it would also be fair to consider that perhaps The Beach Boys began when Carl and David started playing their guitars together in 1959. Shocking but true. After all, it was the Chuck Berry/Dick Dale guitar format that became the early signature sound of The Beach Boys. Carl and David even wrote an instrumental song together in early 1961, 'Blue City', that, although unrecorded, became a staple of The Beach Boys' live set in 1962. When Brian began to formulate his own original material, among the first people he worked with on developing his songs were Carl and David. On numerous occasions, the two budding guitarists sat beside Brian at the piano, learning his chord progressions and playing along. David clearly recalls Brian teaching him the chords that later became 'Surfer Girl' long before there was a band called The Beach Boys. Although each of the occurrences listed above were important steps in the formation of America's band, picking one moment that definitively kick-started them is impossible. But one thing is for certain: all of the instances of Beach Boys beginnings listed above occurred well *before* the mythical Labour Day weekend rehearsals of 1961.

David Marks's place in the creation of The Beach Boys has been permanently downplayed for one basic reason: he's not on the first single. When it came time to record Brian and Mike's new song 'Surfin'', David Marks was left out of the process. 'When they came home with a copy of the record, I was hurt,' says David. 'I was always under the impression that we were a band since I was practising with them. I thought I was part of the band.' When 'Surfin'' inexplicably became a local hit, he felt even worse. But at least David was there to help his friends celebrate. 'We were driving in Brian's car,' says Marks, recalling the famous moment The Beach Boys first hit the radio airwaves. 'Carl and I were in the back seat and Dennis was in the front passenger seat. We were leaving the Foster Freeze on Hawthorne Boulevard and 120th Street, just cruising and smoking cigarettes. We all had just pigged out on ice cream and burritos. All of us were pretty new at smoking,' says David. 'When "Surfin'" came on the radio, Carl started throwing up. I know the story has been told that he threw up because he was so excited from hearing the song on the radio, but cigarettes and too much junk food had more to do with it,' insists Marks. ' "Surfin'" just pushed him over the edge.'

Carl's Hawthorne High classmate, the late Mark Groseclose, remembered in a 1986 interview, 'Carl and I used to sneak off to the boys' head during PE and smoke cigarettes together. The first time I met Dennis Wilson, he beat me up because he thought I was a bad influence on Carl. In my sophomore year in high school, I had wood shop with Dennis. I got to know him pretty good, and that's when I found out they were doing a record . . . and "Surfin'" came out.' When the suddenly in-demand Beach Boys began gigging at local dances, David Marks was on the outside looking in.

Although the pre-David Beach Boys only played a handful of live gigs with Al in the line-up, it tortured David to hear about it. The Beach Boys appeared in public for the first time that December performing two songs at a dance held at the Rendezvous Ballroom on Balboa Island in Newport Beach. Al played stand-up bass, Carl guitar, Dennis slapped a snare drum, and Brian and Mike stood together at a single microphone and sang. 'We didn't know anything about renting pianos at the time,' says Al. 'We were just so green, we'd never played anywhere before. We all had to learn how to play instruments real quick.' A week later, they landed a gig at the Ritchie Valens Memorial Dance in Long Beach on New Year's Eve. 'No disrespect to Al, but I was really hurt and bitter that they were playing without me,' David recalls. 'I was so upset about it that I started lying and telling people at school I *was* on the record.'

Since his connection to the Wilsons and their music was so strong, it seemed a crime to David that he had been left out of their band. And so he continued to tell people he was a Beach Boy, even if he technically wasn't. At school, around the neighbourhood, at the Fosters Freeze – you name it. For a string of frustrated weeks, David kept the lie going whenever the subject of The Beach Boys came up. 'I'm in the band too,' he'd insist to people. 'I wasn't sure if anyone believed me.'

He worried that sooner or later the truth would catch up with him and he'd be exposed as a liar. But in a way, deep down inside of him, David knew his lie was the truth as well. He was a good guitar player. He was part of the neighbour-hood and, in a way, part of the Wilson family. He'd played music with those guys long before they were a band. He had helped them grow into what they were. Somewhere inside of him a consistent voice was telling David he was one of The Beach Boys. It is often said if you envision your goal, strongly and consistently, it will become reality. In a crazy adolescent kind of way, it seems that's just what David was doing. Meanwhile, fate was busy making plans for his future.

4. COME ON A SAFARI WITH US

T he Wilson brothers and Mike Love were forced to deal
with the reality that Alan Jardine was hedging his bets
and thinking about a college degree. Al had a great voice for
harmony, which Brian loved, but his heart was that of a folk
singer, not a rock and roller. The whole rock scene had little
appeal to Al, but that was the stylistic direction that Brian –
and even more so, Carl – felt an instinct to follow. And there
was Al's big concern about security and the future. On one
hand, he loved to sing with Brian and the guys, but on the
other hand he wanted to pursue a solid education and find a
profession that paid well. 'I thought I'd better stay in school
and not be an idiot,' explains Al. That was the kind of guy Al
was; he liked to play it safe. Brian was devoted to his music
at all costs; Carl was devoted to the guitar and to Brian;
Dennis was devoted to meeting girls and surfing; and Mike
was looking for a way to make some quick bread and avoid
the dead-end job he was stuck in. Even if they didn't know it
at the time, The Beach Boys group concept was a perfect
vehicle for all of them, but not so for Al – at least, not yet.

After playing a handful of local dances, Al Jardine became dissatisfied with the results of being a Beach Boy. Even though the 'Surfin'' single had done surprisingly well, its monetary pay-off was minimal, and Al wasn't thrilled with many of the songs the group were adding to their set list. He also reportedly disliked dealing with some of the rowdier patrons that attended the Southern California shows the boys were playing in the earliest days of 1962. Al did participate in a Beach Boys recording session in early February. He also attended a demo session a few weeks later that Brian threw together at World Pacific. Besides Brian and Al, the session included contributions from Dennis, Audree and a friend named Val Polluto. The recording would eventually be released as a single credited to 'Kenny and the Cadets'. At times, it seemed as if Brian preferred the idea of a Phil Spector approach, putting together records with varying personnel rather than an all-for-one, one-for-all group situation. And with questionable camaraderie, without any official press bio, and apparently without any group photos, The Beach Boys really weren't much of a band yet in early 1962.

By the middle of February, Al Jardine had bailed out, assuming The Beach Boys vehicle would not provide him with a viable career. Al resumed classes at El Camino Junior College, and on the side he reformed his folk group The Islanders. The standard Beach Boys myth has Al going off to 'dental school' at some eastern location, but another look inside the door of truth reveals that Al stayed in Southern California, where he eventually landed a day job at an aerospace plant named Garrett Research. Meanwhile, Brian (now on electric bass), Dennis, Carl and Mike performed as a four-piece at the Rainbow Gardens in Pomona. The four-piece Beach Boys lasted only a matter of days. It was quickly decided by Brian that the band needed another guitarist to fill out the sound. Carl knew just the guy for the job. 'When Al left everybody was kind of ticked off,' remembers Carl's friend Ron Swallow. 'And it was like, "Forget Al, we'll get some-body else. Dave's across the street. He can play. Let's have him come over." And it's basically as simple as that.'

'One Sunday night I was in my pyjamas, getting ready for bed, and there was a knock at my door,' recalls David. 'It was Brian, Dennis and Carl. They asked my parents if I could be in the band,' says David. Everything stopped for a little while, and David wondered if he'd really heard what he'd just heard. 'YESSS!!' he screamed as he sprinted around the room, bouncing up and down like a leprechaun on speed. A prayer had been answered, a dream had come true, and a karmic pay-off had been delivered. It might have been a couple of months behind schedule but it showed up as loud and clear as a Fender bar chord. 'Brian started giving my parents a big routine about how negotiations with record companies were looking good . . . he said that the band was going to be signed. Dennis and Carl were prodding my mom to say yes and eventually she did,' remembers David. He had just been officially invited to join what would become one of the most popular recording acts of all time. And David's big lie about being a member of The Beach Boys was forever covered.

If Brian had chosen anyone else to become the fifth Beach Boy, auditions and rehearsals would have been necessary. He'd have been concerned whether the chemistry would be right. But David and Carl had already been playing guitar together for years. Dave and Dennis had already bonded in a lasting way, too. And Brian was a hero to David. Although Murry preferred to keep things in the family, Dave was the closest thing to family available. It seemed only natural for David to slide into the sudden vacancy in The Beach Boys' line-up. He'd imagined himself there from day one.

Brian was well aware that David couldn't sing like Al. His voice was average at best, and Brian had very high standards for his harmony arrangements. But the upside was that David's guitar prowess was sparkling for a thirteen-year-old. Carrie Marks says, 'David has said many times how he and Carl were so in tune with each other that when they picked up guitars and played together, it was like the vocal blend you get when brothers sing . . . they fed off each other instinctively. And, no matter what guitar player they got, none of them would have had the chemistry that he and Carl had together.'

And with David's guitar came a more electric direction for The Beach Boys. 'I was resisting that trend to electric,' admits Al Jardine. 'I just wasn't enthusiastic about it. And as soon as I left they were able to bring that dimension up. They went to Fender equipment, and David was already trained on that.' David's personality fit in well, too. He gave the band another Dennis-style free spirit. His rock and roll aura translated into a good stage presence and photogenic image. At first, Brian may have worried David was too young, but Dave's musicianship ultimately sold Brian. In a way, David Marks was like the local kid who got called up from the minor leagues to the big team. And the season was just getting started.

In late February 1962, David Marks played his first of hundreds of gigs as a member of The Beach Boys. The show was at the Bel Air Bay Club on the Pacific Coast Highway and Dave's feet were barely touching the ground throughout. That same month the 'Surfin'' single peaked in the Billboard Hot 100 at number 75. The earliest known group photo of The Beach Boys was taken at one of Dave's first live appearances with the band. In it Dave is wearing a borrowed sports jacket from Brian that fits him more like an overcoat. But despite his small stature in the beginning, David would grow – both physically, and into his role as a Beach Boy. His face and smile became a familiar element of their early iconic image. By 31 March, when The Beach Boys played a show at the Ontario National Guard Armory with The Vibrants, David had settled into the group nicely. The sound of his sunburst Fender Stratocaster guitar was a perfectly functioning element of Brian Wilson's emerging musical language.

The first Beach Boys recording session featuring David Marks on guitar was held at Western Recorders at 6000 Sunset Boulevard in April of 1962. The five youngsters lugged their gear into a dark and unimpressive room and prepared to let loose. It was that day at Western when Brian and The Beach Boys first connected with their signature sound. There the band re-recorded a Brian Wilson/Mike Love tune that further explored Dennis's thematic suggestion called 'Surfin'

Safari'. An earlier version of the song had been recorded at World Pacific Studios shortly before Al left the band. Brian was reportedly unhappy with the results of that rendition, and asked Carl, David and drummer Dennis to 'tighten up the feel' on this new recording. With Murry and engineer Chuck Britz watching from the control room, Brian counted out the tempo, and on four the group took off. In that moment it all came together for The Beach Boys. The unmistakable guitar synergy that already existed between David and Carl exploded from the studio speakers. Brian liked what he heard.

Compared to 'Surfin'', this was metal. No sign of stand-up bass or folk sensibility on this recording. And the tiny amateurish guitar sound and lazy feel of the World Pacific version of 'Surfin' Safari' had now transformed into something crisp and modern. 'It was Carl and Dave who brought that electric guitar drive into the band,' says Al Jardine. 'And because of that, Brian was able to expand a little bit.' The electric rock format gave Brian the perfect template to work with. 'Brian listened to Chuck Berry, and he knew that Carl and I knew how to play that stuff,' says David. 'And because of that, he wrote a lot of his material with electric guitar in mind.' With David rejoining Carl, an ingrained instrumental chemistry came to life in the studio. With this recording of 'Surfin' Safari', The Beach Boys leaped from the living room to the garage. This was rock and roll, pure and simple. Dennis's drumming is joyous, Carl and Dave's guitars are bright and driving, Mike's lead singing is direct and distinct, and Brian's vocal arrangement is infectious. It sounded like a hit. But for now, it was only a demo.

A second legendary Beach Boys classic was recorded that same day at Western. The brand new song, titled '409', was co-written by Brian and his friend Gary Usher. A cousin of Beach Boys neighbour Greg Jones, Usher had recently arrived from the East Coast and immediately hit it off with Brian. A gifted writer and arranger in his own right, Gary participated in the session like a sixth Beach Boy. Dave had already played guitar on an earlier Wilson/Usher session at Western and knew him from around the neighbourhood. He was comfortable with his presence. Not so for Murry Wilson, who perceived Usher as an outsider. Due to Murry's reservations about him, Usher's days as Brian's main collaborator were numbered. But on that day in April, they were clicking like crickets. Brian and Gary's song concentrated on the American male teen's obsession with cubic inches and elapsed times. Brian later borrowed David's trusty Roberts reel-to-reel recorder and taped Usher racing his Chevy Impala up and down Kornblum Avenue while neighbours screamed at them to knock it off. Edited onto the tape, Usher's car sounded real fine ... even though it was only a 348 and not a 409. Gary Usher would remain in The Beach Boys' sphere long enough to contribute several classic songs to their body of work.

A couple of days after the 'Safari' session, The Beach Boys played the Easter Week Stomp at the Redondo Beach High School Auditorium. On the bill with them were The Vibrants, as well as South Bay favourites The Belairs, who featured the dual guitars of Paul Johnson and Eddie Bertrand. Johnson, a true innovator of instrumental guitar music, has long maintained he was asked to join The Beach Boys as their rhythm guitarist in the band's early days. 'I met them when we did a TV show together,' says Johnson. 'It was on the *Wink Martindale Dance Party* and that was The Belairs' first TV show too. The Belairs had just gone through this incredible summer of '61 where we went from being a bunch of kids playing in our living room to being thrust to the forefront of this huge explosion of surf culture and being embraced along with Dick Dale as being champions musically of the movement.' Johnson remembers riding home from the TV show with The Beach Boys and being treated to an a cappella rendition of their yet-to-be-released song 'Surfer Girl'. I remember being very impressed and thinking, Wow, these guys just might take this a little further,' says Johnson, who subsequently befriended Dennis and Carl and visited the Wilson home. 'I also remember there was this little kid who lived around the corner who was always hanging out.'

Months later, Johnson recalls receiving a phone call from one of the Wilson brothers, who offered him a 'temporary' role in the band. 'When they asked me it was like, "Hey, we're on our way up, as you can see, we are breaking nationally." I remember thinking, Yeah, this would be a great opportunity for me,' says Johnson. He ultimately turned down the offer because he was already in his 'own band' and playing his 'own music'. 'I thought about it and called back and told them, "Thanks, but no thanks." I realised this was not the vehicle for me,' says Johnson. The fact that Paul Johnson was asked to join The Beach Boys at some point should be noted. In fact, Carl and David were both fans of his playing and fantasised together about adding him to The Beach Boys in 1962. However, Johnson's recollection of exactly when 'the call' occurred conflicts with some of the known facts. He maintains that he was asked after 'Surfin' Safari' had been a hit and when the band was already breaking nationally. 'I remember definitely being aware that they had a second record that was on its way up the national charts,' says Johnson. His memory of being asked to 'fill in for Al' in mid-1962 or later, at a time when Al was long gone and when David was already contractually in The Beach Boys' line-up, doesn't quite add up. But Johnson offers this as a possible explanation: 'Maybe David was in the band and they wanted to add me as well.' Skip Hand, who played drums in The Galaxies with Johnson in 1964, recalls hearing about Johnson's offer from The Beach Boys, but isn't clear on the exact details either. 'It either happened when Al first left, or more probably when David left because by that time they'd established themselves real well,' says Hand. Regardless of how and when the offer came to be, Paul Johnson has no regrets about passing it up.

Murry Wilson, who had already appointed himself the dictatorial master of The Beach Boys, wasted little time proving he was a qualified manager. After the shaky, independent Candix Records went belly up, The Beach Boys found themselves labelless and biding their time playing local dances including one at Hawthorne High. They looked to Murry for help in landing a real record deal. With a focus bordering on obsession, Murry energetically hawked the band's demo recordings, including the fresh versions of 'Surfin' Safari' and '409'. According to music industry veteran Don Podolor, it was *he* who paved the way for Murry's ultimate success. Murry knew that Dave Marks had already worked with Don and his brother Richie at American Recorders. In April 1962, Murry was insisting to Podolor that his sons' band, which now included young David on guitar, was destined for fame.

The fact that Dave had previously recorded with and befriended the Podolors gave Don an added reason to try and help these kids catch an industry wave. 'Murry Wilson, who was my friend and called me five times a day, was shopping the demo of The Beach Boys' next record,' remembers Podolor. 'He asked me to help him, and I did my best for him and the boys.' Podolor went to bat for Murry, offering The Beach Boys' demo to everyone he could think of. 'I went to all the record companies and finally I got one of the labels really interested, Dot Records,' remembers Podolor. 'Then I was told soon after that Randy Wood, the president of Dot, had turned it down.' Podolor knew Murry would be calling soon, and he hated having to tell him that Dot, like all the other labels in town, had passed on the group. Don Podolor was well acquainted with the fact that dealing with a pissed-off Murry Wilson was no picnic. He needed to think of something fast.

Gazing out the window of his Vine Street office, Don cringed at the thought of the phone ringing and Murry being on the other end. 'So I looked across the street, and there was the Capitol Records building,' says Podolor. 'One of my friends, Nik Venet, was working at Capitol, and he was using our studio, American Recorders, a lot.' While using Podolor's studio, Venet had run up an unpaid tab that in May of 1962 had grown to over a thousand dollars. The Podolors figured it was worth a grand to get Murry Wilson off their back. Don told Venet he'd waive the outstanding balance if he'd meet Murry Wilson and listen to The Beach Boys' demo. 'So I called up Nik and I basically forced him to take a meeting with Murry Wilson,' says Podolor. 'And from that meeting The

Beach Boys got signed. I forced the meeting and I got them signed. It actually happened because I didn't want to have to tell Murry Wilson that Dot had passed on his group.'

On 10 May 1962, Capitol Records purchased the demo recordings of 'Surfin' Safari' and '409' from Murry Wilson, as well as another great Brian Wilson/Gary Usher collaboration called 'Lonely Sea'. David had witnessed Brian and Usher compose the haunting ballad 'Lonely Sea' one afternoon at the Wilson home. 'What most people don't know is that Gary wrote the music, including the guitar intro,' says David. 'Brian helped with the melody, but mainly his contribution was the great lyrics. Carl and I helped them work out the arrangement on our guitars.' Despite its obvious beauty, 'Lonely Sea' wouldn't see the light of day until the second Beach Boys LP, but Nik Venet declared the other two songs a ready-made single and plans for a 45 release commenced. That summer The Beach Boys were signed to an official Capitol Records recording contract. The agreement with Capitol stated that Brian, Dennis, Carl, Mike and David would each receive an equal twenty per cent share of all advances and royalty money generated by the group's record sales.

David was represented in the contract negotiation by attorney Walter Hurst, who is known as a pioneer in music law. 'He basically wrote the book on music law,' says David. 'He was one of the first guys who really went to bat for the artist.' However, according to David, not everyone was pleased with his representation. 'Murry was not happy with Walter Hurst,' says David. 'Without him protecting me, I think Murry would have found a way to screw me out of my share right away. I'm sure if I'd shown up without Walter, I wouldn't have gotten on the lifetime contract with Capitol. But as long as those records sell I get money, and that's because of Walter.' Ironically, because David was represented by such a forward-thinking attorney, all of The Beach Boys ended up with better contracts.

The label that in the past had done big business with a roster of hallowed show business veterans like Frank Sinatra, Judy Garland, Dean Martin and Nat King Cole was shifting its style to youth-oriented groups. For a time the acoustic-folk-styled Kingston Trio had been the label's top-selling act, but as the decade of the sixties moved ahead, the fiercely electric Beach Boys, and soon The Beatles from Liverpool, England, would be the new sales giants at Capitol. Just ahead was an unprecedented streak of hit records, sold-out performances and screaming fans. In the midst of it all, David Marks would turn fourteen years old in August.

Released as a single that summer, 'Surfin' Safari' became a huge hit, eventually reaching number fourteen on the national charts. Icing the cake on its impressive national showing, the single hit the number one spot on several LA radio stations. '409' proved to be an extremely popular flip side as well. Both recordings are built upon the gritty edge of David and Carl's punky Fender guitar sound and Dennis's primitive beat. Gone was the semi-acoustic aura of 'Surfin'', with its lack of any perceptible edge. In its place was something Dave and Carl had plugged into long before – electric guitar-based rock and roll. The six-string chemistry that had been brewing for a couple of years between Carl and David turned Brian Wilson's delicate harmonies into danceable rock and roll. The result was an exciting texture that spoke directly to the teens who would buy it in droves.

'The first time I heard "Surfin' Safari" on the radio, I was eating dinner with my parents,' recalls Marks. 'When it came on I got so excited that I put my face in my napkin and screamed like a little girl.' Capitol pushed forward with a Beach Boys promotional campaign and plans for a full LP. Capitol's Nik Venet hastily organised a photo shoot for the album cover. Venet knew a bearded character known as Calypso Joe who drove around Hollywood in a Model A Ford truck. 'Nik gave the guy fifty bucks to let us use the truck for the day,' remembers David. Subsequently, Brian, Dennis, Carl, Mike and David drove up to Paradise Cove in Malibu wearing white chinos and blue Pendleton shirts. The classic photos taken that day by photographer Kenneth Veeder beautifully capture the five smiling California boys. The Beach Boys, an old pick-up decorated with palm leaves, a surfboard, and an ocean. One of rock and roll's most enduring images was born.

The Beach Boys appeared outdoors in the Oxnard Plaza on Saturday 14 July 1962 to promote their new single. The band was there to entertain a crowd gathered for the city's annual Diaper Derby, in which infants crawled along in a virtual drag race. The group's appearance was broadcast live on the local KOXR AM radio station. Included in their short set was a cover of The Belairs' guitar classic, 'Mr Moto'. While being interviewed afterwards, Brian announced the band's next single would be a new song called 'Chug A Lug'. Among those name-checked in the lyrics to Brian's 'Chug A Lug' was neighbour Louie Marotta. Louie may have been the first true Beach Boys fan and their earliest and biggest supporter. It was Louie's sister Lois's surfboard that was borrowed for one of the band's very first photos shoots in 1962. Louie was a fixture around The Beach Boys, whether it was accompanying them to a gig, carrying their amps, or just being there. 'We all loved Louie,' says David. 'I became dependent upon him. He was like a security blanket. I would take walks around the neighbourhood at night and tell him stories just to make him laugh.' Louie's laughter was a constant element in the early days of The Beach Boys.

As time passed, the one constant in the old Hawthorne neighbourhood was Louie Marotta in his driveway, working on his car. 'I wasn't into letting my dad teach me how to be an auto mechanic,' says David. 'But Louie did. Louie loved tinkering with old cars. He and my dad had this great relationship, and my dad taught Louie a lot about working on cars.' After nearly everyone else from the old neighbourhood had moved on to different lives, Louie remained in Hawthorne. Even when he got married he stayed in the same place, moving only slightly down the street to another house. In later days, Louie became a kind of ambassador to the stream of curious fans exploring The Beach Boys' original neighbourhood. For decades, when any of The Beach Boys, their families or their fans returned to the old stomping ground, Louie was always there in his driveway working on his car, just as he had been in 1962.

On 28 July, The Beach Boys and Louie set off for one of their frequent appearances at the Azusa Teen Club. While travelling to the gig in Audree's Ford Falcon wagon, the new Four Seasons hit 'Sherry' came blasting through the car radio. Brian had become temporarily obsessed with the tune and its soaring harmonies. On this particular evening he decided on the spur of the moment that the band had to add it to their set list. 'When we got to the gig the first thing Brian did was take us all into the restroom and he taught us the vocal parts to "Sherry",' says David. 'We played it that night and kept it in our set for quite a while. Brian's ability to project his enthusiasm to the rest of the group was one of his greatest gifts.'

That same evening, The Beach Boys' performance of 'Surfin' Safari' was filmed for inclusion in the short film *One Man's Challenge*. The movie was a low-budget documentary examining the growing Southern California phenomenon of teen delinquents with too much time on their hands. In the film, the Azusa club is held up as an example of a place where young people could gather to blow off steam by dancing to their favourite combos. This is the only known performance footage of the Pendleton-shirt era Beach Boys. During the performance David is seen smiling, tossing his surfer cut, and chopping away on his sunburst Fender Stratocaster.

By the middle of summer reports of isolated Beach Boys breakouts in far-reaching AM radio markets began to trickle back to Hawthorne. One stunt by a brash nineteen-year-old Memphis disc jockey named Bob Clark got plenty of attention. While on the air at WHHM, Clark invited anyone with a 409 Chevy to cruise nearby Poplar Avenue one warm Friday night. Hundreds of cars showed up and literally clogged downtown Memphis. While a procession of shiny Chevy Impalas revved their engines and cranked their radios, Clark spun The Beach Boys song '409' for an entire hour non-stop. The resulting publicity gave Clark the number one show in Memphis and gave The Beach Boys a big local hit.

In August The Beach Boys began work on their first Capitol LP. The inevitable power struggle between Murry and Brian was immediately evident when the band initiated the recording process. 'Brian would get the settings in the control room the way he wanted them and then go out into the studio to play with us,' says David. 'As soon as he did Murry would reach over and change everything. Then when he heard the playback, Brian would say, "What the fuck happened?" Murry was forever turning up the treble on everything. That's why those early Beach Boys records sound so bright, and in a way he made them sound better on little transistor radios. But what really made the records so good is that Brian's sincerity came through on them, plus they had really good energy.'

The first Beach Boys LP included nine Brian Wilson originals co-written with Mike Love and/or Gary Usher. Looking back, the material was mostly weak by Brian Wilson standards. But he was only getting started. Standout moments were both sides of the single, which were also included on the LP, a re-recording of 'Surfin'' cut prior to David joining, and the inventive but somewhat silly 'Ten Little Indians'. David's aunt, Andrea Carlo, was given a moment in The Beach Boys spotlight on the group's recording of 'County Fair', when she added colourful spoken dialogue to enhance the track's 'fair' atmosphere. 'I was just about seventeen years old when "Surfin' Safari" was recorded,' remembers Andrea. 'I had a mad crush on Brian, although he didn't know I was alive. He would come over to my sister's house to visit and he totally ignored me. David was about thirteen years old, and he made fun of me because I had such a crush.' Even though Brian ignored her, Dennis typically did not, which led to her voice making it onto a Beach Boys record. 'As Dennis and I grew older, we actually dated,' remembers Andrea. 'Dennis, David and my sister gave me the opportunity to watch The Beach Boys record. I was just there observing the band when Murry asked me to say those silly words in the background. Murry scared me to death! He had a glass eye and he took it out to scare me. I was a nervous wreck.' Andrea is the answer to a trivia question that has bounced around among hardcore Beach Boys fans for decades. Who was the female voice on 'County Fair'? Now we know.

Another great track on the *Surfin' Safari* LP was a roaring instrumental called 'Moon Dawg' written by guitarist Derry Weaver, who originally recorded it with a studio group known as The Gamblers. The original Gamblers recording also featured future Beach Boy Bruce Johnston on piano. At producer Nik Venet's request, Weaver joined the *Surfin' Safari* LP sessions and acted as an auxiliary guitarist to help pad The Beach Boys' sound in places. The group's cover of 'Moon Dawg' is notable for the fact that Carl played the drums on it. Overall, The Beach Boys' first LP is a decent, but not great, effort, although it still sold in very impressive numbers for a debut.

For years, journalists, fans and occasionally even David himself have commented that his voice wasn't included on any Beach Boys records. However, the evidence points to something different. Because Dave's voice was changing almost daily at age thirteen, Brian was wary of using him as a singer. However, there do seem to be several exceptions to the 'Dave doesn't sing' theory. One track that many Beach Boys experts have consistently suggested might possibly feature Dave's voice is the cover of Eddie Cochran's rocker 'Summertime Blues'. Dave himself has a clear recollection of reading those lyrics in the studio. 'I do remember standing around the microphone with Carl singing that song,' says David. 'Brian had wanted each of us to sing at least one song on the album.' David was also regularly featured as vocalist on this song in The Beach Boys' live sets.

In addition, David was trained by Brian to sing the fourth harmony part, the same part as Dennis, in The Beach Boys blend. Since Dennis was busy drumming, David usually sang his vocal parts during the group's live performances. In the studio David also recalls doubling the fourth part with Dennis on occasion. 'Since Dennis and I were the weakest vocally, Brian had the idea if we sang together it would solidify that part,' says David. 'How much of my voice made it onto the records I'm not sure. But I'm definitely in there on a few things.' While writing this book, I consulted the experts that I trust most in disseminating The Beach Boys' individual voices. According to them, the songs that most likely include David on background vocals are the single '409', and from the first LP sessions 'County Fair,' 'Heads You Win, Tails I Lose', and 'Chug A Lug'. But David's true value to The Beach Boys was as a guitarist, and the *Surfin' Safari* LP is full of his bright rhythm riffs.

Around this time, The Beach Boys shared the bill with 'King of the Surf Guitar' Dick Dale at the Swing Auditorium in San Bernardino. It was a wild show that included a riot between the surfers and the hodads in attendance. Dave remembers: 'Dick Dale and his Deltones were the official surfer band; the surfers adopted him. He actually invented the "surf sound". He had these big fat strings on his guitar, and played through a reverb unit and big Fender amps, though he didn't have our vocal thing going, we copped his sound, so the surfers hated us. They would go after us in the parking lot after gigs and try to kick our butts good.' Paul Johnson of The Belairs agrees, 'The Beach Boy vocals were never embraced by the surfers. The surfers listened and thought, Who are these gremmies singing about surfing? The real stuff is the instrumentals. They actually had a little trouble around the beach area getting accepted.'

Jo Ann Marks remembers some very violent incidents at early Beach Boys gigs. 'They did some awful gigs at that time; there were some very scary situations,' says Jo Ann. 'I even got in between them and a group of surfers who wanted to fight them. I stepped right in and said, "Now wait a minute here." It was quite a tussle. Sometimes it seemed like everyone wanted to throw a punch at them. At the time they started out a lot of people were really jealous of The Beach Boys.' During the Swing Auditorium melee, a good portion of the estimated one thousand attendees stormed the stage. 'We were really scared when people were climbing on the stage. We couldn't even play, and ran out the back door,' says David. 'It wasn't too long before we got used to being stormed by audiences, only later it was teenage girls trying to attack us.'

In 1962, angry peers in Southern California wanted a piece of The Beach Boys. The day-to-day reality of being an instant celebrity in the middle of a public school social structure was difficult. 'Unlike bragging about being on "Surfin'"' when I wasn't, I was now afraid to tell anyone at school I was in The Beach Boys,' says David. 'Surfin'' had been an out-of-the-blue local hit, and most of the boys' classmates felt good about it. But national recognition increased the societal spotlight and waves of jealousy cropped up. 'The real surfers resented us,' David explains. 'They felt we were phonies and exploiting their sacred surf. Back then, surfing wasn't just a sport. It was more like a cult or a lifestyle, kind of like Hell's Angels with surfboards. Dennis fit in with the surfers because he was tough and liked to fight, and he did actually surf,' says David. 'But the rest of us didn't.' Suddenly high-school-age girls were making a fuss over the skinny, fourteen-year-old pop star, and he paid a price. The surfers, greasers and jocks practically stood in line to beat him up. It didn't help that he was a Beach Boy alone. Since the border between Hawthorne and Inglewood school districts was Kornblum Avenue, David had to attend a different school from Carl and Dennis. 'Thankfully Steve Love, Mike's younger brother, went to my school,' says David. 'He stepped up to the plate and helped to protect me from some serious ass-kickings.'

On 25 August The Beach Boys performed at the Reseda Jubilee in the baking hot San Fernando Valley. They shared the bill with Southern California favourites Jan and Dean, and actually provided instrumental backing for the popular vocal duo. Brian was a huge fan of their music and looked up to Jan Berry as an innovator in the realm of pop vocal music. The Beach Boys and Jan and Dean's musical paths would intertwine in numerous ways over the coming decades. On this sweltering day in 1962, Jan and Dean were probably the better known of the two acts, but their friends from Hawthorne would eventually eclipse them for ever.

Due to the success of 'Surfin' Safari', which was screaming up the national Top 40 that September, The Beach Boys' local performance schedule began to heat up. The William Morris Agency's Marshall Berle, whose uncle really was TV legend Uncle Milty, became the band's first official booking agent.

'He got us a gig playing at Milton Berle's daughter's birthday party,' recalls David. 'Uncle Milty surprised us with twenty bucks each and told us we did a great job. After that we played a bunch of private parties for TV stars and wealthy people.' One such event was the sixteenth birthday of local debutante Hellen Stillman on 15 September, which actually garnered The Beach Boys a mention in the society section of the *LA Times*. Marshall Berle also booked the band into a series of high school dances, store openings and radio station promotions. Lacking enough original material to fill long sets, the band turned to cover versions, some of which remained staples of their act for many years. 'We did a lot of R&B songs, like "Riot in Cell Block #9", "Papa Ooh Mow Mow", and "Barbara Ann",' remembers David. Although David's voice was rarely heard in the studio, he was regularly featured as a lead vocalist on live covers including Richard Berry's 'Louie Louie' and Wilbert Harrison's 'Kansas City'.

In October 1962, the same month The Beach Boys' *Surfin' Safari* LP was released nationally, the group began a regular weekend residence at the Hollywood nightspot known as Pandora's Box. Located on the Sunset Strip, the club provided the group with their first serious showcase in front of LA's hipster elite. For David Marks, Pandora's Box represented a crash course in the realities of show business. 'You'd walk in there in the afternoon, and the smell of old alcohol and cigarettes would overwhelm you,' remembers David. 'We played there every weekend for a while. After playing there I felt like an old man at fourteen, like I'd been playing in stinky bars all my life. It's where we first got turned on to iced cappuccinos.' It didn't take long before the club was packed with a cross-section of beatniks, fringe actors, working musicians, go-go dancers and curious teens all mingling together to experience Southern California's newest surf-pop sensations. Among those who squeezed into Pandora's Box to see The Beach Boys were teenage sisters Marilyn and Diane Rovell, and their cousin Ginger Blake. The trio, who would soon be known as The Honeys singing group, were immediately taken by the five Beach Boys. 'David really looked like a

THE LOST BEACH BOY

surfer type to me,' recalls Marilyn Wilson-Rutherford. 'He always kind of nonchalantly played his guitar, not really focusing on the audience. He was a carefree teenager in my eyes.' As legend has it, it was at Pandora's Box that Brian spilled his hot chocolate or iced cappuccino (depending on who you ask) all over Marilyn's lap, indirectly leading to an epic love affair that resulted in some of pop music's best-loved songs.

On 27 October 1962, The Beach Boys performed for the first time at the legendary Hollywood Bowl. The concert was hosted by veteran television personality Art Linkletter. Joining The Beach Boys on the all-star bill were actress Debbie Reynolds, singer Jimmie Rodgers, comedian Soupy Sales, teen sensations Shelley Fabares and Paul Peterson, and singing groups The Rivingtons and The Castells. One of the show's most memorable moments came when Reynolds smashed her acoustic guitar and leaped into the pool in front of the Bowl's stage. This was the one and only time David performed on the Hollywood Bowl stage, although The Beach Boys would return to play there without him several times in the years ahead.

At the same time the 'Surfin' Safari' single was peaking nationally at number fourteen, The Beach Boys received word that the song had sailed to number one in, of all places, Sweden. The group was still shaking its collective head over that on 3 November, while they filmed an appearance for Bob Eubanks's *Pickwick Dance Party*, a TV show that aired on KTLA every Saturday afternoon. In front of the delighted teen audience, the boys performed 'Ten Little Indians', the song now scheduled to be their second Capitol single. That same week, David, Carl, Dennis and Brian, who were still minors, attended California Superior Court in downtown Los Angeles to have their Capitol Records contracts legally approved by their parents. The court ordered that any and all future changes or adjustments to the original Capitol Records recording contract could only be made with the court's approval. It was also ordered that at least 25 per cent of their future royalties be set aside in trustee savings accounts, to be handed over at age 21.

That December, The Beach Boys performed at a pre-football game pep rally at the University of Southern California and then at the grand opening of the new Cinnamon Cinder nightclub in Long Beach. Following those local engagements the band embarked on their first extended tour of California. With dates booked in Santa Barbara, Bakersfield, Fresno, San Jose, Merced, Stockton and Santa Cruz, the group was away from LA for over two weeks. The band set out across California with their bodies and equipment distributed between Mike love's Volkswagen and Audree's Ford Falcon wagon. Although the 'Ten Little Indians' single flopped, becoming The Beach Boys' only non-hit single of the David Marks era, the tour itself proved to be wildly successful, and the band made a surprisingly large profit. For fourteen-year-old David, life on the road turned out to be an adventure beyond his wildest dreams.

The overwhelming freedom of being a teenage sensation let loose on the waiting world gave David's folks some well-founded concerns. 'Before we left on the tour, my father put his arm around Mike's shoulder and said, "You are the oldest . . . keep your eye on the little bastard." My dad's arms were about as big around as Mike's legs. I think he scared Mike into a sense of obligation to try and keep an eye on me,' says David. Mike became David's designated road roommate. While more or less trying to keep David out of trouble, Mike also educated him in some less than prudent ways. 'Mike kept a bottle of vodka in his sax case,' remembers David. 'I was constantly sneaking hits off the bottle. One day I found some rubbers in there and asked him what they were. That night, when he brought a girl back to our room, I figured it out for myself. I spent many a night trying to fall asleep with a pillow over my head to hide the visions of some girl and Mike in the next bed with his white ass going up and down on her.'

After having been coddled as an only child by his mother who, according to Dave, had unsuccessfully tried to keep him from running wild with other children, he suddenly found himself increasingly independent from his parents due to the sudden rise of The Beach Boys. David took the change in his stride. 'I didn't feel any different because my attitude was just the same,' he says. 'I was arrogant. I felt like nothing could touch me. Becoming famous just made all of those tendencies a little worse, I suppose.'

According to Dave's mother, The Beach Boys' success made Murry Wilson's tendencies more extreme as well. 'Murry was just awful right from the start,' says Jo Ann. 'He had to control everything. What should have been a joyous time, when the boys became so successful, was not, thanks to Murry. He just had a way of taking the fun out of everything. Audree was just the opposite of him, she was the sweetest person, and everybody loved her. But Murry was a tyrant.'

Murry was missing when The Beach Boys' tour reached its conclusion in Santa Cruz, having returned to LA the night before. The absence of Murry's controlling presence left the group in a mood to party. Carl's best friend, Ron Swallow, remembers, 'They did the show in Santa Cruz and the concert went great. After the show we were at a hotel down near the beach, by the Santa Cruz boardwalk.' Dennis had apparently told everyone, including the fans, that The Beach Boys were having a party in their rooms after the show. 'A bunch of people ended up coming over,' says Swallow. 'Some guys came that had their girlfriends with them, and the girls ended up being more interested in the band than their boyfriends. We were upstairs with the girls and standing out on the balcony, and these guys were down in the parking lot.' The group of college-aged boyfriends became increasingly irritated that the band was occupying their girlfriends' attention. First they began verbally harassing the group. Soon they were threatening to come upstairs and give The Beach Boys an ass-kicking. David and the others knew this wasn't going to end pleasantly. What the young men in the parking lot hadn't expected was that one of The Beach Boys lived for moments like these.

'Dennis was a hothead, anyway,' says Swallow. 'And when he heard these guys were making threats he said, "OK, fine, I'll go get them," and he went marching down the stairs.' Swallow tried to reason with him. 'I said, "Dennis, come on, we'll get the police to take care of it." But Dennis just said, "No, I'm going to take care of it myself." ' Just as one of the angry boyfriends came charging up the stairs, Dennis met him with a crushing kick to the testicles. 'He got him good,' says Swallow. 'He kicked him hard enough that it actually split open the guy's scrotum.' Dennis looked at the others and said, 'Anybody else?'

With their friend lying on the ground screaming and bleeding from his crotch, the rest of the boys backed off. An ambulance was called to collect the fallen combatant and the Santa Cruz police also showed up to question witnesses. Dennis was required to return to Santa Cruz at a later date and appear before the judge. 'It was thrown out on the basis that Dennis was not the aggressor but was protecting himself and others from an attacker,' says Swallow. With the Santa Cruz incident serving as an intense finale, the first Beach Boys tour was over.

Upon returning to Southern California, The Beach Boys celebrated their first Christmas as Capitol recording stars. On 27 December, the group performed at a 'Surf Fair' held at the Santa Monica Civic Auditorium. The fair consisted of daylong screenings of spectacular surfing films and performances by local groups including Shenandoah's Folk Singers and The Surfside Four. After their concert appearance Dennis and David invited two cute female fans to join them at the Santa Monica pier amusement centre for rides and snacks. 'We ended up making out with them under the boardwalk,' says David, 'just like in the song by The Coasters.'

As the year 1962 came to a close, David Marks found himself firmly strapped into The Beach Boys roller coaster. For the moment, the ride was nothing but fun. The terrifying twists and turns that his future held were still around life's big blind curve. David had no clue what was coming next. For now he was just holding on tight and enjoying the ride.

5. SITTIN' ON TOP OF THE WORLD

In January 1963, The Beach Boys gathered for the recording session that would produce both sides of their next single. Brian chose to combine Chuck Berry's 'Sweet Little Sixteen' musical format with surfing lyrics. The result would prove to be a launching pad to massive international fame for The Beach Boys. The instant the full band ran through Brian's new arrangement, it was obvious it had the potential to be a hit. With catchy lyrics about being 'gone for the summer' and 'tell the teacher we're surfin'', this tune, more than any, national-ised the surfing craze. It didn't matter if you were landlocked. According to The Beach Boys, if you lived anywhere in the USA, you could wax down your board, plan a route, and go on safari to stay.

The classic single 'Surfin' USA' was recorded at Western Recorders Studio 3 with engineer Chuck Britz attempting to keep Murry at bay. Murry continued to question Brian's every move and aggressively challenged the others to 'fight for success'. Despite the static from his old man, Brian essentially took control of the session and, due to his ingenuity, the group made another huge leap forward. In support of Carl's memorable lead guitar flourishes, David Marks's steady guitar presence was clearly in evidence on 'Surfin' USA'. Dave's chunky reverbed rhythm seductively counters the sweet Beach Boys harmonies with a semi-metallic edge. This recording would eventually become *the* all-time surf music anthem. And David's role in that success should not be underestimated.

According to Jeff Foskett of Brian Wilson's current band, David's performance on 'Surfin' USA' was one key to the record's unique appeal. 'David's rhythm playing on "Surfin' USA" is masterful in its simplicity,' says Foskett. 'People may wonder, How hard can it be to play three chords? True, but it's how one plays those three chords that is the difference between success and something else. You can hear him on the seventh fret striking fiercely on the strings creating an almost "metallic" rhythm sound.' 'Surfin' USA' is rich with the guitar chemistry that Carl and David had perfected by this point. Their funky rhythmic charge was vibrant and danceable, even landing the single on the Billboard Rhythm and Blues charts for a few weeks. With a fantastic harmony arrangement and a great Mike Love lead vocal, 'Surfin' USA' gave The Beach Boys a signature hit that would remain popular for decades to come. If you listen carefully to the song's fadeout, you can hear David throw in some Dick Dale-style staccato downslides for good measure.

The flipside, which also proved to be wildly successful, was another hot-rod anthem called 'Shut Down'. David and Carl's Fender guitars once again made the perfect bed for Brian to lay his harmonies on. 'David's rhythm performance is again very "metallic" but very steady and true,' says Jeff Foskett. The percolating thrust from Carl's muted Fender bottom end picking gives 'Shut Down' a playfully sinister dragstrip-burning rumble. This cut also benefited from Dennis's barely in control but always passionate drumming, a bleating sax solo by Mike, and Brian's usual tasteful bass lines. This was the quintessential garage band Beach Boys sound, and it would take the world on an exhilarating quarter-mile ride. If

THE LOST BEACH BOY

you listen closely to the very last notes of 'Shut Down', you can hear David Marks directly defying Murry Wilson's orders. Murry had let it be known that in the studio, David's role would be limited to rhythm guitar only, while Carl would play all the leads. Since the two guitarists were basically equal in ability, Murry's rule didn't sit well with David. Although Dave had been playing occasional lead guitar during Beach Boys concerts when the band needed to stretch their songs to maximise set length, Murry wasn't going to allow it on the records. The Dick Dale downslides on 'Surfin' USA' are just one example of David ignoring the Murry-imposed boundaries. On 'Shut Down', just as the song is fading out, David again strays from the rhythm-only role and rips off a crisp Chuck Berry-style lead riff on the song's last notes. For decades those few notes have played to millions of ears, giving David a chance to flip Murry the bird endlessly.

With the new single finished, the band was sitting on top of the world. 'When we heard the playback of "Surfin' USA" we knew we had something very special,' says David. 'Brian used to take his rough mixes on acetate to every house in the neighbourhood and play them on all the different hi-fis so he could hear what his songs sounded like on various systems. We thought he was nuts doing that, but now all of the books on the subject recommend doing this. That's just another example of Brian's genius being dismissed as insanity only to find out years later that he was just ahead of his time. When he did this with "Surfin' USA", every time he heard it, he got happier.' Although Chuck Berry would later challenge Brian over the songwriting credit and force him to adjust it, nothing could stop the momentum created by this recording.

For a time the band continued to perform steadily in their vast home state. They often drove for hours across desert or farmland to play one-nighters. It was on one such jaunt through a rural area that David got to live out a fantasy that Brian so beautifully expressed in his song 'Farmer's Daughter'. 'We had just finished playing an afternoon show in some small town in Northern California,' says David. 'There was a cute girl that had been standing in front of the stage during the whole show. After the crowd thinned out and we went out to pack our gear I noticed she was still there. Having the ego I did, thinking I was a star, I thought she was waiting for me. It turned out she was just waiting there for her dad. But I started talking to her and by the time her dad got there she invited me to dinner at their farmhouse down the road,' remembers David. While the teenage waif's father drove them to the farm, David wasted no time making his move. 'I was sitting in the back seat with the girl, making eye contact with her dad in his rear-view mirror while my hand was inside his daughter's shirt,' says David. 'He had no idea. I had dinner and hung out with the family and then they drove me back to our hotel, where I bragged to the guys. Dennis and Mike were getting girls left and right and Carl and I hardly ever did, so this was one of the first times I had something to brag about.' David believes that his enthusiastic description of that evening's events inspired Brian and Mike to write a new song called 'Farmer's Daughter', which would be a highlight of the group's upcoming LP.

Sessions began for The Beach Boys' second LP that January. 'As fast as Brian could write new songs we were in the studio recording them,' says David. The eldest Wilson let it be known that he hadn't been happy on the road, complaining that the noise from the amps was bothering his already damaged ears. But when he was home and working on new music, Brian was solidly in his element. 'We could see a shift in the material he was coming up with,' says David. 'His songs were becoming more melancholy and serious.' Gone were the silly singalongs like 'Chug A Lug' and 'Ten Little Indians' and in their place were bittersweet evocative tunes like 'Farmer's Daughter', 'Lana' and the previously recorded 'Lonely Sea'. As a Beach Boy and friend, David had a bird's eye view of Brian Wilson's impressive growth as a composer. 'I think I was close enough to him at the beginning that I could feel what he was feeling,' says David. 'It was like he inhabited a world of his own, like a fantasy world in his head. When I was a little kid I could hear symphonies going on in my head and I thought they were real. They faded away as I grew older and I polluted my mind with other shit. But someone like Brian, in his childlike state, never lost that. He kept hearing it and he found a way to materialise it. He nailed what was going on in his head. And he was excited and happy to be in that world. If something passed through him like a sound he'd go, "Whoa, I've gotta nail it now!" On the spot, if it occurred in his head he immediately went to it and did it. He'd just rush into the studio and do it. He'd say, "If I don't do it now it'll get away and I'll never do it." That's how he was with his music. It was his world. To have that passion and that enthusiasm is 99 per cent of why he's so great.'

The *Surfin' USA* LP sessions produced nothing short of a classic album. It would turn out to be one of the most popular LPs of the group's entire career. More than any other Beach Boys album, it was a 'guitar' record. No one was thinking of The Beach Boys as a 'vocal' group when this LP was flying out of the stores in 1963. Containing five instrumentals, it was as if Brian decided to turn loose the six-string jam sessions that Carl and David had already been conducting for years. He surrounded them with some great vocal tracks and a vibrant production sound. Although the producer's credit went to Nik Venet, and Murry Wilson hovered over the sessions like a drill sergeant, the band knew who was really in charge. They all looked to Brian for direction, and he never let them down. When the group cranked out two Dick Dale covers with 'Let's Go Trippin'' and a very raw take of 'Miserlou', it was Brian who gave the orders and set the pace. On the latter, David's chopping rhythm perfectly complements Carl's lead perform-ance. The group original 'Stoked' is an all-time surf guitar classic that was made up on the spot by Brian the same day it was recorded. On the wild 'Surf Jam', David again wanders outside of Murry's rhythm-only borders with a flurry of single note picking just before Carl launches into the lead. You can hear Brian screaming at David and the others throughout the raucous performance, challenging them to stay in the groove. And the result was a feast for anyone with an interest in the electric guitar. 'Fortunately for guitar players, the *Surfin' USA* LP has those five instrumental tracks,' says Jeff Foskett. 'It's cool to listen to the two young teenagers fire away on those cuts.'

Flamin' Groovies founder and guitarist Cyril Jordan remembers the impact The Beach Boys' second LP had on him. 'The first records I bought were Chuck Berry's *On Top* and *Surfin' USA* by The Beach Boys,' says Jordan. 'I became crazed about the electric guitar. Then I found out David Marks was fourteen. Hell, I was fourteen then. I couldn't believe it. I didn't have to wait to grow up. He was on Capitol Records. And the rhythm guitar was for me.' Upon its release, the *Surfin' USA* LP undoubtedly influenced an entire generation of guitarists and still stands as the toughest-sounding LP in The Beach Boys canon. If the band had split up in early 1963 and never performed again, they would still be known for having recorded one of the era's defining rock records. *Surfin' USA*, more than any other Beach Boys LP, bears the influence of young David Marks and his Fender Stratocaster guitar. This was the garage rock, or dare I say, punk rock Beach Boys in all their T-shirt-wearing, blue-jean-sporting, barefoot, surfer hair, we-don't-give-a-shit glory. In a year, the self-contained rock band with two electric guitarists and a long-haired, head-shaking drummer would be commonplace. The Beatles opened the floodgates. But in early 1963, The Beach Boys had a unique presence on the national scene because they already had those elements in place. Kids all around California and elsewhere looked at David and Dennis's rebellious visual presence on those first two Beach Boys album covers and the first national momentum of US garage rock lurched forward. Vocal group? I think not. These Beach Boys were an electric rock and roll band, and the coolest one on the continent.

In the midst of the landmark *Surfin' USA* sessions, the group travelled to Arizona for a string of sold-out shows. It was becoming evident that The Beach Boys were known far beyond California, as the Arizona audiences were overflowing. David was paid a total of $169 for the Arizona gigs, a small fortune for a fourteen-year-old. The Beach Boys also stopped by a University of Arizona college fraternity to perform a set at their big annual winter party. It turned out to be an incredibly wild affair with endless waves of hard booze and soft co-eds. 'We were doing the ZBT house in Tucson, Arizona,' remembers Mike Love. 'We went there for one show and we stayed for three days.' Mike had some explaining to do to Elmer when the boys got back to California two days late, and with young David in an obviously tattered state.

As the enterprise became bigger, the boys worked harder, and tensions between them increased. 'It was hard work travelling, all cramped into a car together, driving hundreds of miles to the next town,' says Marks. 'Mike and Dennis had this competition over who was the sex symbol of the group. It was always boiling under the surface and they began to get on each other's nerves.' Brian had no interest in involving himself in the hierarchy of personalities. Most of the time he only wanted to concentrate on writing his songs. 'Carl was the first one of us kids to realise how big we were getting,' says David. 'He knew we were evolving into a business and he buckled down and got very serious. He would get really pissed at Dennis and me because we didn't take the band seriously enough. We just wanted to have fun and play our music. We weren't really aware of the impact we were making back then,' says David. 'We were just kids playing music. We would get glimpses of our success when girls would swarm us after shows, screaming our names. Or we'd get recognised in restaurants and hotels. But we took it for granted. We thought that it happened to all bands.'

Back in LA, Dennis was still providing David with a never-ending string of unforgettable moments. 'One day, Dennis took me out in his rear-engine Corvair,' remembers Dave. 'He wanted to go look at new Corvettes at Felix Chevrolet in downtown LA. While we were going about sixty or seventy on the freeway, Dennis suddenly sneezed and lost control of the wheel.' The lightweight Corvair lost traction and spun like a top across several lanes. David closed his eyes and waited for what he thought would be an inevitable impact. 'By some miracle we didn't hit anything and Dennis gained total control and kept right on going without missing a beat,' says David. 'I guess I had turned completely white because when Dennis looked over at me he started laughing hysterically.' A week later, Dennis's luck ran out when he slammed the Corvair into a cement wall and badly injured his legs. Waiting in the wings to cover for him was Carl's long-time buddy Mark Groseclose. Mark was not only a fine drummer, but he was also an incredible graphic artist with seemingly endless talent. Add to that Mark's legendary sense of humour, and it's easy to understand why he became one of David's most beloved friends. 'Dave and I met when Carl asked me to jam with him and David over at his house,' said Groseclose in a 1987 interview. 'We'd just get together and play a lot of stuff The Beach Boys didn't play. We had a lot of fun. Eventually Bill Trenkle started sitting in, playing bass. It was around this time that Dennis smashed up his Corvair, and I was asked to sit in for Dennis with The Beach Boys. I did four gigs with them. The first one was at the Valentine's Dance at Hawthorne High School. The Beach Boys were just starting to become popular. During this gig, Dave turned to me and said he wished I could play with them all the time and I said I wished I could, too!'

It wasn't that David didn't appreciate what Dennis gave The Beach Boys. He knew he was a major part of the appeal of the band. But David and Mark Groseclose quickly developed a special chemistry that went far beyond music. Their personalities meshed in a way that made David wish they could play together for more than a few gigs. For the time being, Groseclose stuck around, as Dennis's troubles continued. On his first attempt to rejoin The Beach Boys, Dennis fell off the drum riser and re-broke his ankle. On another occasion, he suffered a serious concussion in his parents' bathroom. 'Dennis was dating a girl who would get him reds and he was taking them sometimes to get high,' remembers David. 'He was in the bathroom at the Wilsons' house and he passed out and hit his head on the toilet. The ambulance had to come and take him to the hospital. I remember looking out my window and seeing flashing lights and thinking, What did Dennis do this time? It turns out he really messed himself up, he had some sort of temporary brain damage and his motor skills were impaired. After that he developed a stutter. I don't know how much of that was from the head injury and how much was from the drugs, but we were really worried about him. Nobody knew how long he would be like that or if he'd ever be normal again.'

Dennis eventually recovered from the blow to his head, but his relationship with Murry did not. The elder Wilson insisted Dennis move out on his own for good. Dennis lived with Gary Usher for a time, and then he moved into a small apartment in Manhattan Beach with none other than Mike Love. The thought of Dennis and Mike living together seems insane because of all the legendary battles over girls and lifestyle choices that dominated their relationship in the decades to come. But despite the volatility in store, in 1963 they were still very close friends. 'I remember Dennis and Mike's apartment in Manhattan Beach,' says David. 'It was a four-unit complex right on the beach, and they lived upstairs. There was a constant flow of Cutty Sark and J&B Scotch through that apartment. Dennis and Mike were drinking tremendous amounts of booze. There was always a party going on there with lots of young girls. I remember one night some pretty blonde sat on my lap when I was there. I was so young I wasn't sure what to do. Then she burned my neck with her cigarette just to get a reaction. It was a crazy place with lots of crazy people hanging out but it didn't last long. Mike and Dennis started fist fighting and shit, and they couldn't live together any more.'

That March, as 'Surfin' USA' began its long assault on the US pop charts, The Beach Boys performed a full schedule of concerts throughout California. On 8 March, David was paid $217.50 for a single gig. By 1963 standards, that was a major payday. David's father was literally working his fingers to the bone for weeks to earn that much. On 16 March, The Beach Boys played another wild sold-out show in Hemet, California. The audience was ecstatic throughout the performance, and, for the first time, girls were throwing themselves at the stage. During 'Louie Louie', David cut loose with a long guitar solo that seemed to go on endlessly. Brian and Dennis laughed and encouraged David to keep it going because they knew his soloing was getting under Murry's skin. Murry was literally smouldering at stage right while watching David's guitar marathon go on and on and on. Puffing furiously on his pipe, Murry turned and left the concert early, heading back to LA without a word. Afterwards the rest of the group partied with their adoring fans while Brian spent the entire night in his hotel room on the phone with his girlfriend Judy Bowles.

Between gigs, David was having a terrible time adhering to the rigours of school. He was constantly courting trouble by experimenting with cutting class, petty theft, vandalism, smoking, drinking, and generally screwing up. He was a rock star, after all. In a way, he was just keeping his chops up. And much of the time, trouble found him whether he was looking for it or not. 'I was getting into a lot of fights,' says David. Throngs of jealous teen guys would sarcastically tease David with the exaggeratedly punctuated gibe 'Beeeech Boy'. For a skinny fourteen-year-old boy, being a famous Beach Boy could be like having a flashing target pasted on your head. No longer able to cope with life as major celebrities in a public school environment, Carl and David made plans to attend Hollywood Professional School. Among their classmates at HPS were Marilyn and Diane Rovell, musician Eddy Medora and actresses Peggy Lipton, Ann Marshall and Sue Lyon.

'Hollywood Professional School was an old two-storey building on Hollywood Boulevard that had once been a mortuary,' remembers David. 'The Manns, who ran the school, looked like characters from the Addams Family, and all the teachers were ancient, with gin on their breath.' Children of celebrities and Hollywood producers, as well as a few teen stars like David and Carl, made up the student body. Most days, Carl drove David to school in his new turquoise Pontiac Grand Prix. After a time, they began a routine of cutting class and hanging out at Earl Leaf's home. Leaf, a journalist who covered The Beach Boys and other pop stars, was given the nickname 'Big Daddy'. He basically gave Carl and Dave free rein at his home, where they'd hole up daily to smoke cigarettes, talk about girls, and listen to records.

In the afternoons, Carl and Dave would regularly drop off the Rovell sisters at their parents' home in the Fairfax district. 'The Rovells' house was in a great location, centrally located in the Melrose/Fairfax area,' says David. 'It was a nice big house – not a mansion, but a Spanish villa type of home, and it was very comfortable there. Mae Rovell, Marilyn and Diane's mom, always cooked up a storm, and there was all this wonderful gourmet stuff to eat. She was the quintessential Jewish mother and always had a house full of cakes and great chicken and matzo ball soups. She'd make you eat until you were ready to explode and then you could go out to their nice big couch and fall asleep. It was really a great place to relax and get away from all the hassles of life.' Brian was constantly there too. He enjoyed the Rovell family atmosphere so much that, with Mae's blessing, he eventually moved in full time. And with that, the Rovell home became the unofficial Beach Boys clubhouse.

Twenty-four hours a day, the Rovells had an open-door policy for The Beach Boys and their friends. 'Mae kinda liked it,' says David. 'I think Marilyn's dad, Irv, hated it, but he was always polite and pleasant. Their house was always filled with kids. It was like The Beach Boys camp. Mike and Dennis were always there; Jan and Dean were there a lot, too. Brian was always banging away at the piano, and we would be singing all the time.' David would continue to hang out with the merry gang at the Rovell home long after he'd left The Beach Boys. He felt at home there because Mae always made him feel welcome. 'We didn't destroy the place or break anything, but on any given occasion there were fourteen or fifteen people there,' remembers David. 'There were records playing, lots of joking around, and just generally socialising.' With the teenage Rovell sisters and their female teenage friends hanging about, it was a very nice set-up for The Beach Boys. 'It was pretty innocent,' says David. 'There was no heavy drinking, and no drugs. They were the sweetest people ever in the world, Mae Rovell and her girls. They were just so nice to me.'

On 15 April 1963, The Beach Boys played yet another sold-out concert, this time in Bakersfield, California, where the 'Surfin' USA' single had already made number one on the local KAFY AM radio chart. David was astonished when he was paid $300 cash following the group's performance. The band was ecstatic about the money they were making, the adulation they were receiving, and the fact that their new record was becoming a monster hit. All except for Brian, that is, who became despondent every time the band hit the road. Fighting depression and constantly irritated by the ringing in his ears from increasingly louder concerts, he finally let the others know he was nearing his limit. 'When I found out Brian didn't want to play live gigs any more, I thought, Holy shit, it's over,' remembers David. 'How we gonna do it without him? That was a big concern.'

Brian began to consider re-recruiting his buddy Alan Jardine as an auxiliary Beach Boy. Without Murry's consent, Brian hatched a plan to ask Al to play bass and sing his parts during tedious concert tours. 'Al would come over and rehearse with us, although at first he didn't record with us in the studio,' says David. 'I remember being happy with Al being there because we had been pretty bummed out that Brian didn't want to tour any more. But Al was a good bass player and could make his voice sound just like Brian. We were all relieved. Just having Al in the wings took the pressure off Brian for a little longer,' says David. 'I think it made Brian feel secure knowing Al was there waiting for the call.'

But there was still the problem of Murry. The first time Al showed up to play a gig as Brian's fill-in, he realised Murry was completely in the dark. Murry nearly came out of his skin when he saw Al and no Brian. He immediately got on the phone to Brian and started yelling, 'You're blowing it, son!' To Murry, nothing could be more unprofessional than not showing up for a concert appearance. He railed on at Brian that the fans expected to see the same faces that were on the LP covers, and that they'd paid good money for a concert ticket thinking he'd be there. Once Murry realised that Brian was holding firm, he turned his fury to the issue of Al's monetary compensation. 'I'm only paying for Al for playing live,' Murry said to Brian. 'No studio time. No royalties. Nothing else!'

Temporarily resigned to the fact that Brian was staying home, Murry Wilson arranged a month-long summer tour of the Midwest for the increasingly in-demand Beach Boys. Ironically, Murry decided he needed to stay behind himself to tend to his own business affairs. With that in mind, Murry asked Elmer Marks to act as the group's tour manager. David's parents, caught up in the thrill of their son being part of a hit act, couldn't say no. 'We packed our bags, and the six of us flew to Chicago,' says David. 'The flight to Chicago was my first trip on a jetliner. I was going out on the road to play my guitar . . . just like a real rock star. This was an incredibly cool thing for a fourteen-year-old punk like myself. We were signing autographs, and people were basically making a big fuss over us. The five of us strutted around like kings of the world.'

On 25 April 1963, The Beach Boys' first major tour outside of California began. Upon arrival in Chicago they rented one Chevrolet station wagon and a U-Haul trailer to suit their travelling needs and headed for their first show in Des Moines, Iowa. 'When we arrived in Des Moines, a concerned community board greeted us,' remembers David. 'They told us The Everly Brothers had been there the week before, and if we were going to act like they did, we could just get back on the plane and go home. It turns out they had trashed the hotels and de-virginised some of the local girls.' The Everly Brothers had become one of America's top recording acts in the late 1950s with classic singles like 'Wake Up Little Susie' and 'All I Have To Do Is Dream'. Brian and Mike considered them a huge influence on their own singing style, but in 1963, they became an annoying presence. For weeks, The Beach Boys tour followed the same trail blazed by The Everly Brothers a week earlier, and wherever they went, they were put under a magnifying glass because of the havoc the battling Everly Brothers had wreaked. Ironically, David's parents would later become very close friends with Phil Everly. And soon enough, The Beach Boys would make their own mark as rowdy rock stars. The first date on the tour was booked at Des Moines' historic Val-Aire Ballroom. There The Beach Boys drew 1,870 fans, and each fan paid one dollar to attend. The band was paid a $450 guarantee plus half the gate, giving them a total take of $1,385. The following night, they played a concert in Rockville, Illinois, at the Rockford Teen Club Canteen. Admission was $1.25 for members and $2 for guests. The band attracted a crowd of about 450 teens and was paid $650. Since the stage sound proved to be very bad, they hurried through their set.

On 27 April, the group was scheduled to perform at the Danceland Ballroom in Cedar Rapids, Iowa. There the 'Surfin USA' single was sitting at number two on the local KCRG 1600 AM 'Fabulous Top 50' radio chart and upon their arrival, they found the city buzzing with anticipation about the upcoming concert. The boys were besieged by autograph-seekers as they checked into their hotel that afternoon and that night Elmer collected a total of $1,403 for their efforts. After the show, Dave and Al were given a $6 advance for drinks and food.

The following night, The Beach Boys played the Terp Ballroom in Austin, Minnesota. The audience was relatively small at 510 but their enthusiasm was overwhelming, and the venue's large stage and good sound make for a fun night. Afterwards, when autographs had been signed, the group collected their $500 guarantee and left Austin in a great mood, knowing they had the next day off.

On 30 April 1963, The Beach Boys performed at the Arkowa Ballroom in Sioux Falls, South Dakota. Only 413 fans showed up, and the group was paid a modest $350 flat fee. That night, Al Jardine requested a $20 cash advance, which he used the next morning to buy himself a new pair of pants. Carl was given an advance of $10 and treated himself to a steak dinner.

After sending some of the initial profits back home to Murry at the month's end, The Beach Boys only had a total of $483.31 cash in hand, according to tour manager Elmer Marks's daily journal. The coffers were quickly refilled when the group played the Sports Center Roller Rink in Wichita, Kansas, on the first day of May, however. There, 1,783 fans paid $1.25 apiece and jammed the old rink to see their musical heroes. The screaming from the audience was so loud, the band could barely hear themselves play. Elmer collected a fee of $650 from the rink's manager and reminded the boys they had the following day off. With that in mind, Mike, Dennis and David took three local girls out for hamburgers and malts at a quaint Wichita hangout. Afterwards, they bought some beer and parked at a local make-out spot south of town. The three Beach Boys staggered back to their rooms at 2 a.m. and told Elmer the reason they were so late was because the girls' car had a flat tyre. Elmer noticed several large love bites on David's neck but let it pass without comment.

On 3 May 1963, the band played a large hall in Excelsior Park, Minnesota, where they drew an impressive 1,766 paid fans. The park management informed Elmer that The Beach Boys had attracted the largest crowd at this venue since 1944, and that over 1,000 fans had been turned away at the door. Many of those who couldn't get into the show lingered in the parking lot nearby, just to be close to The Beach Boys. The loyal fans were rewarded after the show, when Dennis and David appeared at a side door to sign autographs. The group collected $1,974.50 for their night's work. Afterwards Dennis was given $10 to replace his pile of shattered drumsticks, while Mike received a $50 cash advance, the most of any Beach Boy on the tour.

The band's wave to fame was in mid-swell. 'When we were on stage, the girls were always screaming, it didn't get any better than that, but we still hadn't realised how big we actually were,' recalls David. It must have been surreal for the merry California gang to be driving through the cornfields of Iowa on the way to their next gig hearing 'Surfin' USA' and 'Shut Down' dominating the radio. They were the hottest teen trend on the airwaves everywhere they went, regardless of how far they travelled from the Pacific's edge. On 4 May, the group played the Duluth Armory in Duluth, Minnesota, where a gang of teenage girls swamped the stage and knocked Dennis completely off his drum stool. Once security restored order, the group – with a slightly tattered Dennis – continued their set. Afterwards, Elmer collected a $600 payment for the show and handed out small advances to Carl and Dennis.

On 5 May, The Beach Boys arrived at the legendary Surf Ballroom in Clear Lake, Iowa. To Carl and David, this was hallowed ground. The Surf is the site of Buddy Holly's last performance, after which he died in a plane crash with Ritchie Valens and the Big Bopper. Since Valens had been a close friend of Carl and David's guitar mentor, John Maus, the occasion took on added meaning. Unfortunately, the experience was marred by a confrontation with the ballroom's management. The Surf's manager, Carol Anderson, took great exception to The Beach Boys' loud guitars and refused to turn the PA up to suit their vocal needs. After the clash with Anderson, the band angrily departed immediately after the show with only a $250 deposit in hand.

Back in Southern California, Jo Ann Marks was receiving some unwanted attention from both Brian and his dad. 'When The Beach Boys were touring without him, and Elmer was out on the road with them, Brian would call me and ask to come over,' remembers Jo Ann. 'He had a romantic interest in me that lasted for quite a long while. It was a little embarrassing. Sometimes his call would come at three in the morning, and this is when he was living with Marilyn. I had to tell him no, and I could hear the disappointment in his voice.' In 1956, when the Marks family first moved into the neighbourhood, Dave's mother was only twenty-seven years old, and very good-looking. As soon as they moved in across the street from the Wilsons, Brian seemed to develop a crush on her. To add to Jo Ann's predicament, Brian's dad also had eyes for her. He kept finding excuses to show up at her door, and was frustrated by her skilful avoidance of him. 'Murry would send Audree and Elmer out on the road with The Beach Boys to look after them,' recalls Jo Ann. 'And while they were gone, he'd be trying to flirt with me. If I saw him coming across the street, I'd lock the doors and hide.'

When the road-weary Beach Boys returned to Southern California on 6 May 1963, following their first Midwest tour, the immense differences between the band's members were underlined on arrival. Mike already had an ex-wife and two young daughters depending on him for income. Dennis had an angry Murry in his face with a stack of bills for hotel damages. Brian clung tightly to the cocoon of his music. Al wasn't exactly sure whether he was in or out of the band. And David and Carl were expected to return to the drudgery of school. The Beach Boys as an act had successfully made their way into the slipstream of national celebrity. They had reached the point of no return . . . and things would never be the same for any of them.

6. SHUT DOWN

In 1963, The Beach Boys became national stars. In that year, David Marks played more than 100 concert dates with the band, from as far west as Hawaii to as far east as New York. He also participated in the recording of three hit LPs and several hit singles that are now considered classics of their era. His face appeared in newspapers, magazines and on television shows across the United States. It would prove to be the peak year of David Marks's personal fame, and it was also the year that his dream ride with The Beach Boys was shut down.

Back in Hawthorne, the boys found a strange combination of adulation and resentment wherever they went. Girls would literally shriek when they recognised one of them, but often their male counterparts simultaneously seethed with anger. 'One day, I stopped into Dino's Pizza, the place in town all the cool kids – like surfers and football players – hung out,' remembers David. 'This big football player started to tease me and make fun of my hair because it was considered long compared to their crew cuts.' David knew that he was about to experience humiliation and provide twisted recreation for older, tougher boys. 'Just as I was about to get my ass kicked, Dennis pulled up in his brand new Corvette Stingray. He walked through the door and saw what was going on,' says David. 'With a real serious look on his face, he stared down at the football player and asked me if there was a problem. I smiled and said no. They all backed down and left me alone,' remembers David. 'Everyone knew Dennis's reputation, and they didn't want to mess with him. I would be left alone when Dennis was around after that.

'However, just because Dennis would protect me from other guys, it didn't mean he wouldn't knock me on my ass sometimes,' says David. One incident in particular, involving a gorgeous girl named Sharon, created a major conflict between Dennis and David. While on a date with her at the Hawthorne Fair, David had already taken a beating for defending her honour. 'A bunch of older guys started pointing at Sharon's chest and yelling "Nice tits", and while I might have been a brat, my father always taught me to stick up for your girl,' says David. 'When I stuck up for Sharon, I got punched out by some asshole.'

Dennis then saw the buxom lass with David, and he immediately noticed her attributes, too. The Don Juan of drummers ignored his young band-mate's feelings entirely, and started hitting on her with his usual confidence. David couldn't take it any more. 'Whenever I would show any interest in a girl, Dennis would move in on her and fuck her. I would get so pissed!' says David. 'So this time I completely lost it and I screamed at him, "Hey, Dennis, you're as crazy as your FATHER!" Boy, did that set him off!' With wild eyes, Dennis instantly forgot about Sharon and went straight after David. Fearing certain death, David closed his eyes and took a nothing-to-lose wild swing at his enraged attacker. He solidly connected with his fist and split Dennis's lip wide open. Unfortunately, the punch barely registered with Dennis. Although he was bleeding profusely, he just kept coming. Dave recalls what happened next: 'He tackled me to the ground and just as he was about to kill me, he looked me in the eye, spat blood in my face, and got up and walked away. I couldn't believe he left me alone.' And Dennis ended up with the girl in the end, anyway.

At the same time David and Dennis were getting violent, Brian was experiencing one of his most peaceful periods. 'Once Brian had left the road, his whole attitude changed,' says David. 'He became the old happy and fun Brian that he had once been. Brian felt more at home living with the Rovells than he did at his own house, and it showed on his face.' To entertain the gang at the Rovell home, Brian bought a movie projector and would rent movie reels used for professional screenings from Hollywood studios. 'He'd get everything set up and play all these great movies for us in the Rovells' living room,' remembers David. 'That was something nobody did back then. Brian was at his happiest when he could just be at home and write music, and then go into the studio and make records. This was a particularly happy time for him.'

At times it seemed like The Beach Boys were just one of the acts that Brian wrote songs for and produced. 'We thought he might totally quit the band because he had so many other things going on in the studio,' says David. Around this time Brian was working on records by Bob & Sheri, The Honeys, Jan and Dean, Sharon Marie, Gary Usher, and The Survivors. The Beach Boys were just one of Brian's many musical interests. As it turned out, Jan and Dean were the only other act Brian was involved with that had any hits remotely rivalling the huge success of The Beach Boys. 'Because we were so successful,' says David, 'Brian was kind of stuck with us, and I think maybe that bugged him a little bit.' Another reason that Brian may have been unable to break out beyond The Beach Boys was his own father. Some have suggested that Murry did what he could to sabotage Brian's success with his other groups by influencing DJs to ignore them, especially those singles that weren't published by Murry's Sea of Tunes company. This tactic is consistent with the mischief Murry had in store for David's own non-Beach Boys releases in the coming year.

In May, The Beach Boys played three sold-out shows in Santa Fe Springs, Long Beach, and at a jam-packed Southern

California Hot Rod Show. The latter event was co-sponsored by the National Hot Rod Association and proved to be such a fantastic experience that it inspired David to write a song about it. His original composition called 'Kustom Kar Show' recounted the experience of playing rock and roll among the chrome and metal-flake set. The Beach Boys found that LA's hardcore hot-rodders were much more accepting of them than the surfers had been. 'They had an easier time with the hot-rodders,' says Paul Johnson. 'It was a totally different situation than with surfing because they weren't perceived as posers when it came to cars.' There was none of the scepticism about their legitimacy, but instead a pleasing acceptance of The Beach Boys' musical celebration of their beloved car hobby. With 'Shut Down' riding high on the local charts, the timing of the car show concert couldn't have been better.

On 24 May 1963, the group performed a major concert at the Sacramento Memorial Auditorium in the state's capital. With Al on bass and Brian home in LA, the show was a milestone in the band's career. This was the first date that saw eighteen-year-old Fred Vail as The Beach Boys' concert promoter. Vail booked The Beach Boys through the William Morris Agency for a flat fee of $750. Fan Jeff Hughson, quoted in the *Sacramento Bee*, remembers the experience: 'It was absolute pandemonium at those [Sacramento] shows. People were jumping off the balconies . . . it was wild. The band rocked, everyone went nuts. They were high energy shows.' The Beach Boys played two separate sets performing nearly every song they knew including an unreleased Brian Wilson tune called 'Surfer Girl'. After the wildly successful concert, Fred Vail got his very first chance to socialise with The Beach Boys, with whom he would become close friends in the years ahead. The band paid for their own rooms at the Mansion Inn on 16th Street, and after the concert Vail, Murry and the group sat down for a late-night meal at the hotel coffee shop. 'David was the youngster, for sure,' says Vail. 'The other guys all seemed a lot older to me. I remember Dave goofed off quite a bit. He was just a typical kid. I remember him throwing food and Murry would tell him to quit it and grow up. David would swear, and Murry just hated it when the guys used that kind of language. He'd get into mischief, but not anything different than other kids his age would have done. Sometimes he'd kind of get carried away with his importance because he was in this famous group. But it wasn't always just Dave who would cut up. Sometimes Dennis would mouth off and Mike too. Carl was clearly the most serious one.'

The day after the Sacramento concert the 'Surfin' USA' single peaked at number three on the Billboard national pop chart. That day, while The Beach Boys prepared for a concert at Inglewood High School, another classic Brian Wilson composition headed towards its place in music history. The song was called 'Surf City', and it was released by Brian's friends Jan and Dean. 'We used to do mini tours with Jan and Dean and back them up instrumentally when they were on stage,' remembers David. 'Jan had a real animal-house kind of mentality. He was always trying to be funny and causing problems. He was a general menace, and always driving like a maniac.' Jan caused a definite problem in The Beach Boys camp when the song he co-wrote and sang with Brian became a massive seller. 'I remember when Jan and Dean's "Surf City" became a hit and that it really pissed Murry off that Brian had given it to them,' says David. 'I didn't get sucked into the jealousy thing but I remember that Carl and Mike were pissed off at Brian about it too. But all of that shit kind of went over my head because it didn't really affect my life as I saw it. I was just a little kid really.'

Around that time, the notorious Jan Berry made even more waves when Jan and Dean joined The Beach Boys for a series of shows in Northern California. With the enterprise becoming more successful, the group now booked flights instead of spending hours driving across the state in cars. As their plane departed LAX that May for The Beach Boys/Jan and Dean shows, Berry let loose his idea of humour in the confines of a commercial airliner. 'When the plane taxied down the runway, Jan began kicking his feet into the air and yelling, "It's a take off! It's a take off! We're all going to die!" He was pounding the pillow against his head and screaming,' says David. 'It was freaking out everybody on the plane. And this was just fun for him. My dad was there and he looked like he wanted to kill him. But Jan continued to act up no matter how many people told him to cool it. He was scaring all the passengers. By the time we were flying over Fresno, the pilot came back and threatened to kick Jan off because he was goofing around so much, screaming and scaring old ladies. The pilot got right in Jan's face and yelled, "I'll land this sonofabitch right in a field if you don't settle down right now!"' Jan's reply was, 'Don't you know me? I'm Jan and Dean!'

Over the next week, The Beach Boys played California bookings in the cities of Bellflower, San Francisco, Oxnard, Palmdale and Bakersfield. The Bakersfield concert was especially notable for the fact that the group backed soul legends Sam Cooke and Lou Rawls during their combined set. They then flew to Texas and played to thousands of fans in Houston. There the group backed yet another music legend. They took the stage and provided backing for bluesman Jimmy Reed during his set before playing a long set of their own. While in Houston, the group recorded radio promotion spots and signed autographs at two local record stores. It seemed that their surfing/car sound had caught on in just about every market in the States. But the gravy train suddenly ran dry for David. According to Jo Ann Marks's records, David Marks received no payment for any Beach Boys concert from this point forward. Murry insisted that to cover growing expenses, the band's profits from concert appearances had to be recycled back into The Beach Boys franchise, of which David had a twenty per cent share. There was also the issue of David being fined for cussing and other acts that Murry considered insubordinate. No one was quite sure if Dave's sudden lack of payments was the result of a group business strategy or due to the constant fines draining away his income. As a result, Murry and David's parents began to clash over financial issues, and the growing tension between them became constant. 'I'd worked all my life and I wasn't going to let anyone fool around with us,' says Jo Ann. 'And because we stood up to Murry, he kind of had it in for David.'

Upon returning to LA, the group quickly recorded both sides of their next single at Western. This time Brian dusted off one of his oldest compositions, the ballad 'Surfer Girl', and the group rose to the challenge of capturing its definitive version. David was already well acquainted with the song because Brian had taught it to him long before there was a band called The Beach Boys. Back then it didn't have 'surfing' lyrics, but it basically retained the same romantic lyrical thrust and musical arrangement. On the recording of 'Surfer Girl', David's guitar strumming is thick and prominent throughout, while Carl's picking stands out clearly on the song's memorable bridge. 'Surfer Girl' would ultimately become one of The Beach Boys' best-loved tunes, in addition to being a huge hit on the pop charts. The other side of the new single was a wonderful new 'hot rod' tune written by Brian and LA disc jockey Roger Christian. The song 'Little Deuce Coupe' had a tremendous harmony arrangement and a great shuffle beat. The instrumental mix was piano heavy although Carl and Dave's bright guitars meshed well with the production. 'Little Deuce Coupe' became yet another major hit and took its deserved place among the upper echelon of all-time Beach Boys classics. And David had played on more than a few of them by now. Although most journalists have dismissed him as a blip on The Beach Boys' historical radar, when you add up all The Beach Boys anthems David's guitar was a part of, one would think he'd be more recognised. And he wasn't done yet.

On 14 June 1963, The Beach Boys travelled to Hawaii for a nine-day tour. Brian again refused to make the trip, and the group was forced to perform their concerts with Al on bass. Elmer Marks once again filled the role of tour manager, and this time, Audree Wilson came along to assist him. Back in LA, Jo Ann would spend most of the nine days hiding from Murry. Also on the Hawaii tour were singers Jackie DeShannon and Dee Dee Sharp, whom The Beach Boys provided instrumental backing for during their respective sets.

To ensure that David would give his all to her songs, the pretty blonde DeShannon regularly flirted with him before her sets. She'd get really close to David in the backstage area, and in her sexiest voice she'd whisper into his ear that she wanted him to play real good for her. Unfortunately, this sex-as-a-weapon strategy backfired, as her attention only made David more distracted and forgetful.

One of the greatest things about the Hawaii tour was that Elmer Marks documented precious snippets of the trip on David's new Bell + Howell movie camera. Included in Elmer's footage are segments of the boys cutting up, hanging out on the beach, and flirting with local girls. Elmer also managed to capture a few minutes of the group performing 'Monster Mash' and several other tunes on stage, as well as footage of Dennis trying to teach the others to surf. As it turned out, Elmer's Hawaii reel is the earliest known moving footage of the band on tour, and, in addition, it provides clear documentation that The Beach Boys were already performing without Brian in 1963.

Staying at the same Waikiki Beach hotel as The Beach Boys during their Hawaii visit was country music legend Red Foley. A working musician since the 1930s and a country music hall-of-famer, Foley was nearing the end of his long musical trail. His body was worse for wear from years of hard drinking, and he'd be dead in only a few years. Carl Wilson was a major fan of Foley's music and was absolutely thrilled to meet the Grand Ole Opry veteran. After first encountering the old cowboy at the hotel lounge, David and Carl were invited up to his room for some serious drinking. 'We spent a fair amount of the night in his room, listening to his stories and guzzling Southern Comfort,' remembers David. 'He was really old and we listened to his stories about the road and drank whisky with him into the night. I had no idea who he was until Carl explained to me that he was a country music icon. I was also surprised to hear he was Pat Boone's father-in-law. He was old and fucked up and had the shakes from drinking too much. But I felt Carl's excitement about being in his presence, and that really impressed me.'

Downing Southern Comfort with Red Foley was only one of the ways the boys passed time between concerts while in Hawaii. 'We drove around the island in convertibles, we rented surfboards, sailboats and motorbikes, and we annoyed all the women on the beach,' says David. They also invited packs of local girls and tourists back to their rooms for nightly parties. At one such party, a drunken David was carelessly sitting on the thin railing of a fifth-floor balcony when he suddenly slipped over the edge. Just as he was falling over the side to what would surely be a crushing landing on the cement below, Mike somehow reached out with one hand and snagged David by his ankle. 'I literally saved his life,' remembers Mike. 'I caught him by the ankle as he was going backwards over the balcony.' In one motion, Mike pulled him back to safety, and he did so without even the slightest break in his conversation with a pretty girl. A shaken David sat on the floor of the balcony wondering what had just happened. Once Mike finished talking to the girl, he turned to Dave and gently warned, 'You better watch it, kid.' David points out how Mike had kept his word to Elmer. 'He sure lived up to his pledge to keep an eye on me for my father that night.'

With another successful tour behind them, The Beach Boys returned home. Brian instantly informed them that a new LP needed to be recorded right away. Several days of rehearsals were held at the Wilson home to learn Brian's new material before the band flew to Las Vegas on 29 June, where they performed another concert and promoted their new single. On 5 July, they embarked on yet another flight, this time to Phoenix, Arizona, for a concert and a local TV appearance. More rehearsals and a concert in Buena Park filled the following week. Finally, the band gathered at Western and commenced recording sessions for their third LP, to be called *Surfer Girl*. To everyone's surprise, Brian hired session drummer Hal Blaine to replace Dennis on his slinky new song, 'Our Car Club'. This was the first time Blaine performed on a Beach Boys session, although Brian had previously used him on his outside productions. Brian initially considered using the basic track for Marilyn and her group The Honeys, but then decided to perfect it as a Beach Boys vocal. David was just thrilled to be playing in the studio with Blaine, who was already known as LA's finest studio drummer. On the recording of 'Our Car Club', David and Carl provided a wicked pulsating guitar texture that perfectly meshed with Blaine's driving backbeat and tom fills. Dennis adequately handled the rest of the LP's drumming, although Blaine was used on timbales to enhance the feel on Brian and Mike's rocking new song called 'Hawaii', written after Mike gushed to Brian about the group's recent trip. With the whole band already functioning at their highest level, Brian also added auxiliary Beach Boy Al Jardine to the instrumental mix on a number of the LP's tunes. According to historian Craig Slowinski, the session tapes reveal Al is definitely there for the tracking of 'Surfer's Rule' and 'Boogie Woodie', on which he plays bass. The melody for the group's rocking instrumental 'Boogie Woodie' is taken from Rimsky-Korsakov's 'Flight of The Bumble Bee', but the feel of The Beach Boys' version is pure Audree Wilson-style boogie-woogie.

Mrs Wilson forever influenced her sons and David by teaching each of them the same piano style during the pre-Beach Boys years. 'David says today that the rhythm guitar he was playing on those early Beach Boys records was actually a boogie-woogie piano rhythm line but with the surf guitar sound,' says Carrie Marks. 'He said by tightening up the rhythm from straight chords to that tight driving style, and by adding the pinky move, he could get a boogie-woogie/rock and roll piano part to sound like surf guitar. David says it wasn't a conscious decision, it's just what came to him, but it was something nobody else was doing at the time, and it became part of the uniqueness and identity of The Beach Boys. It was Audree who taught him how to play that style of music on the piano, and she also taught Carl, Brian and Dennis the exact same piano part. It sort of clicked in David's head how Audree was a big influence on all of the boys musically, much more than Murry; Audree's piano feel was a common musical thread they were all connected to. All of them had their earliest introduction to that music at the same piano bench,

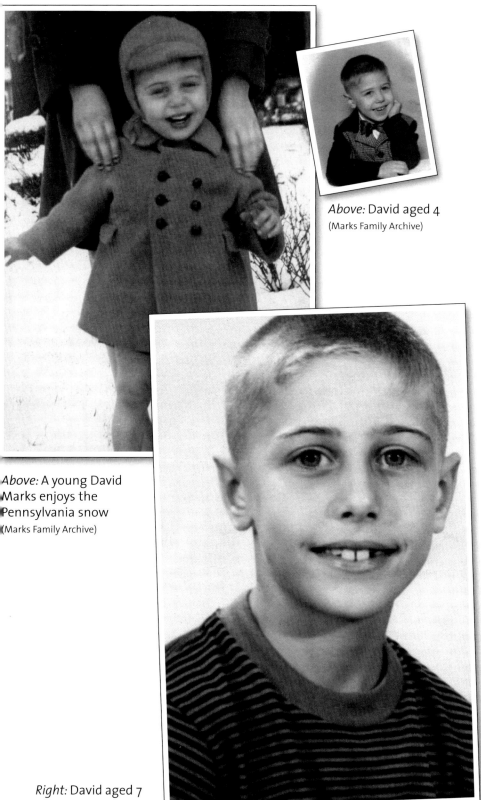

Above: David aged 4
(Marks Family Archive)

Above: A young David
Marks enjoys the
Pennsylvania snow
(Marks Family Archive)

Right: David aged 7
(Marks Family Archive)

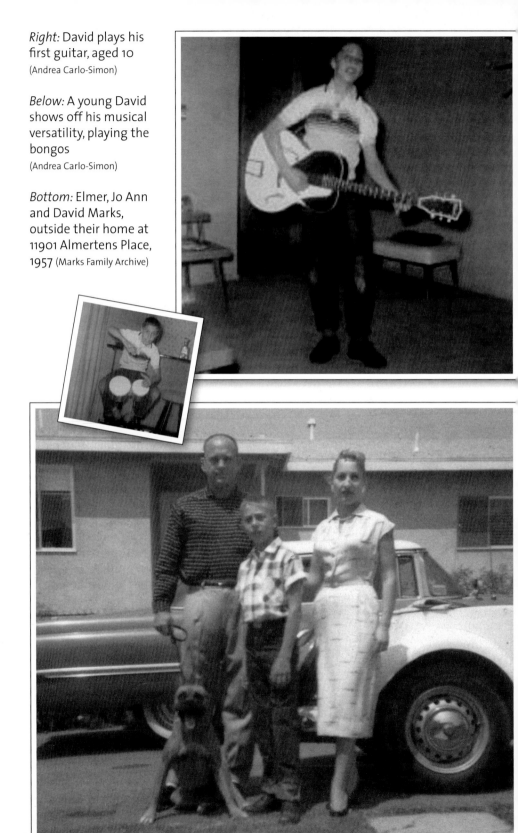

Right: David plays his first guitar, aged 10 (Andrea Carlo-Simon)

Below: A young David shows off his musical versatility, playing the bongos (Andrea Carlo-Simon)

Bottom: Elmer, Jo Ann and David Marks, outside their home at 11901 Almertens Place, 1957 (Marks Family Archive)

Right: Carl Wilson, David Marks, Jo Ann Marks and Dennis Wilson after the Hawthorne Fair, 1962
(Marks Family Archive)

Left: Carl Wilson and Mark Groseclose, 1957
(Kathy Groseclose-Michael)

Below: Two Beach Boys moms: Jo Ann Marks and Audree Wilson chat in front of the Marks home
(Marks Family Archive)

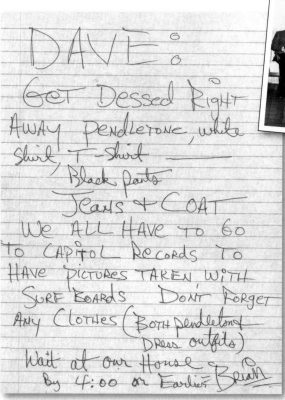

DAVE:
GET Dessed RIGHT
AWAY PENdLETONE, white
Shirt, T-shirt ——
Black pants
Jeans + COAT
We ALL HAVE TO GO
TO CAPITOL ReCords TO
HAVE PICTURES TAKEN WITH
SURF BOARDS   DON'T FORGET
ANY CloTHes (BOTH pendleton
                        DRess outfits)
Wait at our House
By 4:00 on Earlier Brian

Above: The Marks and Wilson families appear in LA Superior Court, 1962 (Marks Family Archive/courtesy of David Beard ESQ)

Left: A note from Brian to Dave (Marks Family Archive)

Below: A pre-Capitol Records Beach Boys perform at the Bel Air Bay Club, 1962 (Capitol Records/Marks Family Archive)

Right: Al, David and Mike playing to thousands in Sacremento in late 1963
(Fred Vail/Treasure Isle Recorders)

Below: The Beach Boys live in Los Angleles in 1962, snapped by Elmer Marks
(Marks Family Archive)

Below: A rare Beach Boys concert poster: Sacramento 1963
(Fred Vail/Treasure Isle Recorders)

 Frederick Vail Productions

PRESENTS

THE BEACH BOYS

THE NO. 1 SURFING GROUP IN THE COUNTRY

Sacramento Memorial Auditorium

SATURDAY, SEPTEMBER 14

—— Two fun filled shows ——

Beach Boy Albums Given Away Free at Each Show
— FREE PICTURES TO ALL ATTENDING —

LATEST RELEASE

rfer Girl
B/W
le Deuce
Coupe

Capitol
CLASSICS

Out Soon!
A new LP
"Surfer Girl"
(SIT 1981)

ADVANCE TICKETS AVAILABLE AT

JACK'S HOUSE OF MUSIC
OPPOSITE COUNTRY CLUB CENTRE and
6749 FAIR OAKS BLVD., CARMICHAEL

CIVIC THEATRE BOX OFFICE
1419 H STREET · GI 1-3163

SOUTHGATE RECORDS
SOUTHGATE SHOPPING CENTER

Camp Malibu

*Dear Mudduh &
Fadduh,*

*Camp is over Satur-
day. Please pick me and
Jeffrey up at noon so
that we'll be home in
time for the Beach Boys
Concert at 2:15. Parents
can get in free if they
come with thier child-
ren.*

ALVIN

*P. S. The Evening Show
is at 8:00 P.M. for any-
one who can stay out
late.*

5 P. M. Pre-teen and Young Teeners 1.25
(Parent admitted free with child)

0 P. M. EVENING ALL SHOW SEATS ADVANCE 1.75 AT DOOR 2.00

Left: Brian and an enthusiastic David in the studio 1962
(Capitol Records)

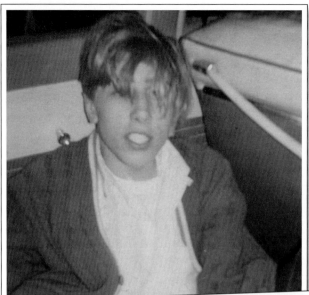

Left: Dennis snaps David on tour in 1963
(Marks Family Archive)

Below: The Beach Boys backstage with Fred Vail, 1963
(Fred Vail/Treasure Isle Recorders)

Left: Dennis Wilson jamming with friends in 1962
(Marks Family Archive)

Right: Jan Berry, Mike Love, a fan, Dean Torrence and Brian Wilson mock the Surfer Girl album cover shot with David, backstage in 1963
(Fred Vail/Treasure Isle Recorders)

Below: The Beach Boys say goodbye to David by tossing him in the pool, October 1963
(Marks Family Archive)

**Meet the Beach Boys: 1 song writer,
1 arranger, 5 singers, 2 guitarists,
1 drummer, and 2 students.**

They started surfing music. With a record called "Surfin' Safari."
And they started hot rod music. With "Shut Down."

The Beach Boys have had one great hit after another. Wild songs
like "Be True To Your School" and "Little Deuce Coupe." Quiet ballads like "Surfer Girl" and "In My Room."

When you know the Beach Boys, this success isn't surprising.
Because they like the kind of music you like. And because they are
five talented and hard working guys. Brian writes and arranges
most of their songs himself. And sings the lead along with Mike.
Carl and Dave play guitar any way you want... rockin' or dreamy
or anything in between. And Dennis sings... while he raps out the
beat on the drums.

With every album, the Beach Boys put their tremendous talent and
versatility on display.

Listen to the Beach Boys on Capitol, and you'll hear what we mean.

For a start, listen to these newest Beach Boys albums:

Top left: No longer a Beach Boy, David
in the early days of 1964
(Marks Family Archive)

Top right: David Marks, 1966
(Marks Family Archive)

Above: David and Mark signing with
A&M Records with their finest Jay
Sebring hairdos (Marks Family Archive)

Left: A 1964 Capitol Records ad shows
that David was still marketed as a
Beach Boy, long after he left the band
(Carol Ann Dreier Collection)

with the same woman, being taught the same groove. Then they each added their own twist but the underlying root was always there. You can't get that magic with just any group of random guys. David finally really gets that after forty-plus years.'

On the recording of 'Boogie Woodie', Dennis, Carl and David heard Brian kick off on the keyboards with the same Audree lick they'd all heard a million times. Like thoroughbreds out of the gate, they all just take off and go. Al was in a separate space, playing bass direct in the booth standing next to Murry. Murry had to tell the others to slow down so Al could keep up with his bass runs. Apparently, Audree never taught him the lick. Al also played bass on Brian's terrific new tune called 'Catch A Wave'. For this classic number, Brian asked David and Carl to create a unique feel with their guitars. ' "Catch A Wave" was more rhythmic,' remembers Brian in his liner notes for the *Surfer Girl* LP's 1990 CD release. 'The guitars were more clean and driving as if to say that they didn't want to stop,' said Brian. 'The piano was played by me and it was perfectly synchronised with the guitars. The three different sounds combined to make one unique sound. I was ecstatic about this.' By bringing Al in to the sessions to cover some of the bass playing, Brian was freed up to concentrate more on playing keyboards, arranging and producing. In fact, the *Surfer Girl* LP is the first to officially credit Brian as The Beach Boys producer. The results are fabulous, especially on the amazing ballad 'In My Room'. Without a doubt one of The Beach Boys greatest ballads ever, 'In My Room' might be the ultimate example of the original six-man Beach Boys line-up hitting their stride. The tune includes a great vocal blend that starts off with the three Wilson boys but then quickly adds Al and Mike to the mix. It also features tender, deep guitar picking from Carl, and lush strumming from David, all of which makes 'In My Room' a perfect Beach Boys cocktail. 'Of the earliest LPs on which David appears, I think *Surfer Girl* is my favourite,' says Jeff Foskett. 'I don't think David's guitar playing is any less prevalent on this record than on *Surfin' USA*.'

On the final night of the *Surfer Girl* LP sessions, David broke out his old Sears Silvertone acoustic guitar to play on The Beach Boys' recording of 'Your Summer Dream'. The session lasted longer than most, and proved to be a gruelling but highly productive affair. After their hard day's night was finally done, David and Dennis continued their nightly ritual of going out for chilli dogs. 'When we were recording those albums and we'd be working every night until 2 a.m., afterwards Dennis and I would always go to this place called Pops that was open twenty-four hours. They had these great chilli dogs that Dennis just loved. We stopped there every night and ate those chilli dogs. We didn't discover Pink's until later.' As Dave and Dennis leaned against the sleek hood of Dennis's midnight-blue Corvette, eating, they reflected on the blurry path behind them. Although the point they had arrived at was far removed from where they were the summer before, Dave and Dennis were basically the same two kids. 'This past year was so damn busy, and I'm so damn tired,' said David. 'It was like ten years jammed into one.' Dennis thought for a few seconds about what Dave had just said and then answered, 'Yeah, it went by like ten years in ten minutes.'

Within days, the group was back in concert action again. A caravan of performers left LA and drove up Highway 101 for a big weekend concert in Santa Maria, California. Joining The Beach Boys on the bill were The Honeys and Gary Usher's Four Speeds. That month, while the *Surfin' USA* LP was sitting at number two on the Billboard album chart, The Beach Boys had literally become a household name. With that in mind, Murry booked another extended tour of the Midwest and Eastern states. As plans for the tour went forward, Murry coldly informed Elmer Marks that his services as tour manager were no longer needed. Instead, Murry had hired 'professional' road manager John Hamilton to fill that role. Hamilton was best known for his stint as a tour manager for The Ventures. Jo Ann and Elmer felt they were being cut out of the loop due to underlying issues unrelated to Elmer's effectiveness on the job. Murry, of course, denied this.

In mid-July 1963, The Beach Boys embarked on their longest tour yet. The group would not return to Los Angeles until the last day of August, making the tour over forty days long. After months of Murry's badgering, Brian finally succumbed to the pressure and rejoined the touring Beach Boys. From this point until his subsequent unravelling in late 1964, the group played the vast majority of its live shows with Brian in the line-up. Al Jardine once again found himself the odd man out for a time. The group minus Mike flew out of LAX on 18 July. For this tour, the usual Chevy wagon and U-Haul trailer set-up was used, but this time Mike drove out in his new Jaguar sedan, which was used to ease the group's cramped conditions while driving from gig to gig. From 19–21 July, the group played concerts at the Ideal Beach Resort in Monticello, Indiana, at the Danceland Ballroom in Cedar Rapids, Iowa, and at the Cobblestone Ballroom in Storm Lake, Iowa. Each show was considered a huge success.

The band was given the day off on 22 July, the same day the 'Surfer Girl'/'Little Deuce Coupe' single was released in the United States. While resting in his hotel room, Mike came upon the idea of using the song 'Little Deuce Coupe' as a vehicle to announce the individual members of the group in concert. Mike's rehearsed patter became a staple of future Beach Boys concerts. 'Some of you have asked how we go about making a record,' Mike would tell the audience. 'First we start with Denny on the drums. Then we add Dave on the rhythm guitar. Then it's Carl on the lead guitar. And our leader Brian fills things out on the bass. When we step up to the microphones to sing, it comes out something like this . . .' And with that, the band jumped into their latest hit single.

While in Iowa, Dennis and David found time to rent a speedboat and go water-skiing on Lake Okoboji. Many locals were aware that two of the famous Beach Boys were on the lake that day, and stories still circulate about their visit. Dennis was an expert skier and had a great time while David towed him around the lake. When it was time for David to take his turn, he was a bit nervous. Dennis was behind the wheel and raring to go. After getting some pointers, David managed to get up on two skis and was doing fine until Dennis began to weave and drive the boat in tight circles like a wild man. Eventually, he had the boat going full speed, with David holding onto the rope for dear life. Then Dennis pointed the boat straight at the shoreline, and only veered off at the last second. David rocketed across the wake and slammed into the shore. With his skis flying in different directions, Dave face-planted in the mud, and then bounced and tumbled to a stop. David stood up, spitting mud and gravel out of his mouth, and began to scream at Dennis. 'Fuck you, Dennis, you son of a bitch! There's a hundred fucking miles of water out there and you had to drive me onto dry land, you asshole!' Dennis could not contain his laughter. As he helped a seething David back into the boat, Dennis asked him, 'Hey, Dave, why didn't you just let go of the rope?' Dave wiped some dirt from his eyes and said, 'Fuck . . . I didn't think of that.'

That evening, the group gathered up a bag of snacks and beverages and settled on a grassy hill overlooking Lake Okoboji. The occasion of the impromptu picnic was to listen to the much-hyped Sonny Liston versus Floyd Patterson heavyweight championship fight on Dennis's transistor radio. Brian was particularly excited about the big boxing match and began yelling at the radio as soon as it commenced. Before the first beer had been opened, Liston knocked Patterson senseless, and the fight was over in less than two minutes. Brian started screaming, 'What happened? I wanted to hear a goddamned fight! That wasn't even a fight!'

On 23 July, the group played a well-received concert at the Roof Garden Ballroom in Arnolds Park, Iowa. Among the other acts that performed there in July were Roy Orbison, The Everly Brothers, and Johnny and the Hurricanes. The next day the group performed another show in Sioux City, Iowa, at the Shore Acres Ballroom. On the drive across Iowa, Brian sang the old song 'Sioux City Sue' over and over, to the point of causing a rattled John Hamilton to ask the others, 'Is he ever going to stop?' Dave quickly answered, 'No he won't!' Brian was notorious for getting fixated on a tune and working it to death, usually at the piano. Cramped in a car and fighting off the misery of touring, all Brian had was his voice, and at times he went into a trance while endlessly humming or singing a melody. Finally, Carl broke the monotony by adding a little harmony, which made Brian smile. Soon Brian was teaching the whole gang intricate vocal parts, and rearranging the old standard to suit himself. And with that, everyone in the car – including Hamilton – sang along to 'Sioux City Sue' all the way to Sioux City.

The Beach Boys played a jam-packed concert in Des Moines, Iowa, on 25 July 1963. After the show, Dennis and Mike decided the time had come for the 'two losers', David and Carl, to become men. At fourteen, Dave already had some heavy petting experience with girls, but he'd always stopped short of going all the way. Although two years older, Carl was even less experienced than David, and he admitted the whole idea of sex kind of scared him. But grizzled tour veteran John Hamilton not only approved of the idea, he actually made arrangements with hookers for the whole group. Dave was cool with the plan, but Carl turned to Brian for a reasonable perspective. Unfortunately, his big brother was too wrapped up in a marathon phone call with girlfriend Marilyn to even weigh in. While Brian stayed behind, the others all piled into the Chevy wagon, bought a bottle of whisky, and drove to a sleazy hotel in downtown Des Moines to keep their appointment.

As Dennis and Mike egged them on, David and Carl finally took the plunge with some local prostitutes. 'Mine was reading the newspaper and said, "Let me know when you're done, kid." Twenty-five seconds later, I was a man,' remembers David. 'After that, Carl had his turn. I guess he took it more seriously than me because when he came out he was crying. The next day we were in Rockford, Illinois, signing autographs at a local record shop. Brian was back at the hotel. He usually had no interest in anything that was happening on the road. He just wanted to be home. As we were signing records, our crotches started itching like mad. We were scratching away, and all the kids lined up to get autographs were looking at us with puzzled faces. Mike and Dennis got up and went to the bathroom and came back with the bad news – we all had crabs.'

Back at their hotel, they treated their worsening lice problem with ointment that burned their skin, causing them to leap around the hotel room naked. Soon they realised they were doing all the jumping in front of an open hotel window, giving guests an interesting perspective on The Beach Boys. Hamilton bought two shopping bags full of whisky and beer to help ease their discomfort. That night, a drunken Dennis painted his penis green, stuck a toothbrush in his butt, and ran down the hotel hallway scaring little old ladies. Murry's decision to replace Elmer with John Hamilton was certainly having an interesting effect.

The group continued along their gruelling path with shows at the Penny Park Ballroom in Omaha, Nebraska, on 28 and 29 July, the Coliseum Ballroom in Davenport, Iowa, on the 30th, and a sold-out show in Waupaca, Wisconsin, on the 31st. When the group returned to play a packed house at the Surf Ballroom in Clear Lake, Iowa, on 1 August, there were no complaints from management this time about their volume. With the tour only a third over, everyone was aware that Brian was miserable and badly wanted to go home, and the aura of Buddy Holly and the Surf seemed to take him to an even darker place. That night he called his dad and talked for an hour. Brian pleaded for a ticket home but Murry refused. He wouldn't even consider why Brian couldn't handle the road and insisted he 'toughen up and be professional'.

On 2 August 1963, The Beach Boys played a fantastic concert at the Prom Ballroom in St Paul, Minnesota. The audience literally swarmed the stage: one female fan tore David's shirt, several other girls tried to maul Dennis, and another tightly hugged Brian until she was peeled off by security. The group rewarded their enthusiasm with multiple encores, a rarity in 1963. After the show, while the others hauled away the group's equipment, a weary-but-wired Dennis sat down at the house piano and played a soothing tune. 'When Dennis was a little kid, he taught himself how to play "Moonlight Sonata" on the piano,' remembers David.

'He'd play that after our shows sometimes when we were breaking down our equipment because there was often a piano on stage. And when he did that it was like a chick magnet. "Look, the drummer's playing the piano!" Any girls that were hanging around would get all excited and rush to the piano bench. They'd all be sitting around him listening to him play. And we'd all be jealous. I failed to recognise it at the time, but he was already blossoming as an artist right then by doing that. He was already tapping into that whole romantic vibe that he nailed so well later on with his own songs.'

On 3 August, it was back in the Chevy for the drive to Austin, Minnesota, and a concert at the Terp Ballroom. Then it was another show at the Kato Ballroom in Mankato, Minnesota, on the 4th, followed by a concert in Harbor Springs, Michigan, on the 5th, another in Waterloo, Iowa, on the 6th, and yet another in Ithaca, Michigan, on the 7th. While slogging through their brutal tour, the group received some incredible news. The 'Surfin' USA' single had found its way into the Top Ten in Australia as well as hitting a modest number 34 in the UK. Murry called and told the boys they were becoming an international hit, and an overseas tour would be in the offing. For now, the group was running on fumes, trying to make it through another exhausting stretch of gigs. They were all sick with colds or the flu, and hadn't had more than a couple of hours of sleep in days. Time was passed on long drives by constantly smoking cigarettes, eating bad food and occasionally swigging bourbon, Scotch or vodka. Unfortunately, getting drunk was the only sure way to relax in a constantly speeding car. Dennis did most of the driving in the Chevy, as it seemed he never got tired, while Mike set his own pace in the Jaguar, often bringing a morose Brian along with him.

Between 9 and 16 August, the group performed at the Cold Springs Resort in Hamilton, Indiana, the Auditorium Theater in Chicago, Illinois, the Palace Ballroom in Old Orchard Park, Maine, the Brewer Auditorium in Brewer, Maine, the Surf Auditorium in Hill, Massachusetts, and the Mountain Top

Ballroom in Holyoke, Massachusetts. On 17 August, the group entered Dave's old stomping ground for a series of shows in his birth state of Pennsylvania. 'There were a few people who came out of the woodwork when we played the Pennsylvania area,' remembers David. 'They'd come up and say, "Hey, Dave, remember me?" It was usually distant cousins or old friends from school.' It struck David that he must be a celebrity when distant relatives or friends with a vague connection to him made a big deal about coming out to see him play.

At the Wayne County Fair in Homedale, Pennsylvania, on 17 August, the group played yet another well-received set. Found among Elmer's items was a quickly scribbled and water-damaged list bearing the heading 'First set for Wayne County Fair'.

Surfin Safari
409
Deuce Coupe – group intro
Runaway
Blue City
Farmer's Daughter
Monster Mash
Movin N Groovin
Silly Boy – Dennis sings, Dave drums
Papa Ooh Mow Mow
Honky Tonk
Shut Down
Louie Louie – Dave sings
Surfer Girl
Let's Go Trippin'
Surfin' USA
Johnny B Goode
Encore: What'd I Say – Carl sings

On 18 August, the group performed at Lakewood Park in Mahanoy, Pennsylvania, on 20 August they played at Reinold Brothers Hall in Transfer, Pennsylvania, and on the 21st it was a show at Westview Park in Pittsburgh. While rushing from gig to gig across Pennsylvania, Dennis and the group were inevitably pulled over by the local police for speeding. The officer informed Dennis that he was travelling at 82 miles per hour in a zone that was limited to 50. He also noticed a few empty beer bottles lying on the floor in the back seat. 'You boys haven't been drinking, now, have you?' said the cop. 'Sorry, officer, but we're The Beach Boys and we're on our way to a big concert,' explained Dennis. Seemingly unimpressed, the cop ordered the group to trail him and another officer to the local station where their fine would be settled. The officers radioed ahead, informing the dispatcher that they'd landed a big one. After dutifully following their motorcycle escort to the Lake Erie police headquarters, the group walked up the steep concrete steps to the station, not knowing what to expect. Upon entering, they found a celebratory atmosphere filled with uniformed Beach Boys fans. Dennis, David and Carl spent the next twenty minutes signing autographs and posing for photos with the officers and their families. After patiently and cheerily satisfying the police department's requests, they were let go with just a warning.

Hurrying to the next gig, David and The Beach Boys travelled right through David's old neighbourhood. That morning the *New Castle Pennsylvania News* ran the headline DAVID MARKS TOURS WITH BEACH BOYS over an article that gushed about the local boy who'd made it big. Thoughts of his mornings at Grandma Carlo's house, his musical 'uncles' Benny and Johnny, and his long-lost playmates at Rose Avenue School flashed through David's exhausted mind. He felt as if he'd travelled to a place a million miles removed from those days, and the road ahead just kept getting longer.

On 22 August 1963, David celebrated his fifteenth birthday in style. After playing a concert at an amusement park in Wheeling, West Virginia, David and Dennis met a flamboyant millionaire. Upon learning it was Dave's birthday, their new friend took them to dinner at his local yacht club, which was situated elegantly on a river. After they had devoured a gourmet meal and a bottle of good Scotch, the man arranged for David and Dennis to enjoy a very good-looking hooker. 'See that girl over there,' the man said, pointing to a blonde beauty that David and Dennis had already noticed. 'You can have her,' the man said. 'She's all yours.' In a flash, Dennis grabbed her and rocketed up the stairs to where the man had told them there was an empty room waiting for them. 'I was a little pissed off, since it was my birthday and Dennis took her first,' says David. 'When he came back downstairs, he smiled and said, "Go ahead, buddy, I warmed her up for you." I had a much better time than I did with the last hooker,' says David. 'I was probably up there for a good ten minutes!' It was a night that David would never forget. Unfortunately, Dennis and David both contracted venereal disease from the experience – not exactly the kind of birthday present Dave was hoping for.

Throughout the entire tour, Mike Love was constantly bugging David to write a letter to his parents, telling him it was the respectful thing to do. Despite the fact that Murry's 'road rules' had been roundly ignored for weeks, Mike was still trying to adhere to Elmer's request that he look out for young David. He badgered him daily about writing home: 'Dave, have you written your mom yet? You really should, you know. They're your parents, after all. I'm sure they're wondering about you. You should take a few minutes and jot a letter to them. C'mon, David, you know I'm right.' David finally got fed up with Mike's endless prodding and sat down to write a letter home. Once he'd finished, he proudly showed the results to Mike. The letter read:

Dear Mom and Dad,

I'm having a fucking great time on the road! We're drinking lots of whisky and screwing whores in every town. My dick is oozing green pus but don't worry, we're all getting penicillin shots soon. I can't wait to tell you about the rest of the things we've done. See you in a week!

Love, David

After a moment of silence, Mike literally fell to the floor laughing. 'That's the hardest I've ever seen Mike laugh before or since,' says David. 'He said the funniest part was that the letter was truthful. After that he never bugged me about writing home again.'

On 23 August, the group performed at Le Soursdville Lake Park in Dayton, Ohio, and on the 24th they played from 7.30 p.m. to midnight at the Midway Ballroom in Cedar Lake, Indiana. The following three days the group performed without Brian, who returned to LA to produce a Survivors recording session and to see Marilyn. It is not clear whether Al replaced him or whether the band played as a four-piece. Brian returned to the road on 28 August to finish the tour. The Beach Boys with Brian on bass performed at the Avalon Ballroom in La Crosse, Wisconsin, on the 29th. The band played two sets in three hours, polishing off the last notes of their encore 'Johnny B Goode' just after 10 p.m.

Brian informed the others that Murry had caught wind of their exploits and was flying out to finish the tour with them. In the past weeks, several hotel managers had called The Beach Boys' office to complain about damaged property. In addition to that, a concert promoter had also called to inform Murry that some members of the band were drinking hard alcohol before and after a show in Wisconsin, and that Dennis had punched him when he confronted them. Murry was livid when he heard the reports, and jumped on the first plane east. The group sullenly packed their gear into the U-Haul and drove for hours to Chicago's O'Hare airport to meet Murry and face the music. To lighten the mood, Brian decided to buy five pipes so that each member of the group could be puffing on one when they met him. When Murry saw the gag he actually laughed a little bit, but then his mood quickly darkened. The first order of business was to fire John Hamilton and put him on a plane home. Murry never admitted that hiring him was a mistake, but it's clear his 'professional' road manager had badly let him down.

The boys and Murry jumped back into the Chevy, with Mike following along in his Jag, and headed for the tour's final gig in Brooklyn, New York. They drove through the night, and along the way all hell broke loose when Dennis boldly informed Murry that some of them had contracted venereal disease from prostitutes. Murry told them he'd never be able to trust them again and admitted he was worried that Jo Ann and Elmer might sue him for endangering their minor son. 'How could you do this to me? Brian, Carl, I thought I could at least trust you boys,' griped Murry. 'Where was Mike when I needed him?' 'Having fun like the rest of us!' said David. Murry gave David a look that made him fear for his life. Murry lit his pipe and puffed away. The band sat silently as endless lonely miles of highway passed by. Finally Murry spoke up again, telling the boys that once they arrived in New York, he'd get their VD problem taken care of. Later, in a note to Audree, he explained, 'I kept $275 [from the box office receipts] because the boys wanted to go to the doc to get penicillin shots.'

Murry continued to puff and verbally pound on the group as they drove. Dennis tried to turn on the car's radio but Murry slapped his hand away. 'You need to listen to me, son,' he said. Smoking his pipe, waving his arms, and listing all the things the group had done to disrespect him, Murry was on a roll. Then he singled out David. He told the others David was the worst example of them all. He got right in David's face and yelled, 'You are unprofessional, you've got a bad attitude, and you need to grow up!'

Finally, David had heard enough. 'We've been out here busting our butts for a month and a half!' he shouted. 'We're making *you* rich. Don't we get any credit for that?'

Murry replied in a superior tone, 'You broke all the rules, my boy. You disrespected me, Audree and your parents. You boys should all be ashamed. I set the rules, David. If you don't like them you are welcome to leave.' And it was at that point that David fired back the words that would change Beach Boys history: 'OK, I quit!'

David was startled by Murry's lightning-quick reaction to those words. He immediately jumped up and gleefully bellowed, 'OK, everybody, you heard that, David quit!' Dave remembers, 'At that moment I wasn't too sure that I really wanted to quit.' But Murry liked the idea, saying, 'Remember this, boys. David quit, that's it, he's out of the band.'

Brian Wilson related his recollection of the incident to *Entertainment Tonight*. 'David got into an argument with my dad on the way to New York in the car and David said, "OK, I quit the group," and Dad said, "Right, I hold you to it," and that was it. He quit! It was a trivial argument and he lost The Beach Boys over it.'

At first, not a single member of The Beach Boys believed David was actually quitting the group. 'All the other guys thought it was too absurd to leave while the band was at the top, so they just dismissed the whole thing,' says David. 'Since they kind of dismissed me, it made me want to leave even more.'

Further along the drive to New York, they stopped for petrol. While Murry was in the toilets, Brian took David aside and told him, 'Dave, you can't quit, we need you.' Perhaps Brian's true feelings were wrapped up in his own desire to stay off the road. Murry's readiness to eliminate David from The Beach Boys was one way to ensure that his reluctant son stayed on the touring treadmill.

Since Murry was an employee of The Beach Boys organisation as their manager and since David was a 20 per cent owner of The Beach Boys franchise, technically, Murry was David's employee. There is no easy way that Murry could have fired David from The Beach Boys. If that had been the case, then David could have dragged Murry and the group through some very difficult legal wrangling. But by bringing the issue to the fore himself, David opened the door, and while Murry kept his foot lodged in it, his sons hoped it would quietly close again. The coming months were a mysterious time in Beach Boys history. David would still be a Beach Boy, but one who wanted to leave the group. While the other Beach Boys tried their best to discourage him from leaving, Murry Wilson did whatever he could to accommodate David's wish. He saw an opening, he took advantage, and then he rewrote history to cover his tracks.

Even though David and Murry didn't exactly get along, David maintains a degree of admiration for the Wilsons' dad in retrospect. 'Murry was a hard-assed businessman, and without him, there would have been no Beach Boys,' says David. 'We fought a lot, but I was an arrogant little kid who wanted fun and didn't regard it as a business. I found out the hard way the bastard was right!' Fred Vail agrees, 'Murry was not unlike any other father of the era. He'd been through the Depression. He'd been through tough times. He knew what it was like to earn a living. He knew what it was like to be the breadwinner for the family.' At fifteen years of age, David had a difficult time buying into Murry's militaristic routine. He remembers the drill: 'Murry would tell us over and over, "It's a business. It's a business. Straighten up. You've got to be serious. Quit fooling around. It's not a party, it's a business!"' But David has never been one to confirm the endless stories of Murry's physically abusive side. 'I didn't see it at all,' says David. 'I saw an occasional slap and one major scuffle between Dennis and Murry one day in the Wilsons' garage. My dad had to go over and separate them. That was the only physical violence I ever saw in the Wilson family.'

On 30 August 1963, The Beach Boys played the final concert date of their marathon tour in Brooklyn, New York. The show was held at the enormous Fox Theater and was hosted by radio legend Murray the K. Joining The Beach Boys on the concert's incredible all-star bill were Little Stevie Wonder, Ben E. King, Gene Pitney, The Shirelles, Smokey Robinson and the Miracles, The Drifters, The Dovells, The Angels, The Tymes, Jay and the Americans, The Chiffons and Randy and the Rainbows. It was definitely The Beach Boys' highest profile concert yet. Despite Murry's epic rant about rule-breaking, the tour was clearly the band's most successful to date, as it provided a gargantuan influx of cash. Following the New York concert, Murry and the boys immediately caught a red-eye flight back home and had little time to rest once they arrived. That night the weary group performed in front of thousands of fans at the big 'Show of Stars' concert held at the Los Angeles Sports Arena. On the bill with The

Beach Boys were Jan and Dean, Marvin Gaye, The Righteous Brothers, The Olympics, Darlene Love, and a new artist named Wayne Newton. David spent the 24 hours following the show in bed. During the tour he'd had a head cold, stomach flu, food poisoning, electrical shocks from bad equipment, alcohol poisoning from too much booze, a throat infection from too many cigarettes, crabs from one hooker, the clap from another, and had lost more than ten pounds from his already skeletal frame. His parents were greatly concerned that he'd never be the same. He wouldn't. Soon enough, Carl's phone call awakened Dave from a solid day and night of sleep. He informed him that new Beach Boys recording sessions started tomorrow at Western and that rehearsals began in thirty minutes. David rolled out of bed, ran across the street, and stepped right back into The Beach Boys pressure cooker.

Brian rose to the challenge of Capitol's request for yet another Beach Boys LP, cooking up some excellent material. The new sessions would yield another bumper crop of Beach Boys classics including 'Be True To Your School', 'Spirit of America', 'No-Go Showboat', 'Cherry Cherry Coupe' and 'Ballad Of Ole Betsy'. As the new recording sessions commenced at Western, there was no issue of David having quit the group. He plugged in and played his guitar parts as requested by Brian. At one point during the sessions, David asked Brian if the group could record his own original composition, titled 'Kustom Kar Show'. David felt his song was perfect for the car-themed LP, and Brian listened to David's run-through with interest. But with Murry glaring over his shoulder, Brian ultimately turned down the song, telling David, 'You're not ready yet.' Throughout the sessions, Murry gave David the silent treatment. 'He simply acted as if I wasn't there,' says David. Murry used Carl as a go-between, which actually suited David just fine, but probably wasn't such a nice thing for Carl. The issue of David quitting the group wasn't mentioned by anyone until David himself brought it up – and before long, he got into the habit of bringing it up daily. He'd ask Carl, 'How many more shows do I have to play?' Carl would just laugh and ignore him. Today, David regrets having put Carl in such a weird place. 'Carl was the guy who lobbied to get me into the group, and now I was pressuring Carl to help me find a way to get out,' says David. 'That must have driven him nuts.'

But David didn't let up. He kept reminding Carl he wanted to go. And for a time, Carl kept acting as if David was only joking. On 4 September, the group flew to Denver, Colorado, for a sold-out concert. Brian hated to be away from the studio with so much pressure on him to produce hit songs but he was on stage that night. On 7 September, he was there again when The Beach Boys took the stage in Salt Lake City, Utah. It was that day in Salt Lake when Brian and Mike composed one of their greatest songs, another Chuck Berry-styled rocker, which was titled 'Fun, Fun, Fun'. Brian was so excited about the new tune that he had the band rehearse it several times as soon as they returned to LA. They tried it as a slow blues, a fast rocker and an in-between combination of the two. David fell in love with Brian's arrangement and Mike's lyric, which was built around a story Dennis had told them all. Unfortunately, Brian decided to shelve 'Fun, Fun, Fun' until later, since he still wasn't sure which tempo was right for the song.

Sessions for the next LP, to be titled *Little Deuce Coupe*, continued in Hollywood. There has been confusion among Beach Boys historians as to whether David actually played on the group's fourth LP sessions or not. There is clear evidence that he learned the material. I witnessed him demonstrate, over four decades after the fact, the exact fingering on several of these obscure songs without having tried it since 1963. Even though the end dates for David's initial Beach Boys tenure will be legally backdated to a date just prior to the *Little Deuce Coupe* sessions, it's a very good bet that David was there. A legal strategy was more than likely designed by Murry to avoid having to pay David his royalties for certain songs – like the hit version of 'Be True To Your School', which he gets nothing for. Today David still receives royalty payments for playing on some but not all of the *Little Deuce Coupe* LP. After-the-fact tampering with the time frame of

David's 'official' Beach Boys departure has only added to the confusion over his participation. But to simplify: as the *Little Deuce Coupe* LP sessions were being recorded and when it was mastered, David Marks was still a member of The Beach Boys. This fact is clearly documented by the gigs, TV shows and promotional appearances he made with the band throughout September 1963.

David and The Beach Boys played a hugely successful concert in San Diego, California, on 9 September. So many fans were turned away at the door that another show at a larger venue was immediately booked there for the following month. Back in LA the group appeared on KHJ TV's *Starstudded Back to School Special* hosted by Bob 'Gilligan' Denver. On 14 September, the band flew north for another successful concert at the Memorial Auditorium in Sacramento, California. There the group reunited with Fred Vail, who was quickly becoming their most effective promoter. That evening, the group played two shows to a frenzied house. The early show began at 5 p.m. and the late show started at 8 p.m. Free Beach Boys LPs and promotional photos were given away to many of the show's attendees. On 20 September, the group performed in Long Beach, California, and on the 21st they flew north to Portland, Oregon. Brian was juggling a full concert schedule, as well as composing, arranging and producing the new LP. Al Jardine once again stepped in to relieve Brian for at least a few of the September shows, and again Murry complained about it and forced his reluctant son to get back on stage. The pressure was clearly getting to Brian. But Murry chose to ignore the warning signs.

On 24 September 1963, The Beach Boys filmed their first national television appearance. To date they had already performed on television more than a dozen times, but every one of those appearances was on a local teen dance show, or a local variety show. This time, The Beach Boys would appear in primetime in front of millions of viewers across America on the CBS television network's popular *Red Skelton Show*. The group was asked to perform their signature hit 'Surfin' USA.' For a second number, Murry suggested they sing something the adult segment of the audience might enjoy. It was decided that a harmony-rich version of the standard 'The Things We Did Last Summer', written by Sammy Cahn and Jule Styne and recorded by Frank Sinatra (among others) would do the trick. The group was absolutely thrilled about their first big TV appearance – until they were told to visit the wardrobe department. The good news: you're on national TV. The bad news: you'll be wearing sailor outfits. The Beach Boys were dressed up in ridiculous costumes with white calf-length, bell-bottomed pants and horizontally striped shirts. Even under those embarrassing conditions, they managed to mime a spirited performance of 'Surfin' USA' with Mike Love shimmying away with one of Skelton's pretty dancers.

Another guest on Skelton's show the same night as The Beach Boys was legendary film star Shirley Temple. One of David's most unforgettable show business memories came when Temple approached him and politely asked for his autograph. As it turned out, she wanted the autograph for her daughter, who was the same age as David and a devoted Beach Boys fan. The Skelton appearance is yet another sign that David was solidly a Beach Boy in the period after his clash with Murry. If Al Jardine had been poised and ready to replace him, one would think the group's first national TV appearance would have been the perfect place to slide him back into the line-up. But the evidence suggests that in late September, The Beach Boys were still betting that David would remain with them for the long haul.

On 28 September, the boys performed in front of 10,000 screaming fans at the Cow Palace in San Francisco. Before the show, David and the band joined a large contingent of TV and movie stars, including Annette Funicello, Frankie Avalon and Doug McClure, for a pre-concert dinner party. 'I was a little bit star-struck when I sat near Annette at dinner,' says Dave. 'I'd been fantasising about her since I was a little kid, and now she was right there, talking to me. All I could do was mumble and drool a little. She probably thought I was an idiot.'

With his nerves bothering him before the hugely anticipated San Francisco appearance, Brian drank too much champagne at dinner. 'Our opening song that night was "Surfin' Safari",' remembers David. 'Brian was sick from the champagne and he threw up right on stage. He turned around and projectile vomited towards the drums and then turned back towards the audience and kept singing. He never missed a note.' Now that's rock and roll!

The Beach Boys played a matinee concert in Fresno, California, on 29 September, and flew directly to Seattle, Washington, for an evening show afterwards. The Seattle appearance was another major concert in front of thousands of young fans. Promoted as the 'Cavalcade of Stars', the performance was held at the legendary Seattle Opera House. Sharing the bill with The Beach Boys were Freddie Canon, Nino Tempo and April Stevens, Dee Dee Sharp, Ray Stevens, The Wailers, The Viceroys, Gail Harris, and once again, 'Little' Stevie Wonder. Jim Valley of The Viceroys remembers that night: 'The concert began and right before the intermission, The Beach Boys took the stage. Pandemonium, they were incredible. Wow, excitement, screaming teenagers like Jim had never seen before. A prelude to Beatlemania. Jim's eyes spun like Mr Toad's! Maybe someday Jim could be in a group like that.' Valley would go on to become a star, playing guitar for Paul Revere and the Raiders.

David recalls his first personal encounter with soul legend Stevie Wonder the day of the Seattle concert. 'Carl and I were outside the hotel, waiting for the limo to take us to the show, and it was raining a little bit,' remembers Dave. 'I was standing on the sidewalk looking around, and all of a sudden Stevie Wonder is there, holding on to my arm. I said, "Oh, hi, Stevie, how's it going?" He said he was fine. Then the limo pulls up and we all get in, and Stevie's mom gets in with us too. And he held onto my arm the whole way. I don't know if things were mixed up and they thought I was his valet or something. I don't remember what we talked about; I just remember he never let go of my arm until we got inside the concert hall. I went out to the front row to watch him perform during his set and it was great. His spit was spraying all over the first few rows of people. I guess those are the kinds of things you notice when you're fifteen. And he was younger than I was, which was rare, because I was always the youngest one wherever we went. I dug his music but I got a little closer to Stevie than I was really comfortable with that day – first he kept grabbing my arm, and then he spat all over me.'

With their international profile rising daily, Murry was making plans for an Australian tour because yet another Beach Boys single, 'Surfer Girl', had just reached the Top Ten there. But for David, the hourglass was running out on his Beach Boys dream. 'I started feeling some extra pressure from Murry,' says Dave. 'He was having some disputes with my mom about money. None of us in the group cared about money. I mean, we all had nice clothes, and just about anything we wanted. But my mother clashed frequently with Murry over my position in the group because she thought I could be a star, or more of a focal point. I guess I was popular with the girls back then. Murry only wanted the Wilsons to be the stars. He used to give Brian a really hard time about giving Mike all the lead vocals. Murry wanted me to be more or less in the background too. So he started picking on me over little things like the way I carried a suitcase, or about me not smiling on stage, or for playing my guitar too loud. He'd come right up on stage during shows and change the settings on my amp and I'd change them right back. I was getting a little pissed off about it all. My dad told me to stick it out and I'd be a millionaire, but I told him to forget it. The fact that my dad wanted me to stay made me want to leave even more.'

Carl's friend Ron Swallow witnessed what may have been the final straw between Dave's parents and Murry Wilson. 'I can remember the day they were all there in the Wilsons' living room,' says Swallow. 'It was like a stand-off between Murry and Dave's mom and dad, and it became very intense. Dave's parents told Murry, "We want to be part of this management team; he's our son, we're going to be involved from that point of view," which was the last thing that Murry Wilson was gonna hear. This was Murry's band. He took possession of it early on. And every time Dave's parents would say, "This is gonna happen or that's gonna happen," Murry would say, "No, it's not, no, it's not." Murry basically said forget it. And while all of this is happening Dave's just sitting there. His eyes were big, looking at this whole thing. Carl's there, I'm there, and we're all watching this happen.' Dave's parents were delivering a final ultimatum and Murry wasn't going to budge. When it became obvious that Murry had no interest in compromise, Dave's parents finally pulled the plug, with Jo Ann saying, 'OK, that's it! He's out of the band. He's got his own group now anyway. You just watch us.' Murry quickly bellowed his parting shot, 'Go ahead! He'll be nothing.'

Ron Swallow remembers the moment clearly: 'I can still see Dave's mom and dad walking out the front door, walking across the grass, and across the street with Dave walking behind them with this posture like, "What in the hell just happened?"'

But deep down David knew what had just happened was inevitable. 'In retrospect, I think I was purposely sabotaging the situation,' he says. 'I always felt alienated because I wasn't in the family. I was a lot younger than the other guys, and I knew they didn't take me seriously.' David had already begun to write his own music, and none of The Beach Boys had any interest in listening to it. Dave says, 'I'd begun rehearsing with my own band. I was pushing my weight around with them. I guess I was trying to be Brian. I taught them my own arrangements the same way Brian had taught The Beach Boys. I changed their name from The Jaguars to Dave and the Marksmen and they were happy about that. In the back of my mind I was sure that when I left The Beach Boys I would be a success because of my affiliation with them.'

Drummer Mark Groseclose remembered in a 1986 inter-view, 'While David was playing with The Beach Boys, me, Bill Trenkle, Gene Fetko, Ed Gauntt and Dennis Herbst put a little band together called The Jaguars. We played a lot of local hops and were having a lot of fun. One day David tells me he's leaving The Beach Boys and wants to start a group of his own with me as his drummer. Anyway, either David took over The Jaguars or we inherited him from The Beach Boys. We rehearsed our butts off and became very good in a short time.' The Jaguars were rechristened Dave and the Marksmen and began rehearsing four days a week in Dave's parents' living room. 'I made certain that those guys understood that I was gonna tell them what to play, and what to sing, and what to wear,' says David. 'And they agreed, because they were actually thankful. They realised that I was in one of the biggest bands in the world and that I had connections in the music business. When I started rehearsing and writing for the Marksmen I was actually still in The Beach Boys. I remember playing Brian my songs and he wasn't that interested, which is understandable. He was into creating his own music. I'm sure as time progressed Brian might have been more interested in my music if I'd stuck around. But I wasn't willing to wait around and see. I really wanted to pursue things with the new group and because of that I was willing to leave The Beach Boys.'

In a way, Al Jardine would be the individual to benefit most from the turn of events. However, in the short term, he too would fall victim to Murry's less-than-balanced approach to The Beach Boys' business affairs. From this point forward, Beach Boys history would be rewritten in a way that nearly eliminated David from the story. He'd regularly be described as a quick 'fill-in' while 'original' Beach Boy Al Jardine took a stab at higher education. Anyone on the inside knew this was fantasy.

Dave's final word on Murry: 'He couldn't control me like he could his sons, and that definitely bothered him. If I had been a nice kid like Al, and cooperated and did what I was told, it would have been a different story. But I wasn't a nice kid; I was difficult. He wasn't lying, but he ended up taking advantage of that. Murry was very smart in his own way.' Just as Al Jardine had never been mentioned in any official Beach Boys press release or bio between February 1962 and October 1963, David would also find himself virtually deleted from the 'official' Beach Boys story. But at the time, he really didn't give a damn.

On 5 October 1963, David Marks performed his last concert with the original Beach Boys in San Diego, California.

After the show, The Beach Boys ceremonially tossed David into a swimming pool, giving him a kind of reverse baptism. The group had several photos taken to document the moment. David knew he was leaving The Beach Boys at the very top of their game. When he joined the group they were virtually unknown outside of Southern California, they could barely get any bookings, and they had no record contract. When Al Jardine replaced David as the fifth Beach Boy in October 1963, he rejoined a group that was already riding high. Beach Boys historian Peter Reum ponders: 'Did Brian have hits based on momentum back in the sixties? Definitely.' The momentum that would result in the future glory of 'I Get Around', 'Pet Sounds' and 'Good Vibrations' was well under way by the end of 1963. Unfortunately for David, he would receive little credit or financial reward for the hard work he put into helping build that momentum.

The *Little Deuce Coupe* LP, the band's fourth, was released that October featuring a group photo on the back cover that still included David. 'Be True To Your School' backed with 'In My Room' was released as a single on 28 October. This was the last new Beach Boys single to feature David on guitar. 'Before David signed a "release" from his Capitol contract, "Be True To Your School" had already been released as a single,' says Carrie Marks. 'I don't think it's a coincidence they chose the very business day before that session as David's retroactive end date. It sure made Murry and the boys a whole bunch of extra money by not having to give David his twenty per cent of another Top Ten song.' And as each new bit of information came to light during the research for this book, the degree of the raw deal Dave was given only seemed to grow.

As for the transition from David back to Al, there is at least one person who disputes the idea that this was a direct swap. Danny Hamilton, younger brother of ex-road manager John Hamilton, claims The Beach Boys first offered him the position as David's replacement. In the book *Smile, Sun, Sand & Pet Sounds*, compiled by Stephen J. McParland, Danny Hamilton stated: 'Their rhythm guitarist Dave Marks was either kicked out of the group, fired, or left. They heard about me from my brother John and my other brother Judd who was working with The Ventures as their lead singer when they would perform live. So The Beach Boys flew me down [from Wenatchee, Washington] to audition to replace Dave Marks.' As is the case with The Belairs' Paul Johnson's story about being offered a position in The Beach Boys, Hamilton's story might be fundamentally true, but the specifics of his recollections don't really fit into the timeline and known facts. Hamilton claims he rehearsed with the band for 'three months' in the summer at their Hawthorne home. We know from looking at The Beach Boys touring schedule there was no three-week gap, let alone a three-month-long stay in Hawthorne. The only extended break in 1963 was the few weeks between David's last gig and Al's first show back.

On 1 November, The Beach Boys turned in a horrible set at the Hollywood Bowl with Al Jardine on rhythm guitar. The group's second-ever appearance at the Bowl was marred by very bad sound and an overall dismal performance. It also didn't help that Al was playing a Gibson guitar, which demolished the all-Fender vibe that had become The Beach Boys standard. Shortly afterwards, Al purchased a Stratocaster like David's to more accurately recreate David's guitar parts. That task was something Al would have to get used to. He would spend the next thirty-five years of Beach Boys concerts regularly playing the rhythm parts David originally recorded on the group's beloved string of early hits.

The first Capitol promotional photos featuring Al Jardine among The Beach Boys line-up were taken in November 1963. That same month, David signed an amendment to The Beach Boys' July 1962 recording contract. The amendment would be backdated to the very date David told Murry 'I quit', on the drive to New York. The agreement stated: 'Capitol has been advised that on August 30, 1963, David L. Marks ceased to be a member of the group performing as The Beach Boys,' adding that, 'David L. Marks is hereby released and discharged by the signatories hereto' – Brian, Dennis, Carl, Mike, and Capitol vice-president F. M. Scott III – 'from any and all obligations and/or liabilities for or in connection with masters unrecorded as of 30 August 1963.' David was led to believe by Murry that he was signing a legal, fair and binding document. However, upon closer inspection, what he signed was far from that. The 'release' was never approved by the same court that originally approved David's Capitol agreement in September 1962. In fact, it was not approved by any court.

A year earlier when David was brought before the judge as a fourteen-year-old to have his Capitol contract approved, the Los Angeles Superior Court clearly ruled that unless any future changes to the contract were approved by the same Superior Court, the terms of the original Capitol contract were in full force until 28 September 1967. This means that David had a fundamental claim to twenty per cent of all royalties for anything released by The Beach Boys until that date. Unfortunately for David Marks, he was completely unaware of that until 2006 . . . and because The Beach Boys pulled a fast one on him again in 1971, he still gets nothing.

At fifteen, after helping to build The Beach Boys franchise at the expense of his own concert earnings, his high school education, and two key formative years of his life, David was given no settlement, no small percentage of the business, and wasn't even paid artist royalties for all of the material he performed on. Instead, Murry and The Beach Boys took control of his rightful twenty per cent share of future royalties and kept quiet about it. And Alan Jardine, who was the obvious heir to David's share of the business, was instead hired as a salaried 'sideman' and remained in that capacity until 1973. 'Murry just refused to give me an equal share,' says Al. 'That was my punishment for leaving in the first place.' And while David's twenty per cent of the franchise was 'absorbed' under the table, The Beach Boys business just kept booming.

Although David was now physically gone from The Beach Boys operation, for a time, in many ways, it was as if he hadn't left at all. He still regularly hung out at the Rovells' house with the whole gang. He still rode to school with Carl.

He still jammed with Carl and Dennis, and even played in public with them at an impromptu performance at Hollywood Professional School in 1964. And David still looked like a Beach Boy, even as their image changed. When the band updated their hairstyles, David changed his, too. It was Carl who initiated the band's shift to haircuts given by Hollywood's well-known stylist Jay Sebring. 'Carl knew all the hip places for that kind of stuff,' says David. 'Jay would do our hair with peppermint shampoo and hairspray.' Photos from the period reveal David's hairstyle was the same as Dennis, Carl and Brian's. It's as if he was still a Beach Boy in 'image' and was compelled to maintain a similar look. David sees it more simply, 'I just did what they did.' And by taking on his own musical responsibility and direction, like Brian had, David was simply imitating his hero. On a sad note, hairstylist Jay Sebring was one of the unlucky people slaughtered by the Manson family in the summer of 1969.

David would one day realise his action of quitting The Beach Boys had lasting consequences. 'People always assumed I was fired or kicked out, because what stupid idiot quits a situation like that? I didn't think about it at the time, but in retrospect, I can see how that may have affected other people,' says Dave. 'I was selfishly ploughing through life, not thinking of anyone else, and quitting this and grabbing that. I realise that Carl and Dennis were probably somewhat resentful because I didn't really have to leave but I insisted on it.' What had begun as a simple friendship between neighbours, and an innocent musical connection, had transformed into a serious business, and it now threatened to splinter the bonds made as little boys. 'As far as I can remember they all cared very much for David,' says Marilyn Wilson-Rutherford. 'But he was just not on the same page as the other members.' Though the friendships endured for a time, the trauma of what had occurred between the Marks and the Wilson families launched their lives into two different directions. In time they'd become as separate and disconnected as they had been before David moved in across the street. For now, everyone just moved on to the next act of an epic drama.

On 22 November 1963, President John F. Kennedy was assassinated in Dallas, Texas. Within months, The Beatles would eclipse The Beach Boys as Capitol's hottest-selling act but in the end Brian and The Beach Boys would rise to the challenge. Their music would not only greatly influence The Beatles, it would also create a lasting niche in the hearts of future generations of music fans. The year 1963 ended with the charts full of Beach Boys LPs and hit singles featuring David Marks on guitar. The songs he recorded with the boys would continue to receive radio play and critical acclaim while remaining consistent sellers for the next four decades. Due to all the original releases, compilations and reissues of The Beach Boys' classic early material, David Marks never completely went away. To this date hundreds of Beach Boys LP and CD titles have been issued internationally that include David Marks somewhere on them.

7. MARKED MAN

The sound shot across Kornblum, down 119th, and right through the Wilsons' screen door. Like a big block mill slowly waking up, turning over and exploding to life. First there was a series of bass drum thuds, a floor tom thump, and then the quick whistle of feedback from a switched-on PA: 'We're testing.' There was twanging and tuning of guitar strings, and a bass sensation you could feel in your bones. The audio signals seemed to alert the entire Hawthorne neighbourhood on that mild afternoon in January 1964. Something exciting was happening.

Louie Marotta pulled his head out from under the hood of his car, wiped the grease off his hands, and strode towards the sound. Greg Jones ambled out of his house and into the open air, meeting Louie on the corner of Almertens and Kornblum. From inside his garage, Gary Hallmark peered down the street. He looked over towards the corner and grinned at Greg and Louie. Five-year-old Paula Bondi slid off the corner fire hydrant and ran across her lawn, giggling. Several youngsters poured out of Gil Lindner's 'Little Store' and ran towards the sudden excitement. Within minutes, a pack of kids had gathered on the walkway in front of the Markses' home. They could clearly see what was happening inside Dave's open front door. Smiling and strumming his cherry-red Fender Jaguar guitar, David Marks made eye contact with drummer Mark Groseclose and nodded. Mark's hands went blurry. He lit into a tight, crisp snare roll. Then the pedal hit the metal. A glorious wall of reverbed Fender chords literally tore through the air. The kids out front swam headfirst into the torrent of sound, wide eyes soaking in the action through the Markses' living-room window. The pavement on 119th vibrated as the Marksmen fired up David's original song, called 'Sheriff Of Noddingham'. It was a killer.

Sounding like a steroid-laced Dick Dale cocktail with a Link Wray chaser, the arrangement was brutally electric. A buzz-saw lead figure, played by Dave, fuelled the onslaught. Thick, dual rhythm guitars, played by Gene Fetko and Ed Gauntt, were held down by Bill Trenkle's subterranean bass line and drummer Mark Groseclose's incessant flailing. The sound was so muscular it could straighten hair. So penetrating it could clean teeth. The crowd of youngsters outside the Marks home grew larger. Several curious adults drifted to the perimeter, some shaking their heads and covering their ears. Windows rattled, cats scampered. The kids were in heaven.

Across Kornblum, the screen door of the Wilson residence flew open, and out stormed Murry Wilson. He purposefully strode to the corner of 119th and Kornblum, and stopped to light his ever-present pipe. Then he walked a few more steps, slowly, head cocked, eyes on the Markses' home. Murry stood alone, twenty feet removed from the spontaneous celebration taking place in front of Dave's front door. The kids were whooping and the music was furious. Puffing away on his pipe and intently listening to the powerful music pouring forth, Murry was sizing up the moment at hand.

Another resident from down the street, a diminutive, moustachioed shoe salesman named Dan Derusha, wandered up and stood next to Murry. Causing a momentary distraction from Murry's deep concentration, Derusha tapped his thick shoulder and shouted, 'Aaayyy ... are those your boys, Murry?'

The question hung there for only a second. 'No!' Murry answered firmly. After pausing for a few more seconds to listen, he turned back to Derusha and grinned slyly. Murry then pointed toward the Markses' home, and in an emphatic tone, blared, 'That's the kid who quit The Beach Boys! Not bad, huh?'

As Dave and the Marksmen filled the neighbourhood with joyous rock and roll that afternoon, Murry Wilson slowly walked back home. He paused in front of his door to relight his pipe, and bent down to pick up the newspaper lying there. As he stood on his front step and scanned the day's news, Murry continued to listen, and he continued to think. Later, he told friends that he hated to admit it but he was genuinely impressed by the Marksmen's tightness and, of all things, their 'professionalism'. He'd never thought of David as having what it took to be a frontman. But there he was, 'the smart-mouthed little punk', leading his own band. It seems Murry Wilson realised that day that just maybe he'd need to find a way to impact the career of Dave and the Marksmen. And for David, that wasn't going to be a good thing.

That same month, The Beach Boys flew to Australia for their first international tour. Dave was almost too busy to notice. Immersed in the process of writing, arranging and rehearsing material with his new band at fifteen years of age, David was the man in charge. This show was squarely on his shoulders. And so was the bill for it. Dave's Beach Boys money would help grease the rail to rock and roll glory for the Marksmen. At least, that was the plan. Although his parents were essentially in control of his modest royalty income until he turned twenty-one, David's hand was always welcome in the cookie jar. 'They just kind of doled out some of the royalty money to me when I needed a guitar or some equipment for my band,' says David. The money financed recording sessions, publicity photos and stage clothing for the new group. David also used some Beach Boys money to buy a sharp 1964

Pontiac Tempest sedan for his mother. Still, with Elmer on disability from a work-related injury, Jo Ann maintained her day job even while she helped manage the new band's affairs.

An independent producer named Russ Regan, whom Dave had met while playing with The Beach Boys, stopped by one evening to listen to a Marksmen rehearsal. Regan was the man who actually came up with the name 'Beach Boys' for their first single, back in 1961. Upon hearing Dave's new group, he immediately recognised the band's potential and voluntarily became their agent, co-publisher and executive producer. Within days, he pitched the Dave and the Marksmen concept to the newly formed A&M records. Co-owners Herb Alpert and Jerry Moss were interested right away, mostly because of Dave's past association with The Beach Boys. Seemingly overnight, Dave and the Marksmen became the first rock group signed to A&M Records.

A session was booked at Western 3 to record the debut Marksmen single. Both car-themed tunes for the group's first A&M release were written by and would be produced by David. He asked The Honeys to come in and sing background vocals, while Chuck Britz manned the soundboard. Britz teased Regan about sitting in 'Murry's chair' when the two settled into the familiar control room. The recording session for 'Cruisin'' and 'Kustom Kar Show' ended up being something close to a Beach Boys auxiliary gathering. Even Dave's Aunt Andrea pitched in, reprising her speaking role. This time, her voice graced 'Cruisin'' in much the same way as it had 'County Fair'.

'I was just watching the Marksmen record and David asked me to sound sexy and say, "Drive daddy drive",' remembers Andrea. 'I think I had to repeat the take several times, as I didn't sound sexy.' As a group, the Marksmen were very well rehearsed, and their session went smoothly, giving them a satisfactory result. 'Cruisin'' is a bluesy dance-beat number with a very direct adolescent theme about kids with time on their hands and money to burn. Dave's lead vocal wasn't pretty; instead, it projected a sneering, juvenile-delinquent edge. While the guitar sound had a similar texture to what one might expect from a former Beach Boy, the recording was tougher, with a less polished sound than Dave's old band. The song's lyric and its raw performance were much closer to the reality of early-sixties suburban teen decadence than anything The Beach Boys had recorded to date.

'Kustom Kar Show', which Dave had previously offered to The Beach Boys, was an up-tempo rocker with a live party-atmosphere production style. It possessed a 'live' ambience similar to Gary U.S. Bonds's 'Quarter To Three', complete with shouts and chatter from the imaginary car show's imaginary teen audience. The Honeys and Aunt Andrea provided the whoops and screams while Dave's guitar blazed and Mark's drumming roared along underneath all the crowd noise. The song has a great celebratory lyric that is catchy enough to make one wish The Beach Boys had recorded it. Brian's harmonic touch might have turned this tune into a hot-rod classic.

Around the same time they were recording tracks at Western with Chuck Britz, Dave and the Marksmen also cut several songs at American Recorders with Don and Richie Podolor. Included in the sessions were versions of Dave's original instrumentals 'Travelin'' and 'Sheriff Of Nodding-ham'. The Podolor recordings were never committed to vinyl, but allowed the Marksmen to develop their material in a friendly environment. After sitting untouched for thirty-eight years, versions of both were finally released by the independent Sundazed Records in 2003.

Once The Beach Boys returned from Australia, Dave resumed his daily rides to Hollywood Professional School with Carl Wilson. 'We were driving to school one day and Carl asked me how things were going with the Marksmen,' remembers David. 'I told him I was just in the studio producing some tracks with them, and he teasingly said, "You can't produce shit!" I answered, "On the contrary, Carl, I just produced a big stinky pile of it." Carl was always reminding me I couldn't use The Beach Boys' name to promote my band; he'd just sneak that into conversations on the way to school. For a teenager, he had a really serious attitude about business.'

One night, David and his parents were invited over to the Rovell home to a small dinner party. Most of The Beach Boys were there and, as usual, David felt right at home. After dinner, Brian ceremoniously unveiled his precious acetate of the next Beach Boys single. The song was 'Fun, Fun, Fun', a song David was well acquainted with. However, the powerful new version he heard coming through the Rovells' hi-fi was a mind-blower. 'In a way, it was like "Surfin'"' all over again,' says David. 'I'd rehearsed it with them, but I wasn't on the record. It felt weird. And it was so great. I couldn't believe what a great-sounding record that was.' Upon hearing Brian's beautifully produced recording, Dave got a sinking feeling that his group, the Marksmen, would never sound that good.

That February, as the Marksmen continued to rehearse their original material, they heard about something called The Beatles. 'No one was sure what to make of them at first,' says David. 'They were this strange-looking British group who shook their heads a lot. It took me a while to get used to the fact that they didn't put any reverb on their guitars. That dry guitar sound seemed so odd to me at first. But once I got used to that, I absolutely loved them.' While Dave's group was preparing to play their first local gigs to support their upcoming A&M single release, Beatlemania seemed to eclipse everything around them. Suddenly, David wasn't an ex-member of the world's biggest rock band; he was an ex-member of yesterday's news.

Around the same time, David received a phone call from a fellow musician who lived in the Northwest named Paul Revere. David had already heard about his hard-working group, Paul Revere and the Raiders. 'They wore these revolutionary war period costumes, and they were just starting to get big on the West Coast,' says Dave. When he picked up the phone, Revere got right to the point, saying, 'Dave, do you want to be a Raider? We need a guitar player and I'd like it to be you.' David thought about it for a few seconds and replied, 'Sorry, Paul, but I have to say no thanks. I've already got my own band, the Marksmen.' And that was that. Paul Revere and the Raiders became one of America's most popular acts of the mid-sixties, but David has no regrets. 'I just couldn't see myself in tights and a three-cornered hat.'

In the meantime, the Marksmen were already fielding offers for local gigs, including one very prestigious booking that never happened. 'We had the chance to become the house band at PJ's in Hollywood at $1,000 a week,' remembered Mark Groseclose in 1986. 'But our parents thought our education was more important and wouldn't let us.' Actually, it was co-rhythm guitarist Ed Gauntt's parents' objections that caused the Marksmen to pass, and the other boys resented it. PJ's was simply one of Hollywood's hottest clubs in 1964; it was there the rocketing career of Latin folksinger Trini Lopez had recently been launched. It was due to Lopez leaving his regular PJ's gig for bigger bookings in New York that the slot became available to Dave's new group. Instead, the Marksmen declined, and a fiery LA band called The Standells were given the job. The Standells would use their PJ's exposure to great effect, recording a live LP there and becoming a major hit act. They scored a national smash with their garage-punk classic single 'Dirty Water' in 1966. Ironically, The Standells' drummer, Gary Leeds, would leave the band during their PJ's residence and join The Walker Brothers, which also featured David and Carl's original guitar mentor John Maus.

That March, The Beach Boys released their *Shut Down Volume 2* LP, the first Beach Boys LP without Dave Marks's photo on the cover. David feels his guitar is probably on the LP somewhere, as he remembers rehearsing a couple of the tunes and perhaps recording them as well. But *Shut Down Volume 2* is by and large the first Beach Boys LP without David's presence, both in image and in spirit. I remember seeing the LP cover, The Beach Boys' first with Alan Jardine pictured on it, in the stores in 1964. I immediately thought to myself, Who in the hell is that little blond guy? Like many Beach Boys fans, I had grown accustomed to seeing David's face on those album covers. In a way, it was shocking that he was suddenly gone, and with no explanation. It was like losing a family member. It seems silly now, because bands change personnel so often, but back then there weren't that many rock bands with a back catalogue. Most Beach Boys fans had never heard of Al Jardine in March 1964. No one saw the *Shut Down Volume 2* cover and said, 'Cool, the guy on "Surfin'"' is finally back, thank God that Marks kid isn't replacing him any more.' As far as Beach Boys fans were concerned, Al was the replacement and the rumours about David began.

Where did he go? No one knew. One of my sister's friends told me he'd gotten a girl 'in trouble' and was kicked out. I asked her what she meant by 'in trouble' but she wouldn't say. I assumed it must have been something bad. One thing was for sure, The Beach Boys' outward image changed once Dave was gone. They didn't look as much like surfers any more. In fact they didn't really look like a rock and roll band any more. At least, that was my impression. The Beatles seemed so much cooler. I hoped that none of The Beatles got a girl 'in trouble' and were replaced some dorky-looking guy. Sorry, Al, I was only seven years old, but that's what I was thinking back then. It seemed like The Beach Boys went from being cool to being square overnight . . . except for Dennis. It was obvious that, no matter how many dorks surrounded him, he was still cool. Such are the memories of these events from my pre-adolescent consumer's perspective.

The reality is that when Dave and the Marksmen released their debut single in March 1964, very few people even noticed. The 'Cruisin'' backed with 'Kustom Kar Show' single on A&M hit the market precisely at the height of Beatlemania. So much for good timing. And David wasn't getting any help from The Beach Boys connection. They were in panic mode themselves, trying to fight off the Fab Four's incredible assault on the music industry. In the meantime, Dave and the Marksmen appeared on two local Southern California TV shows, *The Lloyd Thaxton Show* and *9th Street West*, to promote their new single. While 'Cruisin'' managed to garner some California radio airplay, it wasn't nearly enough. And when David finally heard it on the radio, he knew it wasn't good enough to become a big hit. 'I kept telling the other guys in the band, just hang in there, we're going to be a success,' says David. 'But really I knew deep down the first time I heard our song on the radio that it was basically over. KDAY had a contest where you voted for the best new single on Sundays and "Cruisin'" came in third or fourth. There were all these great records out by people like The Beatles and The Four Seasons. I knew in my heart that ours fell short, quality-wise.'

Still, the Marksmen found many venues more than willing to book them. Their live show was well rehearsed and tight. 'The fans loved our shows, and most of the shows were packed,' says David. Local radio stations were giving Marksmen gigs good promotion and despite the lack of a hit, things were starting to take off. For a while it seemed Dave's feeling about it being 'over' just might have been wrong. But it was very clear that no impact was being seen in record sales. Rumours filtered back to David that Murry Wilson might be part of the problem. The story according to some is that Murry was calling certain disc jockeys and telling them to avoid playing 'Cruisin'' – that is, if they wanted anything extra from The Beach Boys. Murry was reportedly using his power and influence to choke off any attention that Dave's record might have received on its own merits, just as he had reportedly conspired to dampen enthusiasm for Brian's non-Beach Boys productions. But Murry was about to reap what he had sowed. Only six months after getting his wish of eliminating David from The Beach Boys, Murry was about to be eliminated himself. That April, as they recorded vocals for what would turn out to be their first number one record, Brian and The Beach Boys fired Murry as their manager. His hard-nosed style had finally run its course with Brian. And Murry, without The Beach Boys to manage, was a very scary thing. First, he spent a month in bed, severely depressed. Audree Wilson once described the period as the worst time of her life. But when Murry finally got out of bed he was in a fighting mood. He wanted to compete with The Beach Boys. And the first weapon he thought of fighting back with was David.

Meanwhile, the Marksmen were just releasing their second A&M single in June 1964. Both sides were written by David and drummer Mark Groseclose. The A-side, 'Do You Know What Lovers Say?', was an attempt at a Four Seasons-style pop song. It had a catchy enough hook with a falsetto harmony line but overall the song was a dud. It lacked the challenging edge of the first Marksmen single by a long shot, and sounded like a sell-out to convention. The B-side, however, is simply one of the most bizarre recordings of its era. Entitled 'Food Fair', it tells of a brand new craze that's sweeping the land. 'It's not cars or surfing or battles of bands' but 'soups and salads and steaks and roasts' not to mention 'fifty-seven kinds of dessert'. It tells of a place where 'the cupcake queen fell in love with the angel food baker', and where 'Elvis Pretzel's singing up on the stand with the vegetable man'. This is truly one of the most absurd recordings I've ever absorbed. You think The Beach Boys' 1967 post-acid meltdown 'Smiley Smile' was unusual? In the context of 1964, 'Food Fair' was even weirder. It was either a horribly misguided grasp at a novelty hit or something so utterly original it was light years ahead of the norm. I tend to go with the latter. 'I think "Food Fair" was a definite indication of us trying to push the envelope,' says Bill Trenkle. This track would have been perfectly at home on Frank Zappa and The Mothers of Invention's *Freak Out* LP, which was still years in the future. Dave and Mark somehow nailed the same sharply silly-satirical point of view that Zappa became known for later in the decade. Even the way they enunciate their words and plough through the raucous R&B backing parallels the early Mothers feel. This was David and Mark letting their senses of humour and creativity off the leash in a head-shaking two-minute setting. How the Marksmen managed to convince Herb Alpert and Jerry Moss to stick it on a single is unexplainable. Of course, the song proved to be instant commercial suicide.

Without The Beach Boys to focus on, Murry Wilson was looking for new blood. He came up with the idea that he'd create another Beach Boys-style group, but this time clean-cut and controlled. He set his sights on the Marksmen, who had been tossed out like rotten salami by A&M after the 'Food

Fair' incident. Murry offered the suddenly labelless Marksmen another shot at fame and fortune, but only on his terms. 'There came a point in time where Murry tried to produce us because he was kicked out by The Beach Boys as their manager,' remembered Mark Groseclose in a 1986 interview. Murry set up and financed a recording session at Western, hiring Glen Campbell and Hal Blaine to fill out the Marksmen's sound. The project hit an immediate snag when Dave and his band couldn't cope with Murry's insistence on recording his own compositions. As soon as the session was under way, David knew they had made a big mistake by shacking up with Murry again. 'We really didn't want to be involved with Murry,' says Groseclose. 'He even offered us the chance to become The Sunrays and we turned him down on that too. I guess he got really mad at us because I think he blackballed us and many radio stations wouldn't have anything to do with us after that.'

David and Mark had good reason to believe Murry was causing them trouble behind the scenes. 'I heard later from Roger Christian that Murry blackballed me in the business,' explains David. Christian was both a high-profile LA DJ and a Brian Wilson collaborator. Roger had recently written the classic lyrics to 'Don't Worry Baby', which was one side of the latest Beach Boys single. 'Roger was very specific in his description of Murry's tactics,' says David. 'He'd call radio stations and say, "If you play David Marks's record, you won't get the next Beach Boys exclusive." So he put a damper on my career.' Others suggested that Murry was threatening to take away something even more tangible . . . like payola. There were DJs like KHJ's Sam Riddle who reportedly claimed when a Dave and the Marksmen single was added to the KHJ playlist, certain 'perks' provided by Murry were suddenly pulled. 'Murry was in a terrific position to barter with these people,' says Bill Trenkle. 'And he usually got what he wanted.' But even if all this was true, it's doubtful that this 'blackball' strategy would've had any major effect on the first two Marksmen singles. The simple truth is that neither was commercial enough to be hit single material. However, the same cannot be said for the third Marksmen release, which was still months away from being recorded.

In July 1964, 'I Get Around' became the first Beach Boys song to reach number one on the Billboard charts. Dave's old group had done the impossible and shaken off The Beatles' death grip on the US music scene. Around the same time, David was spending many of his free days with Dennis again. Dennis would often take David along with him when he was courting the lovely Carole Freedman, the woman who would become the first Mrs Dennis Wilson. 'We'd go fishing or camping and stuff back when they were first dating,' says David. 'He'd tow his fishing boat behind his Jaguar XKE, which I doubt was very good for the Jaguar. But somehow all three of us would squeeze into the two-seater. I'd be crammed behind the seats all folded up. Looking back, I don't know why I was there. I felt like the big ugly teenage son that was a third wheel. But Dennis insisted I go with them. Dennis just loved having his friends around.'

As The Beach Boys continued to tour without David, they were often faced with questions about him. Puzzled fans would regularly approach members of the group and ask, 'Whatever happened to David Marks?' Dennis's favourite answer became, 'He got sucked up the tailpipe of a 409.' And Brian would say, 'He died in a surfing accident.' Rumours abounded as to what really happened to David. One of the more sensational explanations was that he was thrown in jail for murdering a fan. As the years went on and Dave faded into obscurity, the rumours of his whereabouts continued. One tale that seemed to get the most play with fans was that David had died in a car accident. Some even believed the song 'A Young Man Is Gone' on the *Little Deuce Coupe* LP was The Beach Boys' vocal farewell to the late David Marks. In fact, the song was about James Dean, and the only thing late about David was his homework at Hollywood Professional School.

One day in August, Carl phoned David and informed him that he was planning to fly up to San Francisco at the weekend to see the California premiere of the new Beatles movie, *A Hard Day's Night*. 'It wasn't showing in Los Angeles yet and

Carl couldn't wait to see it,' remembers David. 'He was really into The Beatles and he wanted me to go with him, so we got on a plane at LAX and flew up. Fred Vail came down from Sacramento and met us there.' David had been a fan of The Beatles too but he wasn't crazy for them like Carl. Until he saw *A Hard Day's Night*, they were just one of the groups he admired. However, once he viewed the movie, like Carl, he became all Beatles, all the time. David instantly changed his hair, his clothes, and bought a Vox amp and a Rickenbacker twelve-string guitar just like George Harrison's.

The Marksmen felt the winds of change as well. The first major overhaul was when David replaced rhythm guitarist Ed Gauntt. 'Ed didn't really fit in,' says David. 'He was a nice guy, maybe too nice. One time, he accidentally walked through the plate-glass sliding door at my parents' house and got all cut up. Blood was squirting everywhere. He nearly cut his head off. We had to wrap him in a tourniquet and call the ambulance. That incident might have put a damper on his role in the band.' His replacement was twenty-one-year-old Denny Murry, who could barely play the guitar. 'Denny Murry was a guy who was hanging around Hollywood trying to make it in show business,' says David. 'He had this crusty old drunken and half-crippled manager who came by the house one day and introduced him to us. Denny was much older than we were. He drank and smoked and he was rough, and he got us in a lot of trouble. He sang like Elvis and played a little guitar, and we really liked his name, Denny Murry, because of The Beach Boys thing. He didn't have a place to stay, so he moved in with my parents and me. It wouldn't have been the same without Denny. He made it a well-rounded rogues' gallery.'

The band didn't have to wait long before landing another recording contract. Again, it was Russ Regan who gained the Marksmen interest from yet another record label. This time they were signed to Warner Brothers Records, meaning David had signed with his *third* major record label by the age of sixteen. On 27 September 1964, The Beach Boys performed 'I Get Around' on *The Ed Sullivan Show*. David, Mark and Denny sat at Dave's house with Jo Ann and watched it on TV.

David loved the song and he could hear what would have been his 'guitar part' in the arrangement, now played by Al. Traces of the old Beach Boys sound still lingered in the new material but Brian was moving far beyond what Dave had been a part of. His new music was very sophisticated and progressive for the time, and David admired that but wanted to record something different. The Beatles and the British beat boom wouldn't really alter Brian's approach, although in the coming years it made him more competitive and challenged him to grow. But Brian still remained fiercely Southern Californian in his texture and style. David was ready to leave The Beach Boys-influenced sound behind entirely. His goal was to create something similar to the new sounds he heard coming from England. And with that in mind, he went to work.

The results of David's new approach were two songs scheduled for the Marksmen's Warner Brothers debut. For the A-side, the Marksmen recorded a song entitled 'I Wanna Cry'. Written and produced by sixteen-year-old David, this song proved conclusively that his talent ran deep. Not only does it nicely reflect the British Invasion sound but it also pushes the sonic envelope into uncharted territory for its time. Instead of regurgitating a Beatles homage, like so many American groups of the day, David's 'I Wanna Cry' is much closer in spirit to the haunting resonance of The Zombies and the droning mystery of The Yardbirds, two groups that very few Americans knew about in September 1964. I doubt David himself had even heard of them yet. But again, as he did previously with the Zappa sound, David somehow discovered the same vibe that was later celebrated by fans of those still relatively unknown groups.

With a longing depth in David's reading of his tormented lyric, 'I Wanna Cry' is simply the best thing Dave and the Marksmen ever did. David's Rickenbacker twelve-string is used to epic effect as he chops away at massive chords set deeply in echo. Mark Groseclose's drumming is also stunning and passionate. He pounds the toms in speaker-rattling Ringo-meets-Phil Spector explosions. David's production is gorgeous, with shimmering ghost-like background vocals that pour subtle drippings of harmony into the mix. Russ Regan tops off the wicked sound with an ethereal falsetto vocal. The fact that David recorded this before there was any major US artist doing anything remotely like it makes 'I Wanna Cry' one of a kind. Darian Sahanaja of Brian Wilson's band and Wondermints fame relates, 'There's an unusual brand of twelve-string in the Marksmen sound. Not nearly as jangly as the Rickenbacker-laced Byrds or Beatles, it still had a West Coast breeze to the tone, but counterbalanced with the urgency and angst found on so many garage records of the time,' says Sahanaja. 'The quick strumming figure he does at the end of each "I Wanna Cry" chorus can only be described as harmonically supersonic, like the final jet engines fired just before blasting into the outer atmosphere.'

The flipside is nearly as great. 'I Could Make You Mine' sounds like an up-tempo cross between The Kinks and Gary Lewis and the Playboys – again, two groups barely out of the chute in 1964. David's vocal is playful, indescribably so, and his courage to be different should be noted. Says Darian Sahanaja, 'When Dave chuckles "Uh-huh" during the breaks on "I Could Make You Mine", he sounds like he *really doesn't give a shit!* And *that* was what the garage band ethic was all about.' Although clearly 'punk' in attitude, 'I Could Make You Mine' maintains a strong British beat vibe as well with David's twelve-string torching through a fantastic solo. The record creates a frantic momentum, with breathtaking stops and starts, and flailing rolls by Groseclose all along the way.

'I Wanna Cry' backed with 'I Could Make You Mine' is such a fantastic single that it seems very odd it went completely without notice in October 1964. Murry's alleged tampering with DJs may best explain why a recording this great received zero attention when it was released. The band toured behind it, David pushed it, the label supported it, the market was ripe for it . . . and still no one heard it. It was completely absent from the radio radar screen, without a trace of airplay anywhere. This record definitely is a harbinger of what bands like The Beau Brummels in SF, and later, The

Byrds in LA, would be celebrated for in the months ahead. It displayed a perfect fusion of American garage sensibility with a heavy dose of the current British influence. David had nailed it before any of them. And to this day, very few people know that he did. At the same time The Beach Boys were enjoying another Top Ten hit with the wonderfully American 'When I Grow Up To Be A Man', David's equally great 'I Wanna Cry' disappeared into oblivion.

On 24 October 1964, Dave and the Marksmen performed at the Sacramento Memorial Auditorium. Also on the bill were Jan and Dean, newcomer Glen Campbell, and The Fantastic Baggys. Fred Vail was the promoter and the concert was recorded for Jan and Dean's upcoming *Command Performance* LP. Around the same time, David was given the opportunity by Warner Brothers to write material for other artists on their roster. In short order, David and Mark landed one of their songs on the B-side of the 'You Say Pretty Words' single by Ramona King. The song was called 'Blue Roses', and they were thrilled to have it covered by another artist. 'We had some fun hearing our own music being played by someone else,' remembers Groseclose. 'Hell, I was only eighteen, and David was only sixteen. It was pretty nice watching a full orchestra and a professional singer do a piece of music we put together.' The ultra-lush song was produced by Joe Saraceno, arranged by Ray Pohlman, and had a string arrangement by Jimmy Haskell. Few people realise that Dave Marks's music had these kinds of industry heavyweights attached to it.

In December, with the new *Beach Boys Concert* LP riding at number one on the Billboard charts, Brian's mental house of cards finally caved in. On the eve of a two-week US tour, he melted down on the aeroplane. The overburdened leader of America's top group was found cowering and crying, saying he couldn't take it any more. The group members and flight attendants tried to calm him, but Brian was virtually inconsolable. As many have described, the rubber band of Brian's psyche, which had already been stretched far beyond its comfort zone, had finally snapped. Murry's strategy of guilting his reluctant son into touring, which began in the summer of 1963, had finally backfired, with lasting results. Within weeks, Brian informed The Beach Boys that he would no longer tour with them, and he virtually stayed away from the road for well over a decade. For a time, Glen Campbell replaced him for live Beach Boys shows, and then in spring 1965, Bruce Johnston became Brian's full-time replacement on the road.

Although David and Murry weren't on great terms, their animosity was put aside for one day in early 1965. Murry's 'Beach Boys-light' project was moving forward as he recorded tracks for his new concept called The Sunrays. Murry wanted to emulate the classic Beach Boys guitar sound, and he hired David and Glen Campbell to do the trick. The session for 'Out of Gas' and 'Bye Baby Bye' went quite well. Murry wrote and produced both tracks, and David and Glen nailed The Beach Boys' six-string style. This was David's first session as a paid studio musician, a role he'd get used to later in the decade. The tracks were released as Sunrays B-sides in March and June 1965 respectively. Murry and the individual members of The Sunrays actually meshed quite well. The band had real talent, including songwriter Rick Henn and guitarist Eddy Medora. But in the end, Murry's vision of duplicating 'his' success with The Beach Boys fell short. The Sunrays only achieved minor commercial notoriety, their career highlight being the regional smash 'I Live For The Sun'.

The Marksmen briefly added a sixth member to their line-up when Dave's buddy Greg Jones brought a friend of his named Art Vincent over to the Markses' house. 'This is Art from Chicago, and he sings his ass off,' said Jones confidently. Vincent had a 1950s hairdo and was wearing a trenchcoat on a typically sunny LA day. But despite the fact that he looked like a hodad, David liked his voice. 'We moved him out of the motel he was living in and into my parents' garage,' remembers Dave. 'He ended up performing at some Marksmen shows and did some recording with us.' Vincent's tenor vocals show up on the Marksmen's cover of 'Baby The Rain Must Fall' and David's ultra-pop original called 'I Heard You

Crying', both of which went unreleased. One night, while Vincent was sleeping, Dave fired a few rifle shots into the side of the garage. 'I thought I'd shake Art up,' explains David. Vincent crawled out of the garage on his belly wondering what kind of madness he'd got himself into. He left the Marksmen soon after.

In early 1965, David laboured in the studio, shaping potential material for his next Marksmen release. David himself was footing the bill for these ambitious sessions. He depended on Russ Regan as his go-between with the label. Among the tracks recorded was the gorgeous power ballad 'Don't Cry for Me', again written and produced by David. His production on this number was truly ambitious and of a quality unheard of for a sixteen-year-old. The arrangement included a lovely string arrangement, booming timpani drums, power guitar chording, and a blazing fuzztone guitar solo. Again, David had progressed ahead of the pack with his sound but later received no credit for his pioneering work. Another massive string-laden arrangement graced David's 'In My Lonely World', and although the composition wasn't one of his best, the production was very progressive for its time. As it turned out, though, all of this work was for nothing; Warner Brothers chose to leave it all in the can.

In the spring, Dave and the Marksmen set out on an 'Easter Tour' of the west. Joining them on the jaunt were Southern California favourites Eddie and the Showmen and 'Queen of the Surf Guitar' Kathy Marshall. The Showmen's leader Eddie Bertrand had split from Paul Johnson and The Belairs in 1963 to front his own group. Starting in 1964, the Marksmen and Showmen were essentially co-managed by the team of Jo Ann Marks and Eddie's father Bert Bertrand, and the groups were booked together on many double bills. The bands enjoyed a family atmosphere on the road and besides putting on great performances, the group members socialised like a travelling fraternity. Members of each group often joined each other on stage, creating an atmosphere of relaxed camaraderie wherever they went. Among the venues played on the '65 Easter Tour were the Veterans Memorial Building in Santa Rosa on

10 April and the San Jose County Fairgrounds on 17 April. There were also dates in San Francisco, Oakland, Fresno, Bakersfield, Reno and Las Vegas. The three acts also appeared on local teen-oriented television shows all around California. David has positive memories of his days on the road with the Marksmen/Showmen travelling troupe. For him, it all ended too soon.

Back in LA, it became clear that major gigs in large halls and auditoriums were drying up for the hitless Marksmen. Warner Brothers unceremoniously cut them loose without ever releasing a second single. Things were beginning to look bleak. The group began taking bookings at local clubs and adjusted to playing in front of fifty people instead of 1,500. On one occasion, when the Marksmen were booked at the Red Velvet nightclub in Hollywood, they crossed paths with a living symbol of rock and roll history. As they were running through their pre-set soundcheck, a familiar flamboyantly outfitted figure with a massive pile of hair and a pencil-thin moustache suddenly joined them on stage. Hopping on the piano and cutting loose with some pure rock and roll was none other than Little Richard. He was taken by the Marksmen's rocking sound, and couldn't resist joining in. For a few memorable minutes David and his group had the chance to play music with a true legend. As quickly as he'd appeared, Little Richard shouted, 'Thanks for the jam, boys! You play real good!' And on his way he went.

David's hope for solo fame was now running on fumes. With little reason to continue, Dave and the Marksmen disbanded in late 1965. 'It was definitely fading,' says David. 'There were less and less rehearsals, less and less gigs. Then we terminated. Mark and I went off to play with Band Without A Name. Bill was drafted and became a military aircraft mechanic. Denny went to Baltimore and became a DJ. Gene got a job with TRW and worked in the aerospace industry before dying in 1969 from complications from asthma.' Dave finally had a chance to reflect on the big picture. It had been three years since he'd been without a tour, a scheduled recording session or a booked engagement staring him in the face. 'I'd really kidded myself. I was very deluded. I thought I was getting jobs and doors were opening for me because I was cute and talented,' says David. 'But it was really happening because I was a former Beach Boy.' For the next three decades, David made practically no effort to trade on his Beach Boys past. From 1965 until the mid-nineties, he only hoped to remain an anonymous working musician. And anonymous he would be.

That December, David attended a dinner party at Brian and Marilyn's new home overlooking Beverly Hills. It was another cinematically gorgeous evening in the Hollywood Hills. On sparkling Indian summer nights like these, Los Angeles literally twinkles like a magic tinsel town. Amid the glitter, Beach Boys guitarist Carl Wilson slid behind the wheel of his impressive new steel-grey Aston Martin coupé. In the seat to his right was seventeen-year-old David Marks. He was used to riding shotgun to Carl as both a passenger and as a guitarist. They had been connected in that way since they were two unknown South Bay pipsqueaks. By this night they were both internationally famous teen musicians, although one was still on the way up while the other was fading fast. Happily poised to go cruising in a newly purchased world-class sports car, Carl turned the ignition. The British twelve-cylinder power plant growled pleasantly. In an instant, they were accelerating into the Disney Magic Kingdom backdrop that regularly appears on the Southern California nighttime horizon. With the adolescent perfume of burning rubber wafting into the stars behind them, it might have seemed like a juvenile delinquent's dream come true. But this particular fairytale was already over for David.

Things had been moving too fast for years now. There hadn't been much time to reflect. As Carl tore down Sunset Boulevard that night, ignoring anything close to a speed limit, he was scaring the piss out of David. 'Carl wasn't as scary a driver as Dennis, but he still had his moments,' says David. 'That night was one of them. Carl was on a real high with fame and money. I'd been there, I knew what he felt like . . . but it was just a memory for me.' That night, underneath the exhilaration of speed and the adrenalin of fear, David was experiencing something even stronger – an undeniable sense of loss. That was something he'd have to get used to. Earlier that night, at Brian's new Beverly Hills home, David's mind had been busy adding a few things up. It had been an eye-opening night. He got to check out the other Beach Boys' expensive new cars, as well as Brian and wife Marilyn's stylish new pad. Brian also proudly played David some of the surprisingly sophisticated Beach Boys recordings he was currently producing. David absolutely loved the classic sound of that new music. With over three years of growing success behind them, it certainly was a good time to be a Beach Boy. Unfortunately for David Marks, he no longer was.

On that night in late 1965, it finally dawned on David Marks that he might have made a big mistake. He had boldly quit The Beach Boys two years earlier. His own brave pursuit of solo stardom, while initially showing promise, had recently faded. In the blazing flash of time that had passed since he was an 'official' Beach Boy, he continued to interact with them socially and, in a way, he still felt like he was a part of them. But then came that night at Brian's. Immediately after hearing those haunting new songs, David wandered out onto the patio and lit a cigarette. He was deep in thought. Dennis Wilson followed him out the door. It was Dennis who may have known David the best of them all – after all, he'd been David's Indian guide and blood brother. He'd got David laid and protected him from bullies. Sensing his blue mood, Dennis asked in a very sincere tone, 'Are you OK, David? Is something bothering you?' David clearly remembers the significance of the moment. 'I said I was fine, but part of me wanted to tell Dennis that I wished I was back in the band . . . but I didn't.' Instead David left the party, rocketing into the night with Carl, and in a way he never looked back again.

That night, when Brian unveiled some of the vocal-less music that would eventually end up on the *Pet Sounds* album, David was astonished. The musical growth that Brian had shown since the time David left the band only two years earlier was unbelievable to him. But David also learned from

Dennis that one reason for the major change in Brian was his recent experimentation with drugs. Still, the music David heard left him briefly wishing he were somehow a part of The Beach Boys again. The only way for David to deal with it was to disconnect. And this was the moment he pulled the plug.

On 3 January 1966, The Beach Boys were awarded Gold Records for both the *Surfin' USA* and *Surfer Girl* albums. A short ceremony was held at the Capitol Tower and photos were taken of the event. Recording Industry Association of America Gold Record plaques were handed out to Brian, Dennis, Carl, Mike and Al. Incredibly, David wasn't notified of the ceremony, nor was he sent any awards for his participation in the recording of the LPs. To this day David Marks has never received a Gold Record from The Beach Boys or Capitol for his part in the creation of those two classic and massive-selling albums – surely one of the biggest oversights in rock and roll history.

Two months earlier, in a reply to an innocent letter from a thirteen-year-old fan enquiring why Dave Marks was no longer a Beach Boy, Murry Wilson replied, 'Answering your question about David . . . how can I put into words so you will understand . . . that ordinarily a fourteen-year-old does not comprehend what the word "business" means. David became difficult and turned in his resignation, which we accepted. From that time on, THE BEACH BOYS went sky high in popularity, because Al Jardine is a fantastic harmonizer as well as musician.' Murry's explanation sounds good on paper, but the fact remains that David's resignation came *after* The Beach Boys' popularity had gone 'sky high' and those two Gold Records should have been his and not Al's. But it was too late. David had completely let go. His only chance for survival was to convince himself and the world that he didn't care.

8. LET'S GO TRIPPIN'

Oh, how the mighty have fallen. In early 1966, David Marks found himself toiling at a regular weekend booking at the Sea Witch nightclub at 8514 Sunset Boulevard. He'd been occupying the tiny stage in Hollywood every Saturday night for several months now. His current group was called Band Without A Name, and to David they were also a band without much hope. At seventeen, David was tired and frayed. The former Beach Boy's eyes were ringed with dark circles, his clothes were wrinkled and dingy, and his once formidable self-confidence was on its last legs. That night, the club held about two dozen patrons, and few of them were paying any attention to the music Dave's band was playing. Sitting on his amp and strumming an anonymous cover tune, David's weary eyes glazed over. He was barely there. He felt like this hand was played out. He needed a new game.

When his night's work came to an uninspired end, David stepped out into the late-night Hollywood air. Lights flickered, cars roared by and partiers revelled. Dave slumped against the club's dirty façade and lit a cigarette. Looking up, he made eye contact with a face he'd seen many times before. David nodded and said hello. The face belonged to a diminutive 'street kid' named Rodney Bingenheimer. The kid later became one of LA's premiere DJs, and would eventually be known as 'The Mayor of Sunset Strip'. In 1966, however, Rodney held no such label. He was just a little guy who hung around the edges of the Hollywood scene. But for David he proved to be the key-holder to another universe – one that held both splendour and horror, one that would change him for ever. That night, Bingenheimer innocently reached out and offered David a small orange capsule. 'Want one?' he asked. Feeling he had nothing to lose, David swallowed the capsule even before asking what it was. Things would never be the same.

David followed Rodney to a 'friend's party' at an apartment across the Sunset Strip. They walked partway up a side street and ducked into a small apartment filled with the type of people that were known around Hollywood as 'freaks'. In San Francisco they called them hippies, but not here. Inside the apartment, the music was loud, coloured lights flashed, and giddy laughter seemed to drip from the walls. For David, it was a short walk to a distant place. Dave finally asked Rodney what was in the capsule he'd taken and the answer didn't faze him at first. 'I'd only heard rumours about LSD, so I wasn't really prepared for what happened next,' remembers David. Within a few minutes, David knew much, much more about LSD. As the drug's initial euphoria engulfed his body, everything around him became slightly liquefied. The growing tingling rush seemed to turn his flesh into a useless gooey mass. David found a chair and poured himself into it. His eyes were filled with saturating light and the corners of his mouth tightened into an endless smile. While sitting there and tripping fiercely, he gripped the chair's armrests as if they were two undulating life rafts. Then someone addressed him from a distant dimension: 'Hey, man, want a hit?' Dave could not come close to forming an answer for the alien species sitting directly next to him. But he eyed the freaky fellow and shared his perpetual smile. His new friend was outfitted with a pirate moustache and devil beard. He was wearing black and white striped pants and satin slippers. His image seared into David's flaming brain for ever. To this day he represents something both hilarious and horrifying. The 'devil pirate' then handed David a strange-looking apparatus with what looked to be a smouldering cigarette butt attached to it. While frying on acid for the first time, seventeen-year-old David Marks also took his very first hit of marijuana.

The order in which David encountered the 'drug experience' somehow paralleled his previous life. Everything seemed to come all at once, with no chance to sort things out in a logical, methodical way. Hit records at thirteen, washed up at sixteen, pot and acid in reverse order on the same night at seventeen. This was David's life. 'My first experience with LSD was intriguingly frightening,' says David. 'I was trying to eat a piece of bread and it kept turning into melting cotton. I found myself on the floor giggling uncontrollably. When the devil pirate pulled out the roach-clip, I was basically gone into the vortex. I knew I was never coming back to where I'd been before.' After the 'freak' party, Rodney continued to lead David further along his magical mystery tour. A stroll through the thick early-morning mist of Hollywood felt like surfing on dirty clouds. Every sound on the street bounced through Dave's eardrums like syrup bubbling through a Fender reverb unit. When Rodney pointed to a door and said, 'Let's go in here,' David blindly followed. Upon entering the door the freakiness didn't subside. Suddenly David realised he was a guest at a full-blown Sonny and Cher recording session at Goldstar Studios. David had previously backed Sonny and Cher as a musician, but that morning, while still peaking on his maiden acid voyage, he was entirely unable to communicate. 'Cher looked like Cleopatra,' says David. 'Sonny looked like he had on a wig and a fake nose. Phil Spector was there, talking a million miles an hour to some black chick that was twice his size. It was all pretty trippy for me in that state. I couldn't even speak to any of them because my mouth didn't work. I lasted about five minutes in there and ended up

LET'S GO TRIPPIN'

running out of the studio because I was seeing fluorescent-coloured, geometric-shaped monsters coming out of the speaker cabinets.'

Once David had descended from his marathon hallucino-genic trip, he openly evaluated the experience. Instead of being frightened away from a return visit to the stratosphere, he was entirely fascinated by the process. It was about as far away from being an ex-Beach Boy as he could go. As a result, David began dropping acid on a nearly daily basis. 'Needless to say, the daily LSD trips altered my way of thinking,' says David. Among those who immediately noticed a change in David was his father, Elmer. 'I got along with my dad pretty well until I reached adolescence,' says David. 'And then I alienated everyone, especially my parents. It got worse when I started taking acid. That's when I started relating to my dad like he was an exhibit in a zoo, and he really resented it. He knocked the shit out of me and broke my nose one day.' But David's experimentation with drugs only continued.

David also continued as a musician, but for the time being it was only a half-hearted involvement. David's current group, Band Without A Name, gave him little to work with. The outfit was managed by LA DJ Casey Kasem and fronted by Casey's nephew Eddie Haddad. Dave's role in Band Without A Name was not as frontman or creator but co-guitarist and backing vocalist. The group's repertoire consisted mainly of watered-down cover tunes. Their live routine churned out an hour's worth of Top 40 knock-offs, R&B dance tunes and rock standards. 'We backed up a lot of hit acts like Sonny and Cher,' says David. 'Casey would book us into teen dances and we'd play a set and then back the headliner for their set. It was awful.' Besides Haddad on lead vocals, Band Without A Name included Dave's buddy Mark Groseclose on drums, Richard Faith on electric piano and Larry Puckett on guitar. 'We played lots of hops in Thousand Oaks and at the Hawthorne Memorial Center, backing up acts like the Teddy Bears, Charles Wright, and Freddy Cannon,' remembered Groseclose. 'We also signed on with Dick Biondi's KRLA

Road Show and played with The Bobby Fuller Four. Dick wanted us to record for him, but Casey told us to record our own stuff and Dick dropped us.'

Among the vast array of notable acts playing the LA club scene at the same time as Band Without A Name was a rising group that featured another Hawthorne prodigy named Emitt Rhodes. 'The first time I met Emitt, he was playing drums with the Palace Guard,' remembers David. 'We played shows with them at a club called the Hullabaloo on Sunset near Vine. Their stage costumes were worse than Paul Revere and the Raiders. But Emitt was really talented, and eventually he made some great records with The Merry-Go-Round and some even better solo LPs. I ended up spending some time at his home studio in Hawthorne.'

That spring, Brian Wilson's masterpiece, *Pet Sounds*, was released to the public. David hadn't spoken to any of The Beach Boys in months. He found himself back in the studio briefly when Band Without A Name was given minimal session time to cut tracks with up-and-coming producer Charles Wright. One of the songs they recorded was a David Marks/Mark Groseclose original entitled 'That's Why'. The dramatic folk-rocker is another example of Dave and Mark's ability to create good original material together. Charles Wright went on to major fame with the Watts 103rd Street Rhythm Band, releasing the classic soul smash 'Express Yourself' in 1970. But the Band Without A Name sessions produced by Wright were never completed and remain unreleased. By the time David and Mark had left the group in mid-1966, only Eddie Haddad remained from the original line-up. A reconstructed Band Without A Name eventually received some notoriety by appearing in the 1967 film *Thunder Alley* starring Fabian and Annette Funicello. They also released a single of the soul cover 'Turn On Your Love Light' on Mike Curb's Tower label that same year. David and Mark played no part in either of those performances. After leaving Band Without A Name, and the music scene in general, Mark Groseclose became an award-winning visual artist whose impressive skills covered animation, graphics, television work, fine art and commercial art. It would be a number of years before he and David reconnected.

There is no shortage of memorable drummers in Dave's story. First Dennis, then Mark, and now there would be two more. Among David's friends who also grew up in the Hawthorne area were drummer brothers Terry and Skip Hand. Sibling drummers are a definite rarity in show business, and both Skip and Terry were good ones. David already knew them from their respective tenures banging the skins for Eddie and the Showmen, but now Terry would become a constant in Dave's life. 'One day, Terry Hand called me up and asked me for a ride somewhere in my new Buick Riviera,' says David. 'We ended up driving around in that Buick for the next two years, taking drugs and listening to The Beatles.' At that time Terry was playing with a talented new group named The Everpresent Fullness, which had signed to White Whale records. The Everpresent Fullness line-up also included guitarist Paul Johnson, formerly of The Belairs. Dave ended up driving several members of the group to San Francisco, where they all stayed for part of the summer of 1966. Putting down his guitar for a time, he became a non-playing member of The Everpresent Fullness entourage. 'That's the group I ended up doing a lot of acid with,' says Dave. 'It was like a hippie entourage. We hung out at the Avalon Ballroom and at the Fillmore. I met Bill Graham. I was just in the background and I drove some of the band around in my car. It was fun for a while.'

When the group returned to LA in August 1966, David continued to habitually drive around town with Hand in his trusty Riviera. 'One night, Terry asked me if I wanted to go over to Lyme's house,' remembers David. 'I had no idea who Lyme was. Terry told me about a local folk duo named Lyme and Cybelle, who had a hit record in Los Angeles. Lyme lived in an apartment in Hollywood on Orchid Street. He wore green clothes and green tinted sunglasses and all the walls in his apartment were painted green.' David soon learned that Lyme's real name was Warren Zevon. As soon as they met, something between Warren and David clicked and they became fast friends. 'I was just one of the people he dug being around,' says David. 'He surrounded himself with writers, artists and musicians. There were photographers coming by. It was like an Andy Warhol scene.'

Lyme and Cybelle eventually broke up, and Warren prodded David to form a new band with him. And David, in turn, prodded Warren to drop the silly stage name Lyme. Zevon had previously called himself Sandy when he was performing solo but David insisted his real name was better than anything he could make up. Warren thought about it, and answered, 'Yeah, I guess I am cool.' David moved into his apartment and began an on-and-off jam session with Warren that lasted for many years. Together David, Warren and Glen Crocker, a friend Zevon recruited from the Berklee School of Music in Boston, formed a group called The Flies. 'We used to put heavy fuzztone on our guitars and bass, and we kind of buzzed like flies,' says David. The Flies made their live debut at Bido Lido's, a 'hippie club' on Gower in Hollywood. Eventually Glen Crocker left Hollywood to return to school in Boston, and The Flies stopped buzzing. But Warren and David remained friends and continued to play music together and hang out socially for seven wild years.

In the late summer of 1966, The Beatles were in Los Angeles for a performance at Dodger Stadium that turned out to be their second to last concert appearance ever. Their new LP, *Revolver*, had just been released in the US, and the city of angels was buzzing about the fact that they were in town. For several days prior to their concert, the Fabs relaxed at a large rental house on Blue Jay Way in the Hollywood Hills. That same weekend, David was hanging out with his friends The Turtles, who were headlining at the Whisky a Go Go on the Sunset Strip. David had known Turtles vocalists Mark Volman and Howard Kaylan since their days in the South Bay surf band The Crossfires. By 1966, The Turtles were already well on their way to becoming a massive hit act. Also in attendance were several members of The Everpresent Fullness, as well as Dave's roommate Warren Zevon. The prolific Zevon was in the midst of writing songs for The Turtles, three of which ended up as B-sides. As the well-received show ended and everyone mingled backstage, word filtered through the entourage that The Beatles had invited them all to a party at their house. David would finally have a chance to meet his heroes.

A three-car entourage quickly departed the Whisky and caravanned into the Hollywood Hills. David's Riviera was packed with bodies and filled with marijuana smoke as a chorus of stoned voices sang, 'We're off to meet The Beatles!' As the merry group wound through the hills to their Blue Jay Way destination, the anticipation built to a giddy peak. 'Upon arrival at the party a man in a windbreaker and holding a flashlight came up to the window of my car and started ordering us around and telling us where we could park,' remembers David. 'Jack Ryan, who played the washboard in The Everpresent Fullness, was in the back seat of my car, and he started mouthing off to this guy. It turns out the guy was an undercover policeman.' Within seconds, a gang of uniformed LAPD were surrounding Dave's car and ordering everyone out. At that point, Dave remembered he had about six hits of LSD in capsule form tucked away in his pocket. Although LSD would remain technically legal in California until later that year, the word on the street was that the LA police were ignoring the technicality and busting anyone found with it. With the thought of going to jail and missing The Beatles in his mind, David made a fateful split-second decision. Just as he stepped out of the Riviera, he discreetly slipped all six capsules under his tongue. 'As the cops were going down the line searching us I could feel the capsules popping open in my mouth one by one,' remembers Dave. Within a minute, the half-dozen doses of LSD had dissolved into David's system.

After searching the entire group, the cops only found one marijuana roach in their possession. Due to their defiant attitudes, Jack Ryan and Terry Hand were hauled away by the police. 'They let the rest of us go for some reason,' says David, 'but they wouldn't let us go in to see The Beatles. I was bummed.' A desperately disappointed Dave and Warren got back into the Riviera and slowly drove back to the apartment on Orchid.

On the way home, David suddenly remembered he had just eaten six hits of acid. He informed Warren that he had a big problem in store. He'd just ingested more LSD than he or any of his friends had ever taken, or even witnessed anyone take. Warren sheepishly pointed out to David that he probably shouldn't be driving. 'Good point,' said David. Soon they were safely home but for David the ride was only beginning. 'I started peaking out on the acid pretty quickly,' remembers David. 'Soon I couldn't do anything but lay on the floor. I laid in the corridor between the kitchen and the bathroom for . . . I don't know how long, for days. I was conscious but unable to move. I remember Warren coming in with different people and going, "That's him. There he is," then he'd leave. Then some time would pass and he'd come back again with someone else: "There he is." I'd hear voices saying, "Can I see him?" And Warren would say, "Yeah, come see him, he's in here." And basically, for two days I was like a neighbourhood tour attraction for people who wanted to see the guy who took the most acid.' Finally, after about 48 hours of intense tripping, David was able to move himself into a sitting position, drink some water and eat a banana. Slowly, David made his way back to reality.

During late 1966, David and Terry Hand volunteered to house-sit for Jim Tucker, guitarist for The Turtles, while his group undertook a lengthy tour. The Turtles were in the midst of enjoying a worldwide smash with their latest single 'Happy Together'. They were selling out concerts across the States and were constantly featured on the radio and television. While Dave was staying at Tucker's house, Turtles vocalist Mark Volman called him. Volman was in a panic because co-vocalist Howard Kaylan had just quit the band and walked out on the tour. Mark pleaded with David to fly out immediately and join The Turtles. Realising he had no reason to refuse the offer, David agreed. 'I got really excited and thought this was my chance to get back into the limelight,' remembers Dave. 'I started packing my bags, I grabbed my guitar, I was nearly out the door . . . and then the phone rang again.' It was Volman. This time he told David to 'forget it' – Kaylan had changed his mind. Despite the false alarm, Mark Volman and David remained close friends for years.

One sunny September afternoon in 1966, David and Warren cruised along busy Sunset Boulevard in the Riviera, listening to music and killing time. As they motored down the boulevard, Dave noticed there was a familiar car parked at Western Recorders. 'That's Brian's car,' Dave said to Warren. 'He must be in there working on something.' Warren put aside any pretence of trying to act cool and began peppering David with requests: 'Can we meet him? Can you introduce me to Brian? Can we go in?' He was bouncing on the seat like a kid on Christmas Eve waiting to see Santa Claus. Dave pulled a tyre-screeching U-turn and said, 'Sure, let's go see what Brian's up to.' Upon entering the studio they found Brian alone in his usual lair, Studio 3, with only an assistant engineer to keep him company. 'Hey, Dave!' said Brian. 'How's your mom?' Dave told Brian she was just fine, and then he introduced an awestruck Warren to him. With an intense sense of purpose, Brian announced he was going to play them 'part' of a new track that he'd been editing and re-editing. The song snippet was impressive and featured some very unique production elements but it was only about thirty seconds long and seemed to go nowhere. Brian asked Dave and Warren point-blank, 'What do you think about this music?' But before they could fully answer him, Brian quickly changed the subject and asked if they had any marijuana. David emptied his shirt pocket, giving Brian all his pot, which wasn't very much. Brian scrambled around the studio and seemed to lose all interest in David and Warren. After a short stay, David told Brian to be sure to say hello to his brothers for him. Brian barely nodded and returned to playing with his track. A month later, while driving in the Riviera again, David and Warren heard a DJ on the car radio announce, 'This is the new Beach Boys song, and it sounds like another big hit!' They drove and listened. Towards the end of the song, Warren turned to David and said, 'Isn't that the thing Brian was working on?' Dave agreed. It was the same track. The song was called 'Good Vibrations'.

During the Christmas season of 1966, 'Good Vibrations' seemed to be playing everywhere. It turned out to be the biggest Beach Boys single ever. And the more David heard the lyrics the more he thought about how the thematic connection pointed directly back to his mom. He thought about how Brian constantly showed up at his folks' house and looked through his mother's books. He remembered Brian regularly asking Jo Ann about what she was learning at the metaphysical philosophy study meetings she was attending with J'nevelyn Terrell and Reverend Bond. And though Dave would often roll his eyes when his mother used the term 'vibrations' to describe how she felt about something, Brian took the whole matter very seriously. It's a safe bet that the influence gained from Jo Ann's spiritual quest set in motion his curiosity about vibrations. And it was Jo Ann who eventually introduced Brian to J'nevelyn, who became his personal astrologer and remained his adviser throughout the 'Good Vibrations' and *Smile* periods. The often-told story credited to Audree Wilson, about dogs and their keen sensitivity to vibrations, has been mythologised and long considered the thematic basis for the song. Jo Ann, who loved Audree, would never want to take anything away from her, and she specifically told me she would never go on the record saying she thought 'Good Vibrations' came from her influence. Now in her mid-seventies, she still complains when something has 'bad vibrations'.

Dave and Terry Hand's multi-year drive in the Buick Rivera continued through the last days of 1966. One night in late December, Dave and Terry found themselves at a small party in Hollywood. It was happening at the upstairs apartment of a sometime girlfriend of Dave's, a go-go dancer named Donna Huntington whose nickname was Choo Choo. Also attending the soirée were several members of a well-known local band who had recently gained much notoriety from playing clubs on the Sunset Strip. Dave had been hearing about them for months but he'd never actually listened to their music. That changed when one of the group members proudly played him a just-mastered test-pressing. It was a hot-off-the-press copy of their debut LP, which was due to be released the following month. After listening to a few cuts, David and Terry both decided the music sounded horrible, and unfortunately they were both too high to care about holding back their opinions. After side one ended, Dave made a crack about the 'cheesy' organ sound that dominated the record. Terry pointed out the singer's 'overdramatic' low voice. The two started mocking the sound, with Dave going, 'Doo doo doo doo' to imitate the organ and Terry crooning 'Baby, baby, baby' at the same time. The band members, who were sitting in the same room, were clearly disturbed by the rude comments and quickly snatched their record from the turntable and began to leave the party. As they left, Dave sarcastically asked the guys what the title of their new album would be. One of them turned and answered, 'It's called *The Doors*, you asshole.' And out the door they went.

As 1966 became 1967, The Doors became superstars. At the same time, Brian Wilson was deep in the process of recording his legendary *Smile* LP, which he would tragically abandon in the spring. Dave heard a rumour from someone in Brian's circle that his old neighbour had briefly considered calling to ask him to play guitar on one of his new songs called 'Surf's Up'. But the mercurial Brian quickly dropped the idea and nothing came of it. David himself was paying little attention to making music anyway. He was basically living off his Beach Boys royalties and getting high full-time. With a large chunk of royalty money released from trust upon Elmer's petitioning of the court, David purchased an impressive apartment building in Hollywood. The building, known as the Beresford, was located at 7231 Franklin Avenue near the corner of La Brea Boulevard. Elmer and Jo Ann took over the day-to-day management of the building, and eventually sold their house on Almertens and moved to Hollywood. In early 1967, with the war in Vietnam raging, David was suddenly drafted. 'I reported for duty and had made up my mind I was going to Vietnam,' says David. 'But my X-rays showed I had an ulcer in my stomach lining. That meant I didn't have to go in until the enemy landed on our soil, which wasn't gonna happen. I got lucky. I think Carl was drafted right around the same time as me.' Carl Wilson would become one of the Vietnam War's first high-profile conscientious objectors.

During 1967, The Everpresent Fullness disbanded amid torturous problems with White Whale Records. The terminally enthusiastic Terry Hand soon had David sold on the idea of forming a new band with him. Dave and Terry recruited bassist and future member of The Byrds John York and keyboardist Garrett Moore for their project. The quartet named themselves The Tender Trap, and moved into a house in Manhattan Beach. Before long they tired of the LA scene and moved north to Pacifica, a small town near San Francisco that perched on the ragged cliffs of the Northern Pacific coastline. Cold, constantly foggy and isolated, The Tender Trap's new environment turned out to be a depressing dead end. 'We rented a big house near the ocean,' remembers David. 'The house didn't have any furniture in it, just some mattresses on the floor and our amps and drums. We wrote a few songs and rehearsed some, but mostly all we did was smoke pot and take acid. After a while, we got really paranoid and buried all of our weed in the back yard. We moved back to LA after only a few months.' As he had with the Marksmen, David financed the entire Tender Trap experiment. 'I always felt kind of guilty about my income from The Beach Boys, and I think that's why I was so free to give it away,' says Dave. 'Everybody always knew when David had money,' says Skip Hand. 'He spent it freely.'

Back in Southern California, David ploughed his two-year-old Riviera into a parked garbage truck and then gave the crumpled vehicle to his father. Elmer spent months meticulously restoring it back to perfection. Soon after the restoration was complete, Dave borrowed the car to drive his grandfather to the local grocery market. On the way home, David smashed up the Riviera again. This time, he slammed into the rear end of another car that was stopped at a red light on La Brea Boulevard. His excuse was that he'd been distracted by a pretty girl on the sidewalk. An unlucky passenger in the other car was already in a neck brace, having been injured hours before when his car had been rear-ended by a fleeing thief in a stolen car. The badly shaken man was just being driven home from the hospital by a relative when lightning struck twice and David ploughed into him. Due to a string of violations and accidents, David soon found himself without a car or a driver's licence.

After The Tender Trap disbanded, David sunk back into the Los Angeles scene. He set up his home base in an apartment in his own building in Hollywood, but spent much of his time drifting and crashing with friends. One day Terry Hand called and insisted that Dave come over to hear a great new singer he'd been jamming with in his garage. David was growing wary of Hand's never-ending enthusiasm, especially on the heels of The Tender Trap fiasco. But Dave always had a tough time saying no to Terry, and he decided to check out the rehearsal. The musician Hand had been raving about was keyboardist/vocalist Matthew Moore from Idaho. Moore was the talented son of a preacher who had already released two independent singles with his band known as Matthew Moore Plus Four. The Plus Four had recently returned to Idaho, leaving Matt in Southern California looking for new people to play music with. After a bit of jamming, Dave became very impressed with Matt's songwriting and voice. Matt, in turn, admired Dave's versatile guitar style. An immediate partnership formed. However, Moore didn't share the same appreciation for drummer Terry Hand, who was left out of plans for a new group. Matt and Dave's new band would be named The Moon.

Matt Moore was intrigued by David's Beach Boys past but found it hard to engage him about it. 'Dave was in pretty weird shape when I met him,' remembers Moore. 'I think the whole Beach Boys experience kind of screwed him up. I used to ask, "Why'd you quit something as successful as The Beach Boys?" He'd always give me the same answer. He'd say, "I didn't want to carry my luggage." I figured there had to be more to it than that, but he always stuck to that story.'

Matt Moore's older brother, Danny, was also a fine singer and songwriter who had played bass in Jimmie 'Honeycomb' Rodgers's band and had written songs with Gene Clark long before Clark was singing 'Mr Tambourine Man' and 'Turn, Turn, Turn' with his group, The Byrds. When Danny Moore befriended David, his first encounter with Dave's mum gave him an instant preview of the years ahead. 'She shook Danny's hand and informed him that he was going to make a lot of money in the music business some day,' remembers David. She was right. Danny Moore became a prolific record producer and session vocalist working with the likes of Kim Carnes, Joe Cocker and Bonnie Raitt. Danny also composed several major hit songs including the 1973 smashes 'Shambala' for Three Dog Night and 'My Maria' for B. W. Stevenson. Danny's 'My Maria' hit paydirt a second time in the nineties when country stars Brooks & Dunn took it to the top of the charts again. David recalls, 'When my mom told Danny that he was going to be successful I was kind of embarrassed and said, "Sorry, my mom's a little strange," but the fuckin' shit came true!'

It was Danny Moore who initially presented The Moon's demo material to his friend Mike Curb at Sidewalk Productions. On the strength of brother Matt's great songs, Mike Curb quickly signed The Moon to a production deal. The band was given the keys to Continental Sound Recorders, a studio that happened to be built by Curb employee Larry Brown. Previously the drummer for Davie Allen and the Arrows, Larry Brown was also a world-class recording engineer and producer. He became a huge asset for The Moon when he took on the role of drummer, engineer and producer for them. With all the pieces of The Moon pie falling sweetly into place, Andy 'Drew' Bennett filled out the line-up on bass.

In the early stages of recording, David and Matt Moore each ingested a large dose of LSD and listened intently to the newly released Beatles LP, *Sgt. Pepper's Lonely Hearts Club Band*. Dave and Matt were mesmerised by it and played the record at extreme volume for fourteen hours straight, while running it through the mixing console at Continental. Needless to say, this experience influenced the direction of The Moon's recording project. Another trippy influence was hit upon while visiting Dave's parents' home. In Jo Ann's pile of reading material Matt Moore noticed a book he'd been familiar with in the past, the same book that had once intrigued Brian Wilson: *The Rosicrucian Cosmo-Conception* by Max Heindel. Matt and Dave began studying the material deeply and incorporated it into the concept for The Moon's musical themes and lyrics. 'We were taking a philosophy correspondence course and learning about the occult,' says David. 'We were heavily into the spiritual realm. Everybody I knew was kind of on that trip. Brian, Carl, even Mike, eventually became deeply involved in the spiritual side of things.'

With his creative juices flowing again, David felt very hopeful about working with Matt Moore. He wanted to support Matt's vision and left the songwriting duties completely up to him. Dave's role in The Moon was as guitarist, co-vocalist, co-arranger and full-time sounding board for Matt's ideas. Mike Curb's silent partner status gave The Moon plenty of freedom to experiment with the recording process. 'We weren't paying for studio time so there weren't any budgetary restraints,' says producer Larry Brown. The Moon had 24/7 access to the studio thanks to Curb. 'We literally locked the world outside and lived in the studio,' remembers Matt Moore. 'We'd eat there, sleep there and record there, sometimes without knowing if it was day or night outside. Can you imagine how cool that was for a bunch of eighteen- and nineteen-year-olds? Our whole life was making that record; there was really nothing else going on in our lives except recording. We were totally committed to that project.' For Dave, it was wonderful to find himself deeply committed to something besides driving around and trying to forget about the past. For the third time in his life, he found a group of musicians who became as close to him as family. 'We couldn't have been any closer,' says David. 'We spent hours, days, weeks together in this small confined recording studio. It was like being on submarine duty.'

THE LOST BEACH BOY

And in that environment, David flourished. Feeling like a serious musician making serious music, David was completely in sync with his art. 'Dave was the perfect guitar player and vocalist for The Moon situation because he had the ability to be patient and, when needed, he could concentrate on the part that needed to be played,' says Matt Moore. 'When called upon to play his guitar he was really intense. He'd just sit there by himself and keep playing his part over and over until he knew he had it the way he wanted. Sometimes he'd be recording his part for hours. We'd just stay out of his way and push the record button when he was ready. We were all like that. Larry and I were definitely obsessive compulsive. We made an excellent team.' David mainly used a Gibson ES335 hollow-body electric during The Moon sessions as well as an acoustic Martin D25 and a nylon string Jose Oribe classical model. Besides adding subtle guitar textures to Moore's keyboard-heavy songs, David came into his own as a vocalist as well. He often added key harmonies and counter vocal lines to Moore's fantastic leads, giving The Moon's vocal sound impressive depth. David was also given the opportunity to sing lead on the tracks 'Brother Lou's Love Colony' and 'She's On My Mind', both written by Jack Dalton and Gary Montgomery of the band Colours. At nineteen, David's voice and musical skills had matured nicely and The Moon project was an excellent showcase for him to utilise them.

By the end of 1967, The Moon's first LP, *Without Earth*, was finally complete. The album was filled with wondrous treasures of psychedelic pop and is simply one of the most underrated works of its time. Matt Moore's vocals are beautifully rendered with a lilting, soulful grace. Larry Brown's gorgeous production is filled with layers of invention. Lush voices, inventively played instruments, flourishes of tape manipulation and percussive effects and sophisticated accents fill The Moon's sound palette with wonderful results. The LP's stately strings, arranged by Robert Klimes, are used to great effect in Brown's production. Songs like the tripped-out 'I Should Be Dreaming' and the regal sunshine pop of 'Someday Girl' were perfect snapshots of their place in time. The best track of all may have been Matt Moore's magical harpsi-chord-driven 'Give Me More'. With its magnificent string arrangement and Moore's otherworldly vocal delivery 'Give Me More' should be known as one of the best pop songs of 1967. The weirdly wonderful 'Walking Around' is another Moon classic, capturing a euphoric reflection of David and Matt's penchant for hoofing it along the streets of Los Angeles. One of the LP's most commercially viable moments was David's lead vocal showcase, the bubblegum-sitar epic 'Brother Lou's Love Colony'. David's vocal remains confident amid a potpourri of surging psychedelic sounds, similar in production style to The Cowsills' 1968 recording of 'Hair'. As an album, *Without Earth* stood tall amid the psychedelic pop class of 1967 and 1968. In its own way, it held up well to The Beatles, Stones, Monkees, Zombies and Pink Floyd releases cut during the same period.

While The Moon was rising, Dave's mum Jo Ann was busy working in the offices of Liberty Records in Los Angeles. The label was best known for launching Ross Bagdasarian's novelty smash cartoon act Alvin and the Chipmunks. The character 'Alvin' had been named after label president Alvin Bennett. Liberty was also the home of many hits by Dave's buddies, Jan and Dean. Among Jo Ann's associates at Liberty Records in 1968 was Zelda Samuels, former companion of the late Sam Cooke and manager of singer Mel Carter. Zelda had strong ties to the LA music business, co-writing the classic soul hit 'Lookin' For A Love', recorded by Bobby Womack. Jo Ann and Zelda became fast friends – both women shared the psychic gift. They also got together and composed a Mel Carter B-side called 'Everything Stops For A Little While', surely making David the only Beach Boy whose mother authored a song recorded and released by a major artist. In the midst of her Liberty stint as assistant to the head of A&R, Jo Ann submitted The Moon's recordings to her boss, chief A&R man and jazz legend Dave Pell. The Mike Curb-financed tape was readily accepted and The Moon signed a two-LP distribution deal with the Liberty-owned imprint known as Imperial Records.

In February 1968, *Without Earth* was released to great critical acclaim but weak sales. With Liberty/Imperial in the throes of financial and political problems, very little was done to promote it: that year Liberty had been sold for $38 million to Transamerica Corporation and was combined with another label, United Artists Records. Transamerica was unfamiliar with the recording industry and squandered a knowledgeable asset when label stalwart Alvin Bennett was fired after six months of trying to right the ship.

The Moon's *Without Earth* became a tragic casualty of the label's internal turmoil. A single of the album's lead track, 'Mothers And Fathers', was released simultaneously with the LP but completely disappeared after garnering little notice. The disappointment among the band members was huge. They had selflessly poured many months of their lives into making the best possible record for Curb and the thought that it was hardly being heard was an extremely painful pill to swallow. The Moon did nothing to reverse the situation themselves, avoiding playing live except for several rehearsals at Drew Bennett's home. Instead of dwelling on the downer of knowing their record had bombed commercially, they just geared back up for another shot at the studio process.

One day in the spring of 1968, while tripping on acid yet again, Matt Moore and David suddenly decided to visit Dennis Wilson. David hadn't seen Dennis in well over a year and wanted to make an attempt at reconnecting with his old friend. Since neither David nor Matt owned a car they decided to walk the nearly twenty-mile trek to their proposed destination near Will Rogers State Park. Just like they'd sung in The Moon song 'Walking Around', they mingled with flashes of sunshine, listened to birds sing, and when they got tired they sat on the corner for a while. They also jumped on a bus for a brief leg of the journey. After hours of tripping along the city sidewalks, they finally arrived at Dennis's home on the west end of Sunset. Some barely clothed hippie girls came to the door and informed Dave and Matt that Dennis wasn't home. The thought then occurred to them that maybe they should have called first. Dennis was off touring with The Beach Boys and wouldn't be back for a few days. Dave and Matt stayed for a short time and smoked a joint with the somewhat spacey but seemingly friendly girls. Later, Dave realised, these were some of the infamous Manson girls that were staying at Dennis's house that year. From Dennis's home, the unfazed pair decided to travel back across town to the Griffith Observatory. They shortened the last leg of the journey by ascending straight up the steep hillside that led to the observatory and ultimately climbed over the large wall that surrounded the grounds. There they flopped down on the grass and initiated a round of cloud-busting. Lying among soft tufts of green turf and dandelions, David told Matt stories about when he and Dennis were kids in Hawthorne. Matt and Dave's penchant for striking out on foot in a psychedelic state of mind became a regular routine that defined the spirit of The Moon period.

In between the recording of the first and second Moon LPs, Dave and Matt went to San Francisco for several weeks. It was Dave's third extended stay in the Bay Area during the 1966–68 period. This time, they landed in a squalid room on skid row while Matt took on a production job financed by his brother Danny. David was also hired by Danny to assist in writing string arrangements for the project. Matt's recollection of David in San Francisco is of someone who just 'laid around while I worked'. 'We'd live on 35 cent cheese sandwiches and LSD,' says Moore. 'Sometimes we'd take acid and just walk around or get on a city bus and just ride it all day, looking at weird people and tripping out. It was cheap entertainment and nobody got hurt.'

David eventually tired of the skid row digs and rented a decent hotel room in a better part of town. One evening he made his way to the Avalon Ballroom, where John Mayall's Bluesbreakers were performing. Their lead guitarist in 1968 was a nineteen-year-old phenomenon named Mick Taylor, who would join The Rolling Stones the following year. Upon entering the Avalon early, Dave found himself briefly jamming with Taylor during his soundcheck. Later that night, Taylor presented him with a custom-made bottleneck slide which Dave still uses on occasion.

Back in LA, before work was scheduled to begin on the second Moon LP, Dave became known around Hollywood as an ever-present street character. 'I bought a really expensive suit and walked all over Hollywood with just the jacket and pants,' says David. 'I wore no shirt, no shoes, and I had really long hair down to my shoulders. I was known around town as "the guy in the suit".' One day 'the guy in the suit' was traipsing along the sidewalk in Hollywood, bare feet slapping along the hot concrete, hair flying in the breeze, nowhere to go, nothing to do, when a familiar voice called out, 'Hey, Dave!' David remembers the moment. 'I turned around and it was Dennis. I hadn't seen him in nearly two years. He was driving a beautiful Rolls-Royce. He said he'd just bought it from John Lennon. He was just driving around, like I was just walking around, and he asked me to jump in with him. The first thing I noticed is that we had on the same clothes. He had a new suit on with no shirt or shoes too and really long hair. He asked me if I wanted to go get some chilli dogs at Pink's, which is something we always used to do back in The Beach Boys days. After that we went back to his house on Sunset and smoked some good pot. There were some hippie girls still living there. He played me the latest Beach Boys record, which wasn't out yet. At the time I remember thinking it wasn't very good. It sounded kind of half-baked compared to The Moon. We played the piano for a while, and then I took off on foot. Luckily, I never saw Charlie Manson, and Dennis never mentioned him to me.'

During the rest of 1968 and continuing into the spring of 1969, the second Moon LP was methodically constructed at Continental. For these sessions, David Jackson took the place of 'Drew' Bennett on bass. Again the process turned into a marathon non-stop affair, with the band virtually living at Continental for another year. Entitled simply *The Moon*, the album was again a near masterpiece of pop invention, and Moore's prolific writing streak showed no signs of weakening. The textures of the band's sound took on a slightly progressive aura, with significant amounts of brass and woodwinds added to the mix. Compared to *Without Earth*, there was a real maturity in the performances, although some of the first album's trippy exuberance was lost in the process. The standout tracks were many, including the lovely and concise 'Lebanon', the gorgeous ballad 'Mary Jane' and the anthemic 'Life Is A Season'. Perhaps best of all was a soulful rocker called 'Softly'. Moore's vocal was nothing short of magnificent, while David injected deliciously played guitar passages throughout. Another momentous track was the alternately eerie and whimsical 'Come Out Tonight', which possessed an intense aura that drew the listener directly into the vibe of the time. David's guitar presence was much greater on the second Moon LP than on the first. His subtle picking style on 'Life Is A Season' reminds one of the unique jazz-rock textures brought forth in the seventies by Yes's Steve Howe. In various places on the album Dave tore up the neck with raw electric blues riffs, while balancing other pieces of the LP with gentle acoustic sounds. His melodic nylon-string approach on the ballad 'Not To Know' was a direct result of his newfound interest in classical-style guitar. Anyone wanting to hear how David developed as a guitarist in his post-Beach Boys years should closely listen to the second Moon LP. Compared to the unimaginative and thin guitar sounds on The Beach Boys recordings of the late sixties, David showed he had travelled far beyond Carl and Al as a player. On 22 August 1969 the second Moon LP was mastered for release. This was also the occasion of Dave's 21st birthday.

Almost as quickly as *Without Earth*, the second Moon album also disappeared off the rock radar. 'Even less promotion was done for the second album,' explains Matt Moore. 'By that time Imperial had given up on a lot of their artists and was closing down shop. We were pretty upset at them for not getting anything going for us.' One bright spot came when certain eastern US college-driven radio markets caught on to The Moon for a short time. Reports of Moon airplay sprung up along the north-eastern seaboard in the late summer of 1969. The single 'John Automation' even became a minor local hit in New Haven, Connecticut, reaching number 45 on the WAVZ AM radio charts. But within a few months, both

Moon LPs had faded into obscurity and, inevitably, the group disbanded. Today there is a small but growing cult of Moon fans from all over the world that maintain a passionate level of interest in their two albums and both Moon LPs are now considered psychedelic-era classics by many respected music historians. The albums were remastered to CD and released as a double set on Rev-Ola Records in 2003, with new liner notes written by pop aficionado Steve Stanley. Considering The Moon phenomenon was completely unrelated to his Beach Boys fame, it illustrated that David Marks indeed stood on his own, apart from his first band, and that he had again made a lasting mark in the music business.

On the heels of his Moon experience, Dave joined the band known as Colours. Songwriters Jack Dalton and Gary Montgomery, who previously had contributed the two songs sung by David on the first Moon LP, were the mainstays of Colours. Their two LPs were released on the Dot label in 1968 and 1969. David was in the line-up as lead guitarist for the second Colours LP, which contained a jazz/rock/blues hybrid sound and featured some great originals, including Gary Montgomery's stunning ballad 'Angie'. Like the first Colours LP, it was produced by Danny Moore. The band's 1969 line-up also included Richard Crooks on drums and part-time Moon member David Jackson on bass. During David's tenure Colours was managed by Forest Hamilton, the son of jazz great Chico Hamilton. David performed live with Colours several times in late 1969, including concerts in Palm Springs and Seattle. The highest-profile moment for Colours came when they were featured in a national Jantzen Sportswear advertisement. Colours, like The Moon, were critically lauded in their time, and today their LPs are valued by sixties pop music collectors. But in 1969, the group found no commercial success. Colours soon broke apart and fell into the massive pile of obscure fragments of sixties rock music history.

In the meantime, Jo Ann Marks's psychic explorations had gained her a word-of-mouth reputation around Southern California. Through the connections she'd gained by working at Motown and Liberty Records, and through her friends Zelda Samuels and J'nevelyn Terrell, Jo Ann became a relatively well-known figure around the entertainment industry. A long list of celebrities with an interest in her psychic ability eventually sought her out. 'All kinds of famous people were coming by to get readings from my mom,' says David. 'Carole King, Tuesday Weld, Tina Turner, Regis Philbin, Peter Marshall, the host of *Hollywood Squares*, John Densmore of The Doors, and many others were all coming by to see my mother. They were literally lined up with appointments to see my mom because she would give them accurate psychic readings and she never charged them a penny. She was taught if you accept money for a reading it automatically negates the forces you are channelling. And she was very accurate in her predictions.'

Dave reconnected with his old Hawthorne childhood pal Greg Jones during this period. 'We weren't that much in touch during our late teens, but one day he showed up at my apartment building in Hollywood,' remembers Dave. 'He was down and out so I let him stay there for a while and gave him my Honda motorcycle for transportation. He stayed for a couple of weeks, I guess. Then he bought a beat-up old car and took the seats out and went to the docks at the Central Market in downtown Los Angeles and would fill up his car with produce and haul lettuce to all the Mexican restaurants. He was good with people, a good salesman, and very enterprising.' Jones ended up becoming a major player in LA's huge produce business. One day, Greg drove David to the home recording studio of another talented Hawthorne resident, Emitt Rhodes. Dave had played some gigs with Rhodes's old group, The Palace Guard, during the Band Without A Name days. 'Back then Emitt was playing drums and wearing a uniform,' says Dave. In 1969, he found a much different Rhodes hard at work on his own great music. 'I was doing a lot of pot and acid and Greg dropped me off at his house one day,' remembers Dave. 'Emitt's bands had already broken up by then and he'd custom-built a studio. I don't remember how long I stayed there but I just watched him work and he was recording some really beautiful songs. He sounded just like Paul McCartney and in the frame of mind I was in that day, I was completely blown away by his stuff.'

Although David was enjoying spending time hanging around with some of his old Hawthorne mates, soon the music bug came calling yet again. Drummer Jim Keltner, who Dave first met when he played percussion on a Moon session, encouraged David to attend a rehearsal for the band known as Delaney & Bonnie. Dave had known Delaney Bramlett briefly when he was still a member of The Shindogs, who were the house band on the sixties TV show *Shindig!* In 1969 Bramlett was preparing to tour with the roots-rock outfit that he'd formed a year earlier with his wife Bonnie. They needed a qualified guitarist to fill out the band's sound and were holding auditions at an LA studio. Delaney was well aware of David's guitar work with The Moon and was intrigued by his finger-picking style. When Dave told him he was interested in the gig, Bramlett handed him a tape of selections from the proposed Delaney & Bonnie set list. Dave quickly learned their material and formally auditioned for the group. That same day, a charged-up Bramlett gave him the good news: the gig was David's if he wanted it. Bramlett enthused to Dave that they were going to be huge. He told him John Lennon had already professed they were his favourite act on the basis of their earlier LP, which had sold about as well as The Moon. But once again, Dave had real hope for revisiting the big time as he joined a project with tremendous potential. After a few rehearsals in LA, David played several Southern California gigs as Delaney & Bonnie's lead guitar player. Everything seemed to be going well. However, before he could get completely comfortable in the role, fate intervened. 'I played guitar with them very briefly,' explains David. 'I thought I had a regular job with them, but after a while Delaney would say, "Dave, you don't mind if Dr John sits in tonight, do you?" Then it was, "Dave, you don't mind if Eric Clapton sits in tonight, do you?" After that, he never called me again.' Clapton became the regular guitarist for Delaney & Bonnie & Friends, who soon after became a major international success.

Despite a seemingly never-ending series of musical setbacks, David stayed very active as a working session guitarist in Los Angeles. Producer Danny Moore regularly hired David to play on his sessions at Paramount Studios, which were constant in the late sixties and early seventies. Danny has produced over twenty LPs for an array of artists during his career, most of them during that busy stretch. Moore maintained a core of session regulars, including the great Jim Keltner on drums, Carl Radle – who would soon join Clapton's Derek and the Dominoes – on bass, Gary Montgomery on keyboards, and David Marks on guitar. 'Dave held up his end of things really well in the studio; he's always had talent as a player,' says Moore. And David was fast. 'One time, there was this little tiny hole where nothing happened in this recording,' remembers Moore. 'I swear it was maybe a beat or a beat and a half long. I asked David to put some guitar in there. I told him you've only got time for a note or two. And we recorded his part and then we played it back and we counted . . . he put fourteen notes in there. And it sounded great. I was amazed.'

Among the Moore-produced projects that feature David's guitar playing are the self-titled Denny Brooks LP, released on Warner Brothers, the Michael McGinnis LP, *Welcome to My Mind*, released on MGM, and the Buzz Clifford LP, *See Your Way Clear*, released on Dot. Clifford, who is best known for the 1961 novelty smash 'Baby Sittin' Boogie' became a very close friend of Dave's in the process of working on his 1969 LP. Buzz and Dave's friendship evolved into an on-and-off musical partnership that has lasted for 35 years. 'We'd get together and write songs and arrange stuff, we'd record it and try to make masters, and then we'd run out of money,' says Clifford.

Also in late 1969, David reunited with his former Flies bandmate Glen Crocker on a project entitled 'G. D. Crocker and Dirty Dog Dave Blues'. Produced by Danny Moore at Continental, the sessions were built around Crocker originals and Robert Johnson covers recorded in a full-tilt jazz-blues style. 'Mike Curb probably financed it without knowing,' says David. The project included Crocker on piano, David on guitar, Richard Crooks on drums, Robert Wilson on bass, and horns arranged by Moon string arranger Robert Klimes. Ray Charles's Raelettes were also brought in to sing background vocals. David wailed away in a bone-dry style aided by the Fender bassman amp he'd had modified by steel guitar legend Red Rhodes. Ultimately, this ambitious and expensive collection of songs went unreleased to the public.

An unwelcome companion that David first met while doing session work in 1969 was heroin. 'While playing a session I caught another musician in the bathroom snorting some lines,' remembers Dave. 'I thought it might be some coke but it turned out it was heroin. The guy gave me a line and I remember going back into the studio and partway through the next take, I had to set my guitar down. I ended up throwing up for an hour in the bathroom and then I felt great for the rest of the day.' Heroin would follow David into the next decade and eventually contribute to his decline.

Following several near hits, a few big misses, and a string of major post-Beach Boys letdowns, David was a very worn-out twenty-one-year-old musician. After scraping around the edges of fame between the years 1964 and 1969 with the likes of Dave and the Marksmen, Band Without A Name, Warren Zevon, The Tender Trap, The Moon, Colours, and Delaney & Bonnie, there wasn't very much passion left in his being. As the tumultuous decade of the sixties neared an end, David felt as if he'd seen and done it all. In less than ten years, he had triumphantly ridden to the very top, crashed to somewhere frighteningly near the bottom, and seemingly visited all points in between. It was time to move on. But move on to what? Where does an emotionally fried musician just reaching adulthood with few other skills turn?

9. TIME TO GET ALONE

O ne night David had a simple dream, and in a way it woke him up again. The dream was about someone else. It was of a little boy unwrapping a gift. The gift was a brand new guitar. The dream touched on the essence of wonder, just an innocent boy and his new guitar. And the boy was happy. The dream reconnected David with why he was a musician. The reason he'd first set out on this path was simply because he loved the guitar and loved to play music on it. By focusing on the underlying simplicity of his dream, David remembered why he was here. The lesson? The boy in the dream was someone else, another person, not David. The dream helped him understand that he'd become disconnected from the child who wanted nothing more than to play his guitar. Now it was time to find his way back.

During the Moon period, Dave had taken a deep interest in learning classical guitar. He'd already been influenced into a classical direction by his pal Warren Zevon. As a young teenager, Warren had been a student and close friend of conductor Robert Craft, a noted protégé, collaborator and biographer of the legendary composer Igor Stravinsky. Zevon actually became acquainted with Stravinsky himself when he'd occasionally accompany Craft to the great composer's home. Since the day David met Warren in 1966, he'd been steadily stoking his interest in classical music, and while with The Moon, David began to implement that influence into his playing. Dave's dream only confirmed that this was the right path to follow. It seemed to point the way back to himself. As a result, David initiated a series of steps towards the goal of becoming a complete musician. The first was when he began to take guitar lessons from the classical master Vincente Gomez, who he was introduced to through his old friend Richie Podolor. His lessons with Gomez gave David momentum. After a time, David came under the tutelage of another teacher, Morris Mizrahi. A respected and established classical player, Mizrahi was married to Dave's cousin Toni. It was Toni, whose real name is Carlita, who was a friend of Dave's first major guitar inspiration, John Maus. Now Toni again provided Dave with the connection to a man who would reveal a fresh universe of guitar knowledge and present him with endless new challenges.

'Mori would torture me with scales and tell me that I was weak because I was complaining about my bleeding fingers,' says David. 'He'd always say, "Pain is good." I learned a great deal about the guitar, and music in general, from Mori. He opened up a whole new world of music to me and was one of the most influential people in my playing.' Within a decade, Morris was dead of heart failure. But in their time together he left David with a reservoir of inspiration and a wealth of musical gifts that remain with him to this day.

Then David took the next big step. His ex-roommate and former bandmate Glenn Crocker convinced Dave to join him at the Berklee School of Music in Boston. Berklee is one of the most prestigious music schools in the United States and was an enormous challenge for someone with Dave's patchy educational background, but he felt as if he was ready to raise the bar in his quest for a serious musical education. In November 1969, he and his girlfriend Roseanne Burchett headed to the East Coast in David's red 1962 Porsche 356B. There they rented a five-bedroom house on the Atlantic Ocean in Scituate, Massachusetts, about 30 miles south of Boston. Scituate was a sleepy little village of quiet conservative types, a good place to shed the emotional baggage of the past few years. But before David had much of a chance to settle in, his old life stampeded right through his new one.

In the post-Moon and Colours period, Matt and Danny Moore had been hired onto Joe Cocker's 'Mad Dogs and Englishmen' tour project, both as full-time backing vocalists in the amazing ten-voice choir. The year-long and much-ballyhooed Cocker world tour was being recorded and filmed for a live LP and movie release, and Matt and Danny were right in the thick of it. David had begun his adjustment to being away from California when the Mad Dogs tour hit the East Coast. 'I was kind of lonesome down by the harbour in Scituate,' says David. 'It was winter in Massachusetts, and I was very cold.' But when the Mad Dogs arrived to play a sold-out concert in Boston, things instantly heated up. David drove to the city for a reunion with his LA friends, who were enjoying the Cocker experience to the hilt. That night, David witnessed a fantastic show and for a moment he fantasised about being back in the rock and roll action. After their incredible Boston concert performance, the perpetually wired Cocker entourage literally took control of the hotel lounge where the band was staying. Downtown Boston's Quality Inn witnessed a raging party that night, one that is still talked about in rock and roll circles today. Piles of amps, keyboards and drums were set up and a booze-fuelled jam session rocked into the night. Besides Cocker band stalwarts like Leon Russell, Carl Radle and Jim Gordon, the marathon jam included guests like Taj Mahal, Jesse Ed Davis, as well as David, who was better known to this crowd as a respected LA session guitarist than as an ex-Beach Boy. When the sun came up, the party finally lost steam. David staggered towards the door with his ears ringing. On the way out, he waved and smiled, and in a slightly slurred voice, he shouted, 'You're all welcome to visit me in Scituate any time!'

A day later, David was astonished to see the Mad Dogs and Englishmen tour bus roll up to his house with the horns blowing. He rubbed his eyes as more than 30 scruffy longhairs streamed from the bus towards his home. Matt Moore remembers the moment: 'I said, "Hey, let's go to the sea and visit Dave!"' The entire Mad Dogs tour entourage, including Matt and Danny Moore, Leon Russell, Rita Coolidge, Jim Gordon, Carl Radle, Jim Keltner, Don Preston, Jim Price, Bobby Keys, a slew of roadies, a gaggle of groupies, and a Jack Daniel's-wielding Joe Cocker himself showed up at Dave's door with a hankering to party. 'They smoked all my weed, drank all my wine, pissed off all my neighbours, and then they left,' remembers Dave. 'They wiped me out and trashed my house. When they left I had nothing. It was all gone. I was weedless and wineless.' Before the bus departed, Matt and Danny invited Dave to come along with them on the tour. David was tempted for a moment, until Joe Cocker stumbled up and shouted into Dave's face, 'Come with us, you bloody bastard, we're all going to hell!' Cocker then turned and vomited into a plant pot on his way out of the house. 'The tour got a little crazy about six weeks in,' remembers Danny Moore. 'The first month was just charming, but after that it got a little weird.' Dave decided it was probably a wise thing to stay put.

After the Mad Dogs incident, the local Scituate residents became extremely wary of David and Roseanne. Their treatment from neighbours turned so icy that the couple began to look for a place to live in the city of Boston. The situation became worse when David nearly ran a local sheriff off the two-lane highway with his speeding Porsche. 'You almost just ran the wrong guy off the road,' said the angry officer after pulling David over. He and Roseanne were hauled into the local sheriff's station, where David was booked for reckless driving. When the head sheriff caught wind that David and Roseanne were unmarried and living together, he warned them, 'Either you two get married or leave town!' Residents of the puritanical community had already complained to the sheriffs' department about their hippie neighbours, and the

Above: Concert poster for Jan and Dean with Dave and the Marksmen (Fred Vail/Treasure Isle Recorders)

Top: Dave and the Marksmen – Ed Gauntt, Gene Fetco, Mark Groseclose, David Marks and Bill Trenkle (Marks Family Archive)

Middle: Dave and the Marksmen on tour in Las Vegas with Eddie and the Showmen – Bob Knight, David, Pam and Denny Murry, Mark Groseclose and Terry Hand (Marks Family Archive)

Right: The Marksmen go Beatles in 1964
(Marks Family Archive)

Below: David, Gene, Denny, Bill, Mark – a rare and candid shot of the Marksmen
(Marks Family Archive)

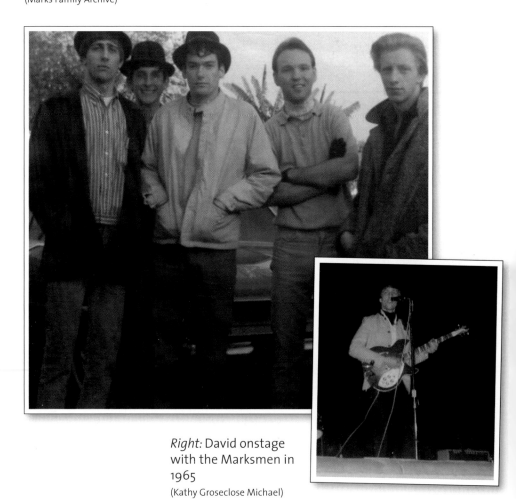

Right: David onstage with the Marksmen in 1965
(Kathy Groseclose Michael)

THE MOON

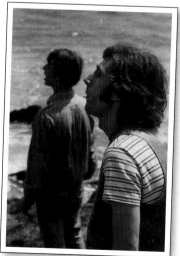

Top: The official Imperial Records promo for the Moon – David Marks, Larry Brown, Matt Moore, Andy Bennett
(Marks Family Archive)

Left: David and Drew – tripping with the Moon
(Marks Family Archive)

Above: The Moon in 1967
(Marks Family Archive)

Above: David with guitar and cigarette in 1971
(Marks Family Archive)

Below: Blazin' on a sunny afternoon, Gary
Montgomery and David, 1972 (Steve Heller)

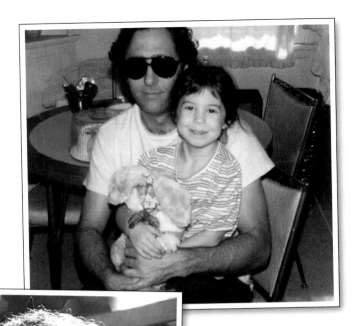

Above: David holding his
daughter Jennifer, 1987
(Marks Family Archive)

Left: Dazed and confused,
David in the early 70s
(Marks Family Archive)

Below: The last photo
taken of Elmer Marks
(Marks Family Archive)

Above: David and his wife Carrie, 2004
(Ann Bulmer)

Above Left: Jennifer, David, Bruce Johnston and John Stamos at John's wedding, 1999
(Jennifer Marks)

Left: David and the other members of the Marks Family
(David Bulmer)

Right: Charlotte Cooper, who was discovered by Jeff Foskett: David is featured on her new album
(Mike prior)

Above: Together again: David onstage with the Beach Boys in Germany, 1999
(Carrie Marks)

Right: David on stage with the Beach Boys in 1999
(Carrie Marks)

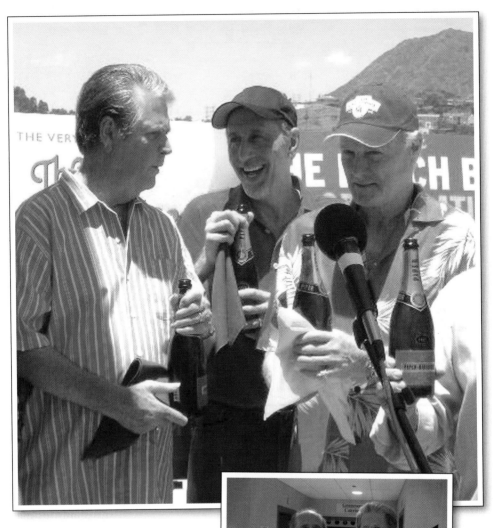

Above: Brian, David and
Mike celebrate at the
Capitol Records rooftop
reunion, June 2006
(Carrie Marks)

Right: Two survivors:
David and Brian
backstage at Brian's Smile
tour, 2005
(Dennis Diken)

Right/bottom: David and
Mike Love, June 2005
(Carrie Marks)

TIME TO GET ALONE

couple was given a clear picture of how unwelcome they were in Scituate. In the spring of 1970, Dave and Roseanne moved to a brownstone apartment on Commonwealth Avenue in Boston.

Once they'd settled into the city, Dave began taking classes at Berklee. But it wasn't that simple. Because he didn't have a high school diploma, he wasn't eligible for enrolment as an 'official' student, but in a special arrangement with the Berklee admissions department Dave was allowed to attend classes in a non-official capacity. Not long after sorting out that problem, Roseanne and Dave broke up and she moved away to Virginia. 'I spent the better part of the next year wandering around Boston alone,' says David.

Dave did, however, become close with a fellow student named Alan Silvestri. The pairing was a fortunate one for David's musical growth. Silvestri was a highly talented artist who would one day compose the scores to some of the highest-grossing action and comedy films ever made. 'Alan taught me how to look at music through scales, which is something I had never thought about before but is the basis for improvising,' says David. 'Alan was energetic and had a real positive energy around him that inspired me.' Although a year younger than David in age, Silvestri became a significant mentor in his development as a musician.

While living in Boston, David naturally maintained his lifelong battle with authority and convention. 'I got a parking ticket every day because I parked in front of my apartment at 206 Commonwealth Avenue,' says David. 'The fines got to be upwards of $700, so they came and towed my car away.' David's prized Porsche ended up in a Boston impound yard, but that didn't faze him one bit. 'It was Thanksgiving night when I found out where it was,' remembers David. 'It was about maybe nine or ten o'clock at night, and it was an outside lot. There was a chain-link fence around it and a locked gate. There was an office trailer with security guys in it, and I could see one of them had a shotgun resting across his lap. I had to wait for the guy who was walking back and forth, making rounds, to get out of sight. Every time he'd pass out of sight, I'd undo another link in the fence with my bare hands. It took a long time to do it. I had to bend each one, and my fingers were getting bloody. After about an hour, I finally got it apart and spread the fence out just enough for a car to get through. I jumped in and started the Porsche and then hauled ass out of there as fast as I could with the lights off. But because the lights were off, I didn't see the concrete curb in front of me. I smashed into it and fucked up the suspension on the Porsche. I still got away and I drove it straight to a repair shop outside of Boston, and left it there. They had it for months. When I finally got it back, like an idiot, I parked it right in front of my apartment again. The police impounded it right away but this time they towed it to a subterranean garage that was heavily guarded. When I finally retrieved the car from impound, my fines were massive.'

Dave eventually became disillusioned with Berklee due to what he describes as 'the stale and frustrated attitudes of the instructors'. He left Berklee behind to study at the nearby Boston Conservatory. Founded in 1867, the arts conservatory was similarly hard for David to enrol in with no high school diploma, and the resident composer, Dr Avram David, nearly laughed him out of his office. 'He made me feel like an idiot for even thinking I was worthy of studying with him,' says David. 'I was extremely upset and nearly in tears. I went into a rant about how I'd worked so hard at Berklee but how the instructors sucked, and how my girlfriend had left me, and how the police had impounded my car, and how I stole it back, and then they took it again, and I went on and on in a very irrational way. I was just blubbering away. Just as I was slinking out of his office he stopped me and said, "OK, kid, if you want to be a composer, write me some music and bring it back and I'll take a listen."' David ran home to his apartment and transposed a composition that he'd already written on the guitar. He plunked out the notes on his electric piano and wrote it out as a chamber piece for choir, piano, strings, flute and trumpets. In the end, he was very proud of the result.

The next day Dave took his original work to Dr David at the conservatory. 'He put the music in front of him and played it on the piano,' remembers Dave. 'It was so beautiful to me because I hadn't heard it played by anyone else and hearing it performed that way brought a tear to my eye.' Dr David begrudgingly admitted the piece was quite good. He agreed to take David under his wing and teach him on his own, but not as an 'official' student of the conservatory because of Dave's lack of high school graduate status. Included in the assignments Avram proposed for David was the task of writing out manuscripts for Dr David's own compositions. 'At the time, I was insulted that he wanted me to do such menial work, but now I realise it was a great honour,' says David. 'Dr David taught me that if I wanted to be a composer then I should act like a composer, talk like a composer and think of myself as a composer. So I kept my manuscripts tucked under my arm as I walked around Boston. I cut off all my hair and I wore military-style boots that came up to my knees, and I hung out in Harvard Square. I settled into the role of the desperate tortured composer quite well.'

Eventually Dr David introduced Dave to his own music teacher, Madame Margaret Chaloff. Madame Chaloff was a well-known figure around Boston who had taught piano and composition to many recognised artists, including jazz legend Miles Davis. 'Madame Chaloff was a psychic and spiritual counsellor, like my mom,' says David. 'Even though she was in her seventies by then, when you looked in her piercing blue eyes, it was like looking at a young girl. She was so vibrant and full of life.' One day, while David was at Madame Chaloff's house, which was right down the street from his own apartment, something unforgettable occurred. A group of twelve of Madame Chaloff's friends had gathered to pray for a woman's son who was hopelessly addicted to hard drugs. 'She had us all get in a circle and pray,' says David. 'Madame Chaloff said she was using each of us as a "battery".' David maintains that the intensity of the prayer circle caused him to experience levitation or an 'out of body' state. 'I could feel the sensation of rising up through the ceiling and being able to look down at us all in the circle below,' says David. 'I know I'd been smoking a lot of pot recently, but it was still an amazing experience.'

One night, Dave went out to see Miles Davis perform at the Jazz Workshop on Boylston Street. Along the way he stopped off at a local doughnut shop to buy a cup of coffee before the concert. There, to his surprise, he encountered the one and only Chuck Berry, who was sitting by himself at the doughnut shop counter. 'Chuck Berry was an idol to me, and I was really excited to see him there,' remembers David. It was Berry who may have been the single biggest influence on David and Carl's guitar style and in turn was a huge factor in The Beach Boys' early success. 'I sat down next to him and told him who I was, and that I had been in The Beach Boys, and that his music had been our inspiration . . . the whole nine yards . . . and he didn't even look at me,' remembers David. Afterwards, Dave realised that mentioning The Beach Boys probably wasn't such a good idea, considering the fact that Chuck had sued them over the writer's credit on the song 'Surfin' USA', a direct lift of Chuck's 'Sweet Little Sixteen'. Ironically, this was the first time in over a year that David had told anyone he'd once been a member of The Beach Boys.

In February 1971, a full symphony orchestra was put together to perform one of Dr Avram David's latest long-form compositions at Boston's Symphony Hall. David attended the performance and was deeply moved by the experience of hearing his instructor's great work, some of which he himself had transcribed. His months of studying with Dr David had centred him musically, and successfully put him back in touch with the foundation of his love for music. The path initiated by his simple dream more than a year earlier, about the boy and his guitar, had led David to exactly where he'd hoped to be. He was learning, composing, growing and not worrying a wit about fame, notoriety or material success. In short, David had completed the journey back to his meaningful essence.

But the times were about to be changin'. After the concert, while walking through the Symphony Hall lobby, David noticed a small poster for an upcoming concert by The Beach

Boys. The mere sight of it froze David in his tracks. While standing there, eyeing the images on the poster, Dave's personal curiosity about the current state of his former mates became too great to ignore. He walked directly to the Symphony Hall box office and purchased a ticket.

On 28 February 1971, David sat anonymously amid the large audience and watched The Beach Boys perform. The experience was bittersweet. 'About halfway through the show I started getting a little misty,' says David. 'I'm not sure why. I think it was because Brian wasn't there, and there were all these sidemen on stage; they even had horns. Something about it wasn't the same and it made me feel kind of sad. Eventually, before the concert had ended, I decided I would just leave because I had to get up early for school the next morning. I was just about out of the lobby when I heard that familiar voice again: "Hey, Dave!" It was Dennis again, just like in LA on the street that time. Somehow, out of all those people, he found me.' With the concert still going, the first thing David asked Dennis was why he wasn't on stage with the group. 'I'm looking for chicks, that's why we have another drummer,' said Dennis. Then he grabbed Dave by the arm and said, 'Come on, Dave, there's *no way* you can leave without saying hi to the rest of the guys.' David realised Dennis was right, and followed him back towards the stage. When David arrived in the backstage area, the group was just coming off stage to massive applause. 'Look what I found!' said Dennis. Carl, Mike and Al warmly greeted David and invited him to join the band for their still-to-be-performed encore. 'It was surreal,' says David. 'I hadn't seen them in years, and suddenly they were putting a guitar in my hands and pushing me up on stage.'

As the band returned to the stage for their encore, a slightly flustered David was with them. With years of physical maturity added to his long frame, few in the crowd recognised he was the same kid from those early album covers. Then Carl introduced him, and the crowd gave David a warm round of applause. Mike mentioned to the audience that David was now living in Boston. Then the group suddenly launched into

'Surfer Girl'. Dave stood with his oldest friends, playing Brian's oldest song again for a couple of strange minutes . . . and then it was over. The crowd went wild as Bruce said, 'How 'bout Dave Marks!' For David, it was a very disorienting moment. 'I had my guitar turned way down and just kind of pretended I was playing,' says David. 'I didn't know why, but somehow it felt kind of wrong to be up there with them. I felt like I was a million miles away from that.'

After the show, David spent some time in Carl's hotel room, watching him give a series of interviews to the local press. Dennis couldn't sit still and was in and out of the room several times until he disappeared completely. Before he left, Dennis and Mike asked David to come back and visit them in the morning. 'I have something to tell you,' said Mike. 'It's important that we talk.' The morning after the Symphony Hall concert, Dave joined Dennis and Mike for breakfast in the hotel lounge. Dave proudly told them about the classical suite he'd been hard at work composing. Dennis teasingly mocked David in his best effeminate lisp: 'Isn't it sweet . . . he's writing a suite!'

After they'd finished their morning meal, Mike asked David to give him a ride to the local health food store. But Mike had more on his mind than granola and wheatgrass. Once they were alone in his car, Mike suggested that David sell his Porsche and give his money to the Maharishi. He then launched into a five-minute sermon about how Transcendental Meditation would change David's life. Dave's first thought was, Why do I want to change my life? But Love was unrelenting. Mike handed David the address of a place known as the Maharishi Center in Cambridge where he could become initiated in Transcendental Meditation. And then he tossed in the clincher: 'You should think about coming back to Los Angeles to rejoin The Beach Boys. It would be the best thing for you.' Although David hadn't thought about anything relating to The Beach Boys in a very long time, they still seemed like his family in a way. David wasn't sure what to make of Mike's offer. It somehow made him feel good and bad at the same time.

Before going their separate ways, Mike invited David to join the group in New York in the next few days. David's head was spinning. The Beach Boys had swept into his life again and given him a lot to think about. In a semi-brainwashed state, he headed straight to Cambridge and became initiated in TM, although he decided to keep his Porsche. Temporarily forgetting about his studies, David dropped everything and flew to New York. There, on the first day of March, he met up with The Beach Boys again. That evening, the group was scheduled to appear on the David Frost television show. David watched their rehearsal and, while sitting in the green room, he played Carl some of the classical pieces he'd been working on at school on Carl's twelve-string guitar. The idea of David joining the band on stage during their television appearance was tossed around by Mike and Carl, but David told them he'd be more comfortable just watching for now. David stood behind the cameras and witnessed The Beach Boys perform 'Forever', 'Vegetables' and an acoustic version of Dennis's 'Lady' for the studio audience. Afterwards he spent a few hours talking with his old California mates and then he headed back to Boston.

On the flight home, David thought deeply about Mike's offer. He was unaware at the time that Mike's main reason for wanting him back in the fold was based on a flawed premise. Mike maintained a great desire to return the band to something closer to their 1963 musical chemistry. The David Frost TV appearance underlined the fact that the Wilsons basically controlled the 1971 Beach Boys. With Dennis and Carl becoming more and more the focal point, Mike was relegated to something less important. Perhaps Mike saw David as a direct connection back to the days when he was more of a leading figure in the band hierarchy. Mike seemed to overlook the possibility that David himself had become a forward-thinking artist and would regard anything close to the old Beach Boys sound as archaic. In fact, David had evolved into a skilled classical and jazz guitarist. To him, even the 'new' Beach Boys sound seemed slightly pedestrian. 'In retrospect, I can see it was an attempt by Mike to hold onto what he saw as the authenticity of the early Beach Boys sound,' says David. 'Brian was all weirded out at that point, and Mike was frustrated because Carl and Dennis were running things and there were no hits happening. He saw me as a bridge back to something closer to what he wanted. And it was wishful thinking on his part, because it was beyond repair at that point. It had evolved into what it was, and even though Mike didn't like it, that's where they were in 1971.'

Later that month, David drove to the Boston Garden to attend a performance by Frank Zappa and the Mothers of Invention. The Mothers' co-lead vocalists at the time were Dave's old friends Howard Kaylan and Mark Volman, formerly of The Turtles. The rotund and hairy pair of singers were now known to Zappa's fans as The Florescent Leech and Eddie (or Flo & Eddie). 'It was a really freaky show,' remembers David. 'They were decapitating baby dolls on stage. But I just loved Zappa's stuff because it was always so progressive and unique.' Once again, during the concert, David was spotted in the crowd by an old friend. 'Mark saw me from the stage and invited me to come backstage,' says Dave. 'We hung out at their hotel after the gig and Mark introduced me to Frank Zappa, who was a hero of mine.' After meeting Frank, Volman took Dave aside and asked, 'What the hell are you doing living in Boston, man?' Dave tried to explain, as he had to Dennis and Mike, about his music, his composing and his education. Volman's somewhat sceptical reaction was another indication that maybe Dave did belong in California after all. All his old friends seemed to think so.

A week later, a random series of incidents filled David's life with an accumulation of what Jo Ann might call 'bad vibrations'. The resulting shock left David in a very paranoid state. 'My apartment was broken into by some junkies while I was sleeping one night,' says David. 'That was really scary. I woke up and there were people crawling out my window. Then, a day later, a guy was shot and killed by the cops on my front steps while trying to rob someone. I was still shaky over those things happening, when suddenly a violent anti-war rally with thousands of militant students came swarming down Commonwealth Avenue right in front of my apartment. There was a full-scale riot happening twenty feet from my bed. It's like all the crazy news clips on TV were happening right where I lived. I kind of got freaked out.' David began thinking about the sunshine in California, his parents, his old friends, and rock and roll. Maybe the Boston experience was meant to be a limited one. He increasingly felt the draw of the west.

By the end of March, David had decided to leave Boston. Something about reconnecting with The Beach Boys and the ensuing flare-up of violence on his street had derailed his passion for completing his education. 'I was in a very weird state,' says Dave. 'I suddenly became unsure of everything again. I packed up the U-Haul and got the hell out of Boston.' On his way back, Dave lingered in the California desert and ended up staying for a few weeks. 'I stopped off at Twenty-nine Palms, a small town in the Mojave Desert near the Joshua Tree National Park,' says David. 'My grandfather had left me five acres of land and a little cabin that was miles out of town when he died. It was very isolated. I hung out in that cabin for a few weeks playing my guitar, drinking beer and contemplating life. I was floating in a confused in-between state. I loved being anonymous in Boston and learning about classical composition. But things had gotten so tense back there that it traumatised me. I didn't want to stay. After talking to Mike and Dennis and Mark [Volman], I felt like I was missing out on something in California. I just wasn't sure what it was.' Dave's cousin Rocky also lived in the desert, a few miles closer to town. While visiting him in March 1971, David began dabbling with heroin again.

After several weeks in the desert, Dave finally returned to Los Angeles and was met with immediate bad news. Elmer had seriously mismanaged the Hollywood apartment building that Dave had purchased back in 1967 with his Beach Boys royalty money. 'He didn't keep enough of the units rented to keep up the tax payments on it,' says David. 'My father wouldn't rent to anyone. No whores, no blacks, no musicians, no actors . . . nobody in Hollywood was allowed to rent an apartment from my dad. That kind of discrimination seriously cuts down on your possibilities for tenants in the middle of Hollywood. So naturally, we lost the thing because we couldn't pay the taxes.' Although Elmer wouldn't accept rent from a long list of gainfully employed Hollywood types whom he perceived as being distasteful, he still allowed a few select struggling artists to live in the building . . . free of charge. Among the tenants Elmer gave free rental to in the 1968–70 period were Dave's friend Warren Zevon and some of the Gold Diggers dancing girls. 'We just got bad advice and we didn't know what we were doing so we lost some good opportunities to make the most of that money,' says David. 'We could have made some lucrative investments, but we screwed it up by not knowing how to manage money that way. It was a shame to lose that Beresford building in Hollywood. It would be worth a pile of money today.'

Only a few days after returning to Southern California, David visited Mike Love at his Manhattan Beach apartment. Again Mike suggested that David consider rejoining The Beach Boys. 'I was really torn about going back,' says David. 'Part of me wanted a steady gig, but I knew there wasn't any way I would fit in with The Beach Boys at that point in my life.' In April, at Mike's invitation, David attended recording sessions held at Brian's house for the next Beach Boys LP, to be titled *Surf's Up*. David watched as background vocals for Carl's song 'Long Promised Road' were recorded. He witnessed the painful process of The Beach Boys trying to coax some vocals out of an uninterested Brian Wilson. 'Brian was laying on his back after chugging a quart of Madori, which is a sweet melon liqueur,' says David. 'Carl held the boom mike down to him so Brian could just lie there and sing. He managed to do a take of the "bop bop" background vocals in "Long Promised Road".' While Brian was still lying on the floor, Al Jardine called Dave over to a display cabinet in Brian's home. 'Al asked me if I wanted to see something funny,' remembers David. 'He was laughing and he showed me a set of china plates that were set out behind the glass. On each plate was the image of Murry smoking his pipe. Al bust out laughing when I said, "Imagine eating your last bite of spaghetti and seeing that face." I then noticed Carl had come over and was listening to Al and me laughing. The look on his face made it clear he wasn't amused the same way we were. He acted kind of hurt that we were making fun of his dad. I'm sure he thought it was just as ridiculous as we did, but when it's your dad you have to defend him.'

Carl agreed to let David rehearse with the band to get a feel for what they were doing. Mike was very adamant about wanting David back but the others didn't show the same enthusiasm – at least, not from Dave's perspective. 'I got the feeling Carl didn't really want me in the group,' says David. 'He told me I could rejoin the band and play bass for them if I wanted. Then he started playing "Help Me Rhonda" and asked me to play along with him on bass. I kind of resented that because I knew I was a better guitar player than Carl or Al. Why should I play bass? Later that same day, Carl sat down at the piano and played one of his new tunes while I fooled around on the bass. I couldn't follow it too well so I just put the bass down and went into the next room and played pool with Brian. After spending a year of intense training on classical guitar and studying with some of the most brilliant minds in music at the time, I just couldn't bring myself to play bass guitar on "Help Me Rhonda".' David spent the rest of the day with The Beach Boys, but refrained from playing music with them.

On 14 April, The Beach Boys appeared at the legendary Whisky a Go Go on LA's Sunset Strip. David again joined the band on stage for part of their set. 'I was still deciding if I should rejoin the group, and they invited me to a gig they were playing at the Whisky,' says David. 'Carl told me to sit in the audience and they would invite me up to play on some of the old surf and car songs towards the end of the set. I sat there until they called me up and I played on a few of the old hits I had recorded with them. Again, it just didn't feel right to me and I just went through the motions. But I was happy to have finally had the chance to play on the Whisky stage where so many of the bands I admired had played in the past. The combined feelings of happiness and of something being wrong left me feeling torn again.' Later that month, David informed The Beach Boys he wasn't interested in a job with them. He thanked them for the offer and wished them well. Dave got the distinct impression that Mike was very disappointed but that Carl took it in his stride. Carl told David it didn't really matter because they already had a guy they liked, named Ed Carter, who could play both guitar and bass really well. 'I ended up being relieved that it didn't work out,' says David. 'I just didn't want to go back to that situation.'

While David was still considering rejoining The Beach Boys, he had his first personal encounters with Bruce Johnston. 'He knew I was hanging around there to see if I wanted to come back to the band, and I think maybe he felt a little threatened by it,' says David. 'I didn't know at the time there was tension there, but I guess there was, since he left the band within a year. Bruce spent a good part of the time I was there being extra nice to me, too nice to me. I remember thinking how strange and creepy it was. He kept telling me he was honoured to be in *my* band. Then I saw him a few weeks later at the Troubadour after I had told them all I wasn't coming back, and I said hello to him and he pretended he didn't know who I was. Funny thing is, he did the same thing to me again in 1997, when I finally went back to The Beach Boys. At least he's consistent.'

Although David didn't rejoin The Beach Boys, he regularly returned to Brian's house to visit him. The one positive in David's flirtation with rejoining the boys was that it briefly rekindled his friendship with Brian. When David stopped by to visit him, The Beach Boys were usually on the road and Brian was by himself, or with Marilyn and his daughters, Carnie and Wendy. 'Brian and I would just hang out and listen to music, or just talk a little,' says David. 'I enjoyed seeing him and Marilyn, but it was obvious Brian wasn't quite the same guy I knew back in Hawthorne. He used people coming over to visit as an excuse to party. Sometimes I just sat there and watched him make phone calls trying to score coke, which he was never able to do any of the times I was there.' One time Dave showed up at Brian's in a truck that Skip Hand's wife had converted into what Dave describes as a 'gypsy-looking camper thing'. 'She had gone nuts and turned from a straight-laced housewife into a hippie chick overnight,' says David. 'She made this truck into an amazing hippie artefact. The truck had a wooden A-frame camper with a shingle roof. It had a sleeper over the cab of the truck with a skylight. The inside had lots of scarves and beads hanging from the ceiling. It looked like the inside of a harem tent. When we pulled into Brian's driveway on Bellagio Road he came running out and said, "Wow, that's a cool camper!" Brian was completely fascinated by that truck and he ran all around it and had to climb inside and check it all out. He just loved it.' Another time Dave went to visit Brian, he found his old friend was in a nearly catatonic state. 'Marilyn buzzed me in the gate and when I drove up to the house Brian was sitting in the back of a long black limousine having his nails done,' remembers David. 'He was in some kind of trance and would barely speak. It got a little weirder every time I went there,' says David. 'But Brian was always kind to me, and I felt a lot of gratitude towards him from when I was a kid.'

Despite having been away from Southern California for a year and a half, David's connection to the LA music scene remained viable. In 1972, while renting a house in Tujunga with his old band-mate from Colours, Gary Montgomery, and his wife Kay, David befriended their neighbour, a fellow musician named T-Bone Burnett. 'T-Bone had rented a house, a big mountain lodge right down from where I was living with Gary and Kay,' says David. 'He was producing sessions for Delbert McClinton and Glen Clark at the time. T-Bone was also a friend of Danny Moore, and we all hung out with Delbert and Glen and worked on their stuff. There was a whole bunch of us that were playing on sessions with each other around that time.' McClinton already had a major claim to fame, as he was credited by John Lennon as being his harmonica-styling inspiration for The Beatles song 'Love Me Do'. Delbert eventually found the top of the pop charts himself, with his 1980 recording of 'Givin' It Up For Your Love'. In 1972, David ended up moving in with Delbert and Glen and playing guitar in their live act around Southern California for a time. 'Delbert always talked like he had a toothpick in his mouth,' says David, 'then he'd blow his nose on my shoe.' David's uncredited acoustic playing appeared on the acclaimed *Genuine Cowhide* LP, released by McClinton in 1976.

Throughout this period, David maintained his friendship with songwriter Warren Zevon. 'I was always jamming on songs with Warren,' says David. 'It seemed like I was at his house every other day, playing music with him. I'd get up in the morning and go there. It was like a job.' Warren told *Goldmine* magazine in 1995, 'I had a friend who had been in The Beach Boys . . . David Marks. He was one of the original, original Beach Boys . . . David and I were hanging around.' By the end of the sixties, Warren's unique songwriting talent had already garnered plenty of notice, but it didn't comfortably pay his bills. It wasn't until Warren was introduced to one of David's parents' friends that he finally found a solid show business gig. Phil Everly, of the legendary Everly Brothers, had befriended the Marks through his and Elmer's shared love of vintage cars. Phil had recently purchased a gorgeous 1932 Packard convertible that Elmer himself had beautifully re-stored. Through that connection, Phil, Elmer and Jo Ann became very close friends.

One day, a drunken David popped into his parents' home and noticed Phil Everly was sitting on their sofa. Surprised to see one of the Everlys in his parents' living room, the first words out of Dave's mouth were, 'You assholes really caused us a lot of trouble on the road back in '63!' Of course, David was referring to the treatment The Beach Boys received when their tour followed that of The Everly Brothers through the Midwest many years before but Phil Everly had no idea what he meant and his perception of David was forever damaged. Despite the permanent tension between Dave and Phil, it was the Marks family who set up an audition for Warren Zevon with The Everly Brothers. Years later, Zevon told VH1, 'I needed a job rather desperately, and I was friends with a guy named David Marks, who was one of The Beach Boys for a while and owned an apartment building. That's what he did with his Beach Boys money, invested in this apartment building and then had the lack of sense to let his musician friends move in and not pay rent. I was living there and through him I met The Everly Brothers and got a chance to play piano for them.' When *Goldmine* magazine asked Warren about getting the Everlys gig, he answered, 'That was also through David Marks . . . I went in and I think they were both there. I just played "Hasten Down The Wind". I said, "Here's a song of mine." And Phil said, "Can you play like [country pianist] Floyd Cramer?" And I said, "I certainly can!" He laughed and said, "You're hired." They were wonderful guys.' Warren became musical director and pianist for The Everly Brothers, a job he held throughout the early 1970s.

One night, David and Warren were out drinking and went into a Japanese bar and restaurant known as the Imperial Gardens. The two of them were already three sheets to the wind when they arrived. Then they drank more. Warren sat down at the lounge piano and announced to the mostly Japanese patrons that his name was Elton John. David perched on a stool at the bar and hooted for Elton. Then he turned and insultingly said to Lyle, the Asian bartender, 'Give me a Jap beer!' An Asian waitress hurried over to drunken David and discreetly told him if he continued to behave like that he was going to find trouble. 'I told her that's good because we're looking for trouble,' remembers David. ' "Give me a double shot of trouble," I said!' The service came fast. 'Warren and I had this running joke about World War II that was very insensitive to the Japanese, but we were acting like idiots because we were way too drunk,' says David. 'I was asking for it, that's for sure.' After swallowing a flurry of bad-tasting Dave and Warren-style humour, Lyle the bartender told them both in no uncertain terms to 'get the fuck out'. But David remained on the stool and levelled one more racially insensitive comment at Lyle: 'I'm not leaving until I get a little nip.'

Before he had stopped laughing at his own stupid joke, David's double order of trouble arrived courtesy of a lead pipe to his skull. He was blindsided by a crushing blow to his forehead, which caused blood to spurt and his body to go completely limp. When David's body hit the floor, Warren hit the door. When he awoke, a group of Japanese men had him by his arms at the top of a steep flight of stairs and were getting ready to toss him. They began a count: 'One, two . . .' 'I said, "Oh, that's OK, I can walk!"' remembers David. 'They all laughed and let me stagger away with blood pouring down my face. They were laughing pretty hard at me, and I guess I deserved it.' Warren, who'd hightailed it out of the bar, met David in the parking lot. The horrified look on Warren's face let David know exactly how bad his injuries were. 'My God, are you still alive under there?' asked Warren. 'I think so,' mumbled David. 'Your face looks like a giant plum, David, and it's getting bigger!' stammered Warren. David's head was partially numb and partially throbbing in pain. 'My skull was like one enormous swollen purple bruise,' says David. 'I looked like a bloodied Elephant Man. Warren rushed me to the emergency room, but they couldn't really do anything for me. They just wiped me down, wrapped me in a big bandage, and sent me home to suffer.' Warren's wife Crystal cared for David for several days until he could manage to feed himself and talk a little. A week later, while drunk again, with his vision partially blocked from his still-healing face, David went through a stop sign and collided with a Jeep. His Porsche was totalled.

Between drunken disasters, David found time to occasionally visit his old neighbourhood in Hawthorne. 'Louie Marotta was still in his driveway working on his car, which always made me feel good,' says David. 'I told Louie about sitting in with The Beach Boys in Boston and at the Whisky. He told me that Dennis still came by to see him at least once a month.' Dave's old neighbour Greg Jones was back living in the area too, staying with a musician friend. 'They had a blues band and I would sit in with them occasionally in bars around Hawthorne,' says David. 'One of the places we played was at the Tropicana Lanes on Century Boulevard.' Bouncing from one jam scene to another and staying high or drunk most of the time, David didn't really care about getting back in touch with himself any more. His Beach Boys royalties came through like clockwork twice a year, and that was just enough for him to get by on. Then in March 1972, David received an additional cheque from Capitol Records for $15,000. The Beach Boys were finally getting paid for the successful lawsuit they had filed against Capitol in the late sixties for underpaid royalties.

When David showed up to collect his back-royalty cheque, he was asked to sign a release. Basically, it entailed pages of legalese describing the process of The Beach Boys vs. Capitol lawsuit and how David's portion of the settlement was arrived at. Everything seemed kosher, unless you looked very closely, something neither David nor his attorney bothered to do at the time. 'I was happy to get some quick money, and so was my lawyer,' says David. But slipped into the multi-page document was a paragraph that seemed to both acknowledge The Beach Boys had left themselves liable to David in 1963, and one that also attempted to remedy any potential legal problem for them in the future regarding their former guitarist. It read that if David signed the document and accepted his payout of $15,000, '*In consideration of the premises, Marks does hereby, for himself and his heirs, executors, administrators, successors and assigns, release, relieve and discharge Capitol and Brian, Carl and Dennis C. Wilson, Michael Love and Alan Jardine, and each of them, of and from any and all manner of claims, actions, causes of action, debts, accounts, covenants, agreements and demands of every kind and nature, in law or in equity, which Marks has or may hereafter have, for or in connection with any matter, cause or thing, from the beginning of the world through and including August 31, 1971.*' It then goes on to say: '*If . . . the facts in respect to which the foregoing release is given turn out to be other than or different from the facts now known or suspected by him, and he expressly accepts the risk that such facts may turn out to be other and different, and expressly waives all benefits and rights granted to him . . .'*. In other words, we know you got screwed, and if you sign this, once you've finally figured out how badly you got screwed, you can never do anything about it. David signed it and immediately spent his share of the settlement on a 50-foot fibreglass boat hull, which he parked in a canyon by the beach in San Marcos. In early 2006, when I asked a well-known Los Angeles entertainment industry attorney how much revenue David might have had a claim to today had he fought for his contractual twenty per cent share of Beach Boys royalties from their August 1963 through September 1967 recorded output, the figure I was given was $10 million.

Now he had a boat hull instead. 'Matt Moore and I bought a boat hull and a trailer together and we made a plan to finish the boat and sail around the world,' says David. After experiencing so many adventures together on foot, the idea of sailing seemed novel to David and Matt. To get their sea legs, they borrowed a friend's boat and sailed off to Catalina Island for a test run. Matt, who had just taken a beginner's course in sailing, instigated the trial trip. The two novice sailors spent most of the voyage verbally fantasising about the glorious destinations they would encounter once their own boat was complete and ready to sail. They reached Catalina without incident, and moored in Babylon harbor. They stayed to party for a few days. Upon their return, things got a bit dicey. First the boat began to take on water due to a 'bad repair' on the boat's tiller. Then, while they attempted to manage the leak, a significant storm broke out and even more water filled the troubled craft. Matt and David spent hours being pelted with wind and rain while bailing their way back to Oceanside. The troubled craft finally crawled into the harbour many hours behind schedule, and they tied it up in an appropriate slip. From there, the exhausted and drenched pair of semi-sailors went out for some hot breakfast at the local coffee shop. Upon returning to their borrowed boat, they were horrified to find that only part of the mast was still above water. While they were eating eggs and bacon, the boat had sunk like a saturated sausage to the bottom of the harbour. After this experience,

Dave and Matt quickly scrapped their ambitious travel plans and sold the boat. 'We thought we couldn't afford it, because as soon as we bought it he ran out of money and so did I,' says Matt. 'As fate would have it, the second we sold it I got a gig playing with David Cassidy, and Dave got another big royalty cheque. But that boat would have probably killed us anyway, so it was a good thing we got rid of it.'

Around this time, Dave received the troubling news that his father had been diagnosed with brain cancer. Never having come to terms with their fractured relationship, this news only added to David's confusion about his dad. David's immediate reaction was to drink even more alcohol and fall further away from truly knowing his father. He also began doing heroin on a regular basis while hanging out with Terry's brother, Skip Hand, and his friends in Redondo Beach. 'There was a lot of heroin, and there was a lot of craziness,' remembers Skip Hand. 'That's what we did, and that's what fuelled us in those days.' The stress of Elmer's condition only added to David's quest to escape reality. 'My dad was starting to go through radiation treatments and needed constant care,' remembers David. 'I was hanging around in really sleazy bars and strip clubs just to get my mind off of it. I was in a horribly destructive place in my personal life at that time.' Over the next three years, Dave's father slowly deteriorated. And David, too, descended into a slow deterioration of mind, body and spirit.

One night, after a disturbing visit to see his badly suffering father, David found himself longing for a connection to a better time. He was fighting depression and grasping for an emotional lifeline. 'I was drinking. I was alone, and I found myself driving near the street the Rovells lived on,' remembers David. He flashed back to the camaraderie and fun that had once filled his days of hanging out there with Brian and the guys. 'I said to myself, I wonder if the Rovells are still living there? I half expected to walk in and see everything still like it was in 1963, with all the guys still hanging out there. Boy, was I tripping.' This was 1972 and everything was different. David was now twenty-four years old. He was an alcoholic and a druggie. His hair was to his shoulders and he had grown a scraggly beard. He looked closer to the Manson family than to The Beach Boys family. There was hardly a trace left of the hopeful fifteen-year-old that had once been so welcome in the family atmosphere of the Rovell home. But David's alcohol-impaired mind clung to a weak thread of irrational hope that his old life was somehow still available to him. And the fact that it was past midnight wouldn't deter him. 'When we were kids, we could come and go at will because Brian was living there, and we'd just all come and go as we pleased,' says David. 'And this one night in the seventies I just showed up at the Rovells' door at two or three in the morning. I must have woken poor Mae up. She came to the door and I don't think she even knew it was me. I was looking different and I was just all fucked up. And I clearly remember she told me, "There's nothing here for you," and she closed the door in my face. It really hit home to me right then, the fact that it was over. That message was really driven home to me, that I'd lost all that . . . it's gone. I knew I'd never get that back, the camaraderie of the Rovell house. And I left and drove around in tears, feeling sorry for myself. It was total insanity on my part to expect her to accept me. It's alcoholism insanity.' And with that, David drove into the night, disconnected from his past, unable to cope with his present, and well into the routine of numbing himself for the foreseeable future.

10. I LOST MY WAY

Towards the end of 1972, a group of Dave's friends, including Buzz Clifford and Gary Montgomery, left LA and moved to Tulsa, Oklahoma. The rich Tulsa music scene had been giving birth to new musical genres and churning out unique artists for many decades. The list of notable musicians spawned in Oklahoma is long and varied, with names like Woody Guthrie, Leon Russell, Jimmy Webb, J. J. Cale, David Gates, Dwight Twilley, Vince Gill and Garth Brooks, to name a few. In Tulsa, Dave's buddies Montgomery and Clifford attached themselves to the remnants of future movie star Gary Busey's former bar band, known as Carp. They renamed the band Mundane Willis and began gigging around the Tulsa club scene. Busey, an Oklahoman himself, had already do-si-doed to LA, where he'd just begun to flirt with the idea of auditioning for acting roles. In 1972, Busey was only known as a rock drummer, but upon meeting Jo Ann Marks he was told that he was destined to become a major film star.

'Gary didn't believe her because he hadn't made any connections as an actor yet,' says David. 'He hooked up with an agent not too long after that. But at the time he met my mom, he was still trying to be a rock and roll drummer. When she told him that he was going to be a famous actor, he said, "Bullshit! Me? A movie star? That's not possible."' Within six years, Busey was nominated for a Best Actor Oscar for his acclaimed performance in *The Buddy Holly Story*.

With many of his LA buddies gone to Oklahoma, Dave briefly moved to San Diego to work for his old friend Greg Jones. 'I took my trailer down to Greg's and parked it in his front yard and he gave me a job in his produce company for a few months,' says David. But, like most things in Dave's life, it was only a quick pit stop in his never-ending escape from reality. He dabbled in everything – jam scenes, relationships, employment, living arrangements, never giving too much of himself to anything for too long. As long as his royalty cheque showed up every six months, he could hit the reset button and start all over again. Dave's only consistent focus was on staying drunk and taking drugs. Sadly, after temporarily regaining focus and commitment in Boston, by late 1972 David was completely off the rails again. He was speeding towards disaster without a care.

On New Year's Eve, after picking up 'some girl', David headed to another party in Hollywood. 'I had no idea who she was,' says David. 'She was just another anonymous girl who came along with me while I did stupid things. I had a 1969 MGC with a big decal of a trout on the driver's door. T-Bone Burnett had sold me the car and he named it the "official trout car".' On this particular night, David was behind the wheel of the trout car in a drunken haze, and was seen maniacally spinning around the intersection of Santa Monica Boulevard and Fairfax. The sight of a dingy, beat-up sports car with a trout on the door, smoking its tyres in never-ending circles in the middle of Hollywood on New Year's Eve was definitely an attention-grabber. Dave kept it going long enough to draw a cheering crowd of onlookers to line the sidewalk. Before long, David's antics were holding up traffic in all four directions. 'I was drunker than shit and screaming and laughing,' says David. 'A cop eventually showed up and pulled me over. He asked me how many beers I'd had. I told him "a million". I ended up getting arrested and thrown in jail.' David was sentenced to two weeks, the first of which was in the less than friendly environs of the LA County jail.

When David was marched to his jail cell, he was greeted by his cellmate for the week, a short, wiry black man with a facial tic and wild eyes. 'He kept lunging at me and hissing,' says David. 'Then he said, "Watch out for me, I'm a rattlesnake. I can strike at any time." I stayed away from him and kept to myself on the top bunk.' Once Rattlesnake noticed David was regularly meditating and doing yoga, he mumbled to himself, 'He's a spiritual boy.' From then on, he stopped hissing. But trouble flared again when a guard caught Dave smoking and shoved him into the back of another scary-looking inmate. 'That guy was ready to jump me, so I thought quick and looked the guard in the eye and put my cigarette out by closing it in my fist,' says David. 'My hand was literally smouldering, but everyone who saw it thought I was crazy and it caused enough of a distraction for me to not get my ass kicked.'

The second week of David's sentence was scheduled to be served at Wayside Honor Ranch in Castaic. The day he was being transferred from his county jail cell, Rattlesnake suddenly piped up. Assuming that his cellmate was being released, he offered to help David with bus fare if he needed it. 'That really surprised me after he'd been so threatening, and I asked him why he was making the gesture,' remembers Dave. 'He said his mother once told him, "You never know when you'll be turning away an angel." That moment sticks with me to this day. It really goes to show you how God speaks to you through people, and usually when you least expect it.'

After a tense week in County jail, David was looking forward to the more relaxed atmosphere of the minimum-security Honor Ranch. However, one stipulation was that he'd have to sacrifice his shoulder-length locks for a military-style haircut. 'I didn't think it was worth cutting off all my hair for a week in a better jail.' Bad choice. Upon his refusal to cooperate, David was sent to an adjacent maximum-security facility where he was the third man in a two-man cell. 'I had to sleep on a paper-thin mattress on the concrete floor until they took it away at 6 a.m. They locked me in that cell for seven straight days without being able to leave once. I was going nuts in there. At one point the guards came by to take us to the showers, which I declined for obvious reasons.' When Dave refused to shower, a fellow prisoner in an adjacent cell began yelling at him, 'What's the matter, hippie, why won't you come shower with us? Are you ashamed of your body?' Later, during lockdown, David teasingly yelled back at him, 'I'm naked now ... I'm not ashamed of my body!' David's cellmate quickly told him in a serious tone, 'You'd better shut up or that guy will hunt you down and kill you!' David shut up.

Almost instantly after being released from prison, Dave was pulled over for speeding, and because his licence was suspended, he faced jail again. 'When I was waiting in court I could see the judge I was going to appear in front of was going to be really tough,' says David. 'I sat there waiting for my name to be called .... and I watched him throw several people in jail with lesser offences than mine.' Faced with the sure prospect of being locked up again, David split court and fled for Tulsa, Oklahoma.

Gary Montgomery kindly flew out from Oklahoma to assist Dave in his escape from LA. The pair rented a car and attempted to tow Dave's 21-foot house trailer all the way to Tulsa. They made it as far as New Mexico before being pulled over in the high desert for – you guessed it – speeding. This time Gary was driving, so David's looming arrest warrant wasn't an issue. The police meticulously searched the trailer for contraband but came up empty. Fortunately, Dave had hidden his large marijuana stash well by stuffing it into the hollow legs of a table inside the trailer. The police eventually let Dave and Gary go. Shaken up from their narrow escape, they pulled off the highway for the night at a local Ramada

Inn. But while pulling into the entrance of the hotel, in pure Cheech and Chong fashion, they forgot about something as basic as clearance height. As the two permanently stoned musicians carelessly pulled Dave's gigantic trailer under the low entryway, a large section of the carport's roof was torn completely off. The *same* cops that had just searched their trailer minutes before happened to be sitting in the hotel coffee shop. While eating their meal and looking out the diner's window, the policemen watched in amazement as the scene outside unfolded. They witnessed Dave and Gary attempt to pull their ten-foot-high trailer under a nine-foot-high carport. With looks of disbelief on their faces, the policemen slowly walked up to David and Gary, who were standing there scratching their heads, with pieces of shredded trailer and carport roof laying all around them. One of the cops looked at the mess with utter disdain and drawled, 'You boys need to get a shorter trailer or find yourselves a taller motel.' The officers then climbed into their patrol car and drove away, but not before saying, 'We'll see you fellas down the highway.' Gary and Dave ended up slinking away from the motel problem after handing over some cash to the owner.

The next day they made it to Tulsa, arriving in a relatively unscathed state. Dave's trailer was parked in the back yard of the home of Gary, his wife Kay and their baby daughter Anna. He lived there for nearly eight months. Dave immediately connected with a clique of musicians he already knew well from Los Angeles. By far the most talented and successful of them was Leon Russell. In 1973, Russell was at the peak of his powers, having already carved out major successes as a session man, songwriter, producer, sideman, solo artist and entrepreneur. An Oklahoma native, he was clearly the king of the early seventies Tulsa scene. 'Leon had this stone church that took up a whole city block,' remembers David. 'It looked like a castle that he turned into a hangout and recording studio. At this point, he'd got a lot of money due to all the hits he'd written and the work he'd done for other artists. He'd have his recording studio running 24 hours a day. He'd have people wandering in and out, and playing all hours, and he captured everything on tape.' The church was located on 3rd and Trenton and it was a virtual beehive of musical activity throughout 1973. Among the musicians who came to visit Leon's church that year were Eric Clapton and George Harrison. For David, his time at the church was spent more as an observer than as a participant. 'I spent quite a bit of time at Leon's place,' says David. 'But I rarely picked up a guitar. I just hung out and watched and listened to what he was doing. The only thing Leon ever wanted to talk to me about was Brian Wilson. He told me all about how he had played piano for Brian on "California Girls" and *Pet Sounds*, and he wanted to know about what it was like when I recorded with The Beach Boys at the beginning. One day at the church he rolled tape and put me through a mock interview about Brian that was supposed to be a joke. I think he was a really big Beach Boys fan, but he kind of tried to play it down.'

Even though Dave didn't play the guitar very much while he lived in Tulsa, he continued to learn about music. His time spent witnessing Leon Russell's creative process was an invaluable experience. Another priceless experience came when a fellow musician named Ike Johnson gave David access to something few white boys from the South Bay had ever dreamed of. Johnson was black, the son of a Baptist minister, and a huge Beach Boys fan, too. When he discovered Dave was *that* David Marks, he was absolutely thrilled to meet him. He proudly took Dave home to meet his family and quickly became very close friends with him. 'Ike was a percussion player and he knew all the musicians in Tulsa,' says David. 'He took me around to all the black clubs where they were playing stuff I had never heard before, like reggae and Brazilian jazz. It was a big deal for me to get to see some of these bands because I wouldn't have been able to just wander into these black clubs without Ike. There was still a lot of segregation in Oklahoma in 1973.' But Ike took David everywhere he went, segregated or not, and Dave found himself in the middle of music scenes where his was the only white face. One night at a Tulsa blues club, Johnson announced to a group of his friends that David was one of the 'original Beach Boys'. One of Ike's older buddies stepped forward and sceptically eyed Dave's scraggly, long-haired mug, and then turned back to Ike and said, 'What the hell happened to him?'

The Tulsa experience intensified when Dave won an ounce of crystal meth in a poker game. He was then followed around for weeks by a never-ending speed-fuelled entourage including Ike and a revolving crowd of Tulsa hippies. The party went on indefinitely until the speed ran out and everyone crashed in David's trailer. 'I had about fifteen people, local band members, politicians' daughters, bikers, Rastafarians, everybody was sleeping in my twenty-one-foot trailer,' says David. 'They just dispersed at their leisure as they woke up, one by one, until it was just me again.' Between visits to Leon's church and club-hopping with Ike Johnson, David also found some time for the local ladies. 'I was visited by practically every woman in town in my trailer in Gary's back yard,' says David. 'I stayed in there, drunk on whisky most of the time, playing the electric piano. I had a Wurlitzer set up on top of the stove and a hot plate set up on top of the Wurlitzer.' He could literally cook and play at the same time. Not exactly a mansion in Beverly Hills, but for a time David greatly enjoyed the simple pleasures that his life in Tulsa afforded him.

That summer, David received word from LA that Murry Wilson had died of heart failure. His emotions were mixed. In a way, Murry was like a second father to David, and the thought of him being gone was a sad thing. The news also forced Dave to think hard about his own dad, who was near death himself. That night David called Elmer and they spoke briefly about Murry and the old days. Deep inside, David still felt traces of bitterness due to the rampant rumours about Murry's efforts to kill his post-Beach Boys career. But he also thought of Murry as the man whose sheer determination had willed The Beach Boys to the top. The thought of a life force as strong as Murry's having departed definitely left a void. That night, in a crowded Tulsa bar, David suddenly rose and hoisted a beer towards the ceiling, shouting, 'Good riddance,

Murry, you fucking bastard!' No one around him had any idea what he was talking about.

Eventually Dave's lawyer called and informed him that his legal troubles in Los Angeles had been cleared up. With the threat of incarceration eliminated, it was now safe for David to return to Southern California. 'Buzz Clifford came by and said he was getting ready to hitchhike back west,' remembers David. 'And I said, "Fuck that, I've got this TWA credit card. Come with me." And we both hopped on a plane and flew back to LA.'

Dave and Buzz temporarily moved in with Danny Moore and began to write new material together. In the meantime, a trio of girls from Tulsa, named Darlene, Connie and Paula, followed Dave and Buzz back to LA in their van. The girls showed up at Danny's door and were basically ready for anything. On the spur of the moment, Dave decided he wanted to go back to Oklahoma for his trailer, so they all piled into Darlene's van and drove the 1,400 miles back to Tulsa.

Over the next few months, David immersed himself in a flurry of recording projects. Buzz and Dave began recording tracks with Danny Moore at Paramount Studios for a proposed joint release. Dave also recorded tracks for what was known as the 'Silvermine' project with Buzz, keyboardist Glen Crocker, guitarist Stanley Hightower, and drummers Terry and Skip Hand. At the same time, Dave also recorded at Blue Dolphin studio with Glen Clark, of Delbert and Glen, and guitarist Don Preston, with Danny Moore mixing the tracks. 'We all just got drunk and coked up and recorded each other's original songs,' says David. 'It was all great but nothing ever got released.' The same can be said for nearly everything David recorded from this point forward.

In June 1974, The Beach Boys' *Endless Summer* LP was released by Capitol Records. With a title suggested by Mike Love, the double LP was a compilation of 1962–65 Beach Boys classics, featuring seven songs from the David Marks era. The release proved to be wildly popular and unexpectedly vaulted The Beach Boys into the realm of American icons.

Immersed in his cycle of jamming, recording, partying and adhering to his avoidance of commitment, David was completely unaware of the ever-growing phenomena of early Beach Boys nostalgia. Not only was he being denied the huge sum of money his original Capitol contract said was rightly his, but he was also denied any significant acknowledgment for the hits he'd played on, and for his part in the group's story. But David Marks paid no attention to such things. Instead, he continued on his wayward spiral of continuous drug and alcohol abuse partnered with sporadic guitar virtuosity. Heroin was now on the intake menu nearly full-time. 'I was travelling in different circles of people and they were all doing heroin,' says David. 'I was indulging in that with about three different groups of people, and none of them knew about each other. There was the beach crowd, the desert crowd and the valley crowd. They were three separate unrelated groups of people, and I travelled in all three circles doing heroin. If one group wasn't happening, I'd just go to the next.'

Dave and Skip Hand spent a period of time in the desert at Dave's cabin in Twentynine Palms, writing music and taking heroin. At first, the drugs were merely an accessory to the pair's musical endeavours but eventually they became the main event. 'I remember Dave and I were doing heroin for about a month straight, then we ran out of money and couldn't keep the drugs flowing,' remembers Hand. 'And one day we both thought we'd come down with the flu. Our mucous membranes were running and we just felt like hell. We're out there in the middle of the desert, the wind was blowing, and we're absolutely stinking miserable with some kind of nasty virus. And then it finally dawned on us both at about the same time: wait a minute . . . could this be . . . addiction? We were both shocked because we really thought it was the flu. We'd been going through heroin withdrawal and we didn't even know it. So we jumped in Dave's van and jammed back to Redondo Beach and bought a spoon of dope, and the symptoms immediately went away.'

David shared some of the dark fun with Warren Zevon when he shot him up for his first heroin experience in the

Redondo Beach 'drug den', which sat right behind the local police station. David and Warren's intense friendship finally imploded shortly after that. While Warren was touring with The Everly Brothers in Japan, he called home late one night to talk to his wife Crystal, whom he missed badly. Unfortunately, David answered the Zevons' phone. Dave was only there to score drugs but apparently Warren didn't believe him. He never spoke to David again.

On 4 July 1974, after spending the previous night and most of the morning partying around Hollywood, David found himself on the street in a physically thrashed state. He slowly walked from Hollywood to Venice Beach, where he sat alone outside a liquor store drinking Club Cocktails. An incredibly similar fate would be in store for another Beach Boy in future years – Dave's old pal Dennis Wilson would become a near fixture on the sidewalks and parking lots of Venice liquor stores in the early eighties – but on this day, it was David who filled the position of tragic ex-Beach Boy. In a deep haze of alcohol and drugs, Dave had sunk very low, although he was still years from his bottom. Somewhere in the fog of opiates, he accessed true emotion and began to think about the people he hadn't seen in years – like Dennis. He decided the only thing left to do was to visit his old neighbourhood and see if any of his long-lost Hawthorne friends were still around. He somehow managed to find a bus that delivered him to the South Bay. He arrived shirtless and strung out. He stopped by the home of an old friend named Lane Sykes. Peeking into Sykes's open doorway, Dave realised he had stumbled into a very bad situation. His friend had just caught his wife in bed with another man. Sykes was extremely agitated and was pointing a .45 calibre handgun at both his wife and her unlucky boyfriend. Then all parties made eye contact with David. He flashed a weak smile and told them, 'I can see you're busy, I'll come back another time.' He attempted to slink away but the enraged husband quickly turned the gun on David and told him, 'Get in there and sit down!' David spent the next thirty minutes reasoning with his frazzled friend, who eventually put the gun down and allowed everyone to leave.

Emotionally exhausted and physically wrecked, David shuffled past Hawthorne High School to the home of his friend and ex-drummer Mark Groseclose. Mark was living at the corner of El Segundo Boulevard and Shoup Avenue, where he shared a duplex with his mother and his little sister Kathy. Dave hadn't seen Mark in years and had made the trek to Hawthorne specifically to try and find him. 'When Dave came to our house to visit after a few years, Mark knew that Dave was in a bad way and on heroin,' says Kathy Groseclose Michael. 'My mom was hanging laundry on the clothes line in the back yard, and there was David, peering over the back fence and saying some strange stuff to her. She didn't recognise him and told him if he didn't stop it she was going to spray him with the hose. Then he said, "Mom, it's me, Dave." He had hitchhiked from Hollywood and had somehow lost $2,000 along the way. Mark, being Dave's true friend, took him in, fed him, gave him rest, and a good talk.' For David, it was a happy reunion. He spent the afternoon and evening celebrating Independence Day in traditional suburban fashion with barbequed food and fireworks. 'It was fun for Mark having David back,' says Kathy. 'They just had something special and were in constant laughter when they were around each other. At one point that night David threw a firecracker and caught Mark's hair on fire. We had a lot of fun.'

By October 1974, the *Endless Summer* LP had risen all the way to number one on the Billboard LP charts. It proved to be the biggest-selling Beach Boys release ever. David remained largely oblivious to the incredible rise in Beach Boys fortunes until his next royalty cheque arrived. Suddenly, David's royalty income had nearly tripled. By the beginning of 1975, The Beach Boys were headlining stadiums across the United States and were voted *Rolling Stone* magazine's 'Band Of The Year'. But it was not a particularly happy period for David and he felt little connection to the individual Beach Boys or their success. The last time David had tried to visit Brian, Marilyn had turned him away at the gate, telling him, 'Brian isn't seeing visitors any more.' On 17 May 1975, at

11.20 p.m., Dave's father, Elmer Lee Marks, died of cancer. 'We didn't think of it as a shock or anything at the time,' says David. 'He'd been sick for so long. He was literally dying for years. He kept having seizures, and then he'd have more cobalt treatments; it was really gruelling. It felt like a blessing when he finally passed away.'

In the summer of 1975, while The Beach Boys were playing to audiences of 50,000 and more, David was gigging at a bar in the San Fernando Valley. Still, the band he was playing guitar in was very notable. They were known as Teddy Jack Eddie and the Night Owl Revue and they spent months performing as the house band at the Sundance Saloon in Calabasas. The band consisted of David on guitar, Gary Busey on drums, Buzz Clifford on guitar and vocals, Glen Crocker on piano, Gary Montgomery on organ and harmonica, Rick Cantu on percussion, and Darrel Leonard on bass. The band earned a reputation as one of LA's hottest bar bands, and the saloon was packed for most of their performances. No one made any point of showcasing the fact that David was formerly a member of the now white-hot Beach Boys. Instead, he was known as a talented guitarist who, although usually in an inebriated state, played his ass off every night when he took the stage. 'People like Leon Russell would sit in with us,' says David. 'A lot of famous people came out to see us. We were kind of hip for a minute within the entertainment industry.' Among the showbiz luminaries who filled the saloon to hear Teddy Jack Eddie and the Night Owl Revue perform were Kris Kristofferson, Barbra Streisand and Bob Dylan. The group also gigged at assorted small venues around Southern California, sometimes sharing the bill with The Moore Brothers Band, which included both Matt and Danny. One night, an unknown kid from Oklahoma named Vince Gill opened for them at the Sweetwater in Redondo Beach and blew everyone away with his guitar skills. Gill then went on to become a huge country music star.

Though their popularity only amounted to a smallish cult following in the Southland, the rocking blues stylings of Teddy Jack Eddie and the Night Owl Revue gave David another brief flash of notoriety. The band's name had been derived from a character Gary Busey had once played on a local Tulsa TV show. David's friendship with Busey proved to be an amusing aspect of the Teddy Jack Eddie experience. 'Gary was a crazy man,' remembers David. 'He liked to do things like ride around on the hood of my car. One time we were driving separate vans on the freeway, going seventy miles an hour, and passing joints back and forth from car to car. Gary would be leaning out the window across the lanes trying to grab the joint. He was nuts, but he was a good musician. As an actor, he played himself pretty much. One night I insulted his drumming, so he quit the band and we didn't talk again for a really long time.' The Night Owl Revue came to an inglorious end, and Busey went on to fame and fortune as a film actor. Gary also built a lasting reputation as a very loose cannon, which eventually thwarted his once-promising movie career.

Another ex-friend of David's who exploded into the limelight during the late seventies was Warren Zevon. After Linda Ronstadt turned Warren's song 'Poor Poor Pitiful Me' into a major hit, Warren scored a Top Ten single of his own, the quirky 'Werewolves Of London,' in 1978. Warren's critically acclaimed LP from the same year, *Excitable Boy*, was a top seller as well. It seemed David Marks found himself in a constant state of being one degree removed from true success. But nothing pleased Dave more than to see a talent like Warren get his due. 'I knew that fame was destined to happen for Warren,' says David. 'He worked hard every day, and finally all the planets lined up just right for him. There were a lot of people in the industry, like Jackson Browne, who passionately believed in Warren. Jackson was one of the big reasons Warren broke through when he did. But if it hadn't happened then, it would have come eventually. He just kept plugging away, and he had a unique gift.'

In the late seventies, David lived and recorded with his long-time friend Terry Hand. They were a mostly hapless pair, constantly staying high, and getting little accomplished. Carrie Marks relates: 'At least Terry's dreams of being a rock star kept David with one foot in music. Terry kept David somewhat focused on trying to make something happen.' During this period, Terry and David wrote and recorded a wonderful song called 'Still Life In Motion'. Under the right circumstances, the song could have easily been a hit record. With its gentle harmonies and relaxed rocking feel it stands up well to the Eagles-style country rock that dominated US radio at the time. But, of course, it only made it to the demo stage, going unreleased until David rewrote the lyrics and put in on his *Something Funny Goin' On* CD in 2003.

While hanging out with Terry at various LA strip clubs, David met a string of exotic dancers and maintained volatile relationships with more than a few. David's royalty money was still flowing decently and he and his stripper girlfriends shared similar interests, like drugs and alcohol. Music began to take a less and less important role in David's life and he slid even further into an anonymous, underachieving freak scene. One night, David's latest girlfriend flipped out after smoking PCP and tried to kill him with a hammer. David fought her off, threw her in his van, and then dumped her in front of the closest police station.

During this period, David would go out of his way to remove himself from his Beach Boys past. He'd regularly instruct people not to introduce him as someone who used to be in The Beach Boys. 'I would even deny it if confronted by someone who asked me about it, and say, "I'm not the same David Marks." It really bothered me,' says David. 'I think I didn't want that kind of attention drawn to me. I was paranoid and withdrawn.' His complete disconnection from The Beach Boys got to the point where David would pick up his royalty cheques without even being cognisant of how the money had been generated. 'It became totally Pavlovian, where the bell would go off and I'd go to the Capitol Tower, pick my cheque up, and proceed to party with whoever happened to be with me at the time,' says David. 'The thought of being associated with The Beach Boys didn't even enter my mind. I was just going to pick up my cheque. It got to the point where I forgot why I was getting that money.' This syndrome went on for years and it proved to be a huge factor in David's push towards killing himself. 'I would have three months of partying and then three months of complete poverty, sleeping on people's floors and begging for money off of my mother to buy vodka. Then for three months after receiving the cheque, I'd be high on the hog again. I'd be buying toys, going to restaurants, and partying and travelling till I ran out of money. Then I'd wait for the next royalty cheque, and that pattern went on. It's an automatic enabling system.' In a late-seventies interview, David was quoted as saying, 'I guess you could say my career is just waiting for cheques.'

Around this time, David nearly died of blood poisoning after cutting his hand on the lid of a cat food can. 'I'd been fasting on tequila at the time and I had no antibodies whatsoever, so the infection set right in,' says David. 'The nurse said if it had been on my left side it would have killed me, because it would have gotten to my heart. As it was I had glowing red streaks from my finger all the way up to my chest. Gangrene had actually set in because I didn't get to a doctor fast enough.' Dave's index finger on his right hand remains partially paralysed due to the poisoning. His dexterity is somewhat compromised when it comes to holding a guitar pick and his finger-picking abilities have suffered somewhat, but it didn't impede his ability to mix a drink and snort a line.

In 1976, Brian Wilson was coaxed back into the studio to attempt to take charge of his first Beach Boys record in nearly a decade. With Brian producing, The Beach Boys scored a Top Ten hit with their nerdy cover of Chuck Berry's ancient 'Rock And Roll Music'. In an interview with John Tobler of *Zig Zag* magazine at the peak of 'Brian's Back' mania, Mike Love was asked about David Marks. 'He is sorely neglected and unjustly so, for he's a fine gentleman, a nice person, and he's also studied classical music at a music school in Boston,' said Mike. 'Now he's back on the West Coast, doing what? I don't know, because I haven't talked to him for the last couple of years.' Despite Mike Love's well-documented sinister side, of all The Beach Boys he was probably the kindest to David

Marks. From the time he joined the band to the present, Mike has consistently shown he has a soft spot for David. 'Mike was the only one who ever bothered to track David down through the years and call just to see if he needed anything, and it was Mike who tried a couple of times to get David back into the band,' says Carrie Marks. 'Remember . . . when they left for their first tour back in 1962, Elmer took Mike aside and told him that since he was the oldest, he had to look after David. I really do believe Mike has taken that to heart as much as he's capable of doing.'

One day in the late seventies, David was visiting his mother's house when the phone rang. It was Mike. He wanted to know where David was living. Jo Ann told Mike, 'You can ask him yourself because he's standing right here.' David and Mike chatted for a bit about the fact they hadn't seen each other in several years, and Dave asked about the other guys and about Mike's family. 'I'm living in Reseda now,' said David. 'Really?' said Mike. 'I'm playing in Reseda soon, why don't you come sit in?' Between Beach Boys tours, Mike was gigging with a side project known as The Endless Summer Beach Band, which included veteran Beach Boys sidemen like Carli Munoz, Daryl Dragon and Mike Kowalski. David's reply to Mike's offer startled him: 'I can't play with you because my guitar's in the pawn shop,' said David. 'You're like a character out of a Charles Dickens novel,' answered Mike. 'Don't worry – if you show up, we'll have a guitar there for you.' David wasn't very interested in revisiting his Beach Boys past but felt he should show up purely out of respect for Mike's olive branch. 'He made the effort to find me, and showed real concern for my wellbeing,' says David. 'Financially, socially, he was on a whole different level than me. He didn't have to do that. I was nearly a bum. I was a footnote in The Beach Boys world. But Mike kept checking in with me anyway. I have great respect for him because he consistently made the effort to see how I was doing.'

With that in mind, David appeared on stage with Mike Love and his band at the Country Club in Reseda. Playing a borrowed guitar, David was only going through the motions and found nothing musically motivating in the set of old Beach Boys hits. Reporters from the *LA Herald Examiner* covered the show and noted David's presence in an article printed the following day. A photo of Dave and Mike on stage together accompanied the article. In attendance that night was Dave's newest girlfriend, a raven-haired beauty named Polly Boutch. During the time they were together, this was the only time she saw David perform on a stage. Instead of regularly working in public as a productive musician and honing his craft in a professional forum, David had devolved into someone who was constantly high, usually alone and hovering over a keyboard with headphones on, or maniacally jamming for endless hours with other anonymous, crank-head guitarists, killing time between drug scores. Playing music became nothing more than a nervous habit to pour excess physical energy into during peak periods of the daily high. Among David's contacts in his ever-expanding network of drug connections were a group known as the 'Wonderland Avenue Crowd', who maintained a notorious drug den in their otherwise quiet North Hollywood neighbourhood. In July 1981, four people were brutally bludgeoned to death as they slept in the residence at 8763 Wonderland Avenue. The Los Angeles Police Department announced that their primary suspect in the grisly killings was legendary porn star John Holmes. In 2003, a successful feature film, *Wonderland*, was released. Starring Val Kilmer, it was based on the events leading to the murders and their aftermath. For David Marks, the story hit very close to home.

Long-time Beach Boys promoter and friend Fred Vail had moved to Nashville in the seventies and earned his living as an independent promoter for RSO Records, among other labels. Fred regularly visited LA on business, but like many people, he'd lost contact with David Marks back in the sixties. One night in 1980, that changed. 'I can remember I was walking down the north side of Sunset Boulevard,' says Vail. 'It was late at night and I was passing by the area on the strip with all the clubs. And I saw this kind of scary-looking guy sitting on the hood of a parked car and he said, "Fred! Is that you?" And I looked and I didn't recognise him, but I walked over and said, "Yes?" And he said, "It's me, it's Dave. Don't you remember?" At that point, I probably hadn't seen him in ten or fifteen years. And I finally recognised who it was and I said, "Dave, I can't believe it's you, it's been so long." I asked him what he was doing there and he said, "Oh, my girlfriend works in this club," and if I recall, I think it was a strip club. He said he was waiting for her to get off work so he could take her home. It was great to see him, but to be honest, I was shocked by how he looked. He was looking pretty seedy. It was obvious he was pretty messed up. I immediately thought of the parallels between him and Dennis, because David and DW had some of the same qualities. We talked for a while, and then I had to go. I really wondered if I'd ever see him again after that.'

Sometimes it seemed he had a death wish. Skip Hand relates a story about riding in Dave's van on the Pacific Coast Highway near Manhattan Beach. David, high as usual, just roared along, ignoring the stop lights at major intersections every half mile or so. 'There's a stretch between El Segundo Boulevard and Rosecrans, and he was going about eighty miles an hour in the van where the speed limit is about forty-five. I started screaming at him, "Dave, please slow down,"' remembers Hand. 'And Dave says, "Are there any cops behind me?" And I looked back and I said, "No, no cops." So he stomps the gas pedal to the floor and soon we're going ninety or ninety-five and he says, "How about now?" And he hits Rosecrans on a red light and goes flying across the intersection yelling, "How about NOW?" And I'm going, JESUS, we made it, and I'm turning white, and he just keeps going faster and yelling, "How about NOW? How about NOW?" Every time he said it, he went faster. We must have been doing well over a hundred. And finally he started laughing and he slowed down a little, and we lived. My God, he was a total nut-job at times.'

One night, David headed out to a nightclub in Manhattan Beach to see a performance by singer Harold Payne. As had become his daily routine, David overindulged on alcohol that night. 'I just drank excessively, almost to the point of not being able to walk, and then like an idiot, I decided to drive,' says David. 'I passed out going about thirty-five miles an hour. When I woke up I tried to start my van and nothing worked, no lights, it wouldn't turn over, so I tried to get out to see what was the matter with it. That's when I realised I was trapped.' Completely oblivious to what had happened minutes before, Dave soon knew he'd been in a serious accident. 'The steering wheel had me pinned down to the seat by my gut,' says David. 'I wiggled and wormed my way free and got out and observed that the concrete light pole I had slammed into was halfway through the van on the passenger's side and the roof was ripped open like a soup can. The pole was cracked in half and leaning over the van. While I'm standing there admiring the damage, a guy pulls up in a Volkswagen and says, "Hop in before the cops get here!" So I did, and he took me home. The next morning I woke up with this pain in my stomach and I had no idea what it was from. I didn't remember what had happened the night before. Just then the phone rang and it was the Redondo Beach sheriff's department. The officer said, "You owe us a light post, Mr Marks, can you please come down and pay us?" That's when it all came back to me. I called Skip Hand and asked him to bring me down there. I have no idea how or why I survived.'

In 1981, David showed up at the offices of Capitol Records to collect his six-month royalty cheque. David was used to it being anywhere from $7,000 to $15,000, depending on how well The Beach Boys' back catalogue had sold over the past half year. There were a few cases when the cheques even exceeded that range, like in the period immediately following the release of *Endless Summer*, when they rose beyond $30,000. But this time, things would be different. Even though The Beach Boys played to as many as 500,000 fans at a time during their yearly 4 July Washington DC concerts, they had lost much of their artistic credibility due to a string of weak LP releases. Unbeknown to David, The Beach Boys' yearly record sales were experiencing a severe downturn. When David arrived at Capitol in the summer of 1981, he was broke as usual and badly needing his royalty fix. He nearly fainted when he was told there was no money for him. 'They said, "Sorry, we gave you too much last time,"' remembers David. '"You don't get one now." That was panic, a complete shock. I had to get a paper round.'

Dave eventually moved to Barstow, where he lived in his van with Polly. 'I just drank Seagram's, did methamphetamine, and played guitar,' remembers Dave. 'My buddy Cash Lowery had become a semi-responsible person with a family in Barstow, and he invited me and Polly out to live with him while we got on our feet.' David and Cash made a routine of jamming on their guitars all night, while Polly became good friends with Cash's wife, Terry, whose nickname was Trip. In the midst of just barely scraping by in Barstow, Polly informed David that she was pregnant with his child.

After surviving a very lean six months, David received a small royalty cheque from Capitol. He and Polly used the money to rent a home in Redondo Beach. In the spring of 1982, Dave and Polly's daughter Jennifer was born. Despite the couple's less than foetus-friendly lifestyle, Jennifer was a beautiful and healthy baby. But after a year of devoted motherhood, Polly suddenly disappeared and left David alone to cope with a one-year-old child. He and baby Jennifer moved in with Jo Ann in Burbank. With constant help from his mother, David committed himself to being a decent dad. Slowly, a personal transformation began to occur. Bit by bit, out of David's core being, a fallible but truly decent person with a good heart began to re-emerge. The daily challenge of being a loving parent became his focus, and the darkness that had engulfed him for years began to recede. 'I think I was a good father who had major limitations,' says David. 'I think a good parent is one who is there, not one who is somewhere else. I read to her every night. It was a little frightening, but it worked out. She's a good kid. My parents raised me to be loyal. So I always cheered for the underdog. I was loyal to my baby. It was a reflex to take care of her. I guess I have a nurturing quality, and that came out with Jennifer.'

Later that year Dave went back to the old neighbourhood in Hawthorne again, and this time his old house was sitting on stilts, waiting to be moved away. Plans for the decade-long Century Freeway project were under way, and part of the area was being dismantled, including the former Wilson home. 'I was in tears, and I fell into Louie Marotta's arms,' says David. 'Louie stayed in that neighbourhood through his whole life, even after they carved it up. He told me that day that Dennis still came by, once a month, and he'd just sit in the driveway watching him work on his car. Louie said Dennis would sit there, drinking beer, and talk to him about the old days.' Dave hadn't seen Dennis in many years, but it felt nice talking to Louie about him and knowing that he just might run into him there someday. 'I could go back there any time and I knew Louie would be in the driveway working on his car,' says David. 'Louie was our anchor. I never saw Dennis, but through Louie I felt like we were still connected, with both of us doing the same thing . . . visiting Louie and hanging out and talking with him. Because of Louie I felt like I still knew Dennis.' The day the city moved David's old house away, Mark Groseclose stopped by and collected two bricks that were left behind at the site. He gave them to David to keep in remembrance of another time. To this day, David still treasures those two old bricks.

On 28 December 1983, 39-year-old Dennis Wilson drowned while diving from a friend's sailboat in Marina del Rey. 'I was in the Blue Dolphin recording studio on Melrose with Buzz and Danny,' remembers David. 'And someone came in and told us one of The Beach Boys had died. My first thought was that it was Brian. But then I found out it was Dennis. I remember that I wasn't surprised. I was hurt, but I wasn't surprised. It didn't hit me for several days until I was alone somewhere and I found myself weeping uncontrollably because I was so sad that Dennis had died. I didn't know he'd been kicked out of The Beach Boys, and was broke and homeless, and had been basically living on the streets. I wish I had run into him, although it probably wouldn't have helped him, but I would have liked to see him again. But it's probably good I didn't run into him, because I would have followed him right into the ocean. I always did whatever Dennis did.' David called Audree Wilson to offer his condolences, and subsequently re-established a relationship with her. The week after the drowning, David and Audree talked about Dennis and all the special times they had shared. 'Before I hung up, Audree said Dennis loved being a Beach Boy and he just couldn't restrain himself from the temptation that went along with that,' remembers David. 'It was very hard for her to accept that he had died so young. She loved Dennis the most; she was his mom.'

What David didn't know at the time, but has learned in recent years, is that towards the end of his life, Dennis had been trying to find him. Dennis's first wife, Carole Wilson Bloom, related a story about Dennis showing up at her door one night. 'He was desperate to find David,' says Carole. 'He asked me to contact anyone that I thought might know where David was. He even wrote me a note to give to David in case I found him. I think Dennis was deeply affected by David leaving the group. He spoke about it many times over the years.'

David understands now that when he left The Beach Boys, it ended up isolating Dennis. 'I was the one in the group who was the most like Dennis,' says David. 'I took some of the heat off of him because I was always in trouble too. We were the ones who were always looking for fun and never taking anything too seriously. I basically learned about life from him when I was a kid, so it's no wonder we were similar. I loved Dennis and I think about him all the time. I'm really sorry I never got to see him again.'

In the mid-1980s, Polly suddenly surfaced and challenged David for custody of Jennifer. Luckily, David was well represented by attorney Larry Waserman. Although Dave was still drinking, he managed to clean himself up for his court appearances. He prepared himself for the case, put on a suit, and showed up on time. Carrie Marks explains: 'I think it speaks volumes about his character that he fought so hard to get custody of Jennifer. So many guys in a similar situation would have been glad to get rid of that responsibility, but David didn't. He loved that little girl so much, and there was no way he was going to let her be raised by anyone else. That's one of the reasons I fell in love with him . . . as messed up as he was, he rose to the occasion and became a pretty good father in spite of all of his faults and addictions. How can you not root for a guy that does the right thing instead of taking the easy way out?' In the end, David was awarded sole custody of his daughter.

Between collecting his shrinking royalty cheques, David was seriously trying to cut down on his lingering substance abuse problems. Although he'd kicked heroin 'cold turkey' several years earlier, a steady drinking habit and occasional cocaine binges continued to plague him. For a couple of months he worked for his old buddy Greg Jones. 'Greg had moved back to LA, where he hooked up with his uncle,' says David. Together they started a company called Village Produce. 'Greg said, "You need money? Take your van and bring it down to the docks at 4 a.m., and I'll load you up with produce, and you can go around to all the restaurants and sell the produce." I actually did it, got my own accounts, and had a regular route. I serviced some of his existing accounts and even landed some of my own. The thing about the Central Market in LA is you can get anything that grows if you know the right people, and Greg and his uncle always knew the right people.' But that job only lasted until Dave's next run-in with the law. Dave explains, 'One morning on the way to the docks, I got pulled over and the cop found a vial of coke between the seats, so I didn't make it to work that morning – I went to jail instead.' Dave ended up serving a short sentence, paying a large fine, and going to drug diversion class.

In October 1986, Dave agreed to get together with two of his former Marksmen mates, drummer Mark Groseclose and bassist Bill Trenkle, for the Southbay Surf Band Reunion in Torrance. The Marksmen shared the reunion bill with The Belairs and Eddie and the Showmen. The reunion concert was considered a big success and provided a fun atmosphere for a nostalgic visit to a time that had passed more than two decades earlier. But on this particular night, Dave was concentrating more on drinking than on reminiscing, and he seemed somewhat detached during the event. His guitar style had evolved into something that was far beyond the 'surf music' sound. It's as if the nostalgia frame was ready for Dave's portrait but his image wouldn't fit into it any more. While his band played early-sixties progressions and textures, Dave's guitar solos sounded closer in spirit to Eddie Van Halen than Dick Dale. In a post-reunion interview with Domenic Priore, he seemed to have little clue as to why people still cared about all this surf music stuff. After the show, David stumbled out to buy some cigarettes and was promptly arrested by the Torrance police for being drunk and disorderly. He spent the night in jail yet again.

Dave's pal Mark Groseclose's own drinking problem had reached the point where his body was giving out too. His eyes were permanently bloodshot, his body was bloated, and his rotted-out teeth were held in with glue. Mark looked nothing like the suave blond drummer who'd once collaborated on great music with David in the sixties. His days were numbered.

In January 1988, The Beach Boys were inducted into the Rock and Roll Hall of Fame along with The Beatles and Bob Dylan. The induction ceremony featured the four living 'original' Beach Boys: Brian, Carl, Mike and Al. As they were inducted, Mike Love launched into an embarrassing diatribe against his perceived foes in the industry. But otherwise, it was a fine night and a big honour for the boys. However, David was not invited to the ceremony or recognised by the Hall of Fame. The only acknowledgement was a tiny mention in the Hall of Fame's Beach Boys display where it reads 'Briefly replaced by David Marks' next to Al Jardine's name. David has never attempted to remedy this, and has paid no mind to it. But in my opinion, leaving out a musician and member who performed on the band's first four LPs, first six hits, first successful tours, and who was an equal member on their first major record contract, is an abomination.

On 29 July 1988, Mark Groseclose died as a result of years of severe alcoholism. He was only 42 years old. Mark's downward spiral began in 1974, when his wife fell into an affair with a co-worker, leading to their divorce. He never recovered emotionally from that break-up. 'It crushed Mark's heart,' says his sister, Kathy Groseclose Michael. 'Mark was in a very bad way because of his alcohol abuse. I remember the night before Mark died, Dave and Terry Hand went to see him in the hospital. David called later to let us know he had seen Mark. He was very sad and lost within himself. I knew then that part of Dave was dying, too. Part of what was alive in him was leaving. David wasn't too far from where Mark was, physically; he was very sick from years of alcoholism too.'

For David, it was an awful experience to see one of his closest friends die of a disease that also held him firmly in its grip. 'Mark had been such a vibrant presence in my life, and was so deeply talented as both a musician and a visual artist,' says David. 'He truly was a genius with his art. It's a tragedy he went out the way he did, but that's what he was determined to do. He was just too sad deep down to pull out of it.' Bill Trenkle, of the Marksmen, concurs: 'Mark was a really special guy in so many ways. He was before his time, and he wore out kinda quick, but he was fantastic while he was here.'

The final word on David and Mark's special connection comes from Mark's sister Kathy. 'When I look back over all of the years that they had together, I also realised just how much Mark loved David, and just what their friendship meant to him as well. There were times they hadn't been in contact for a while, and when they met up again, it was as if only a day had passed. David was there for Mark until the end of his life. He cried, grieved, and held himself for Mark. That, to me, is a true friend.'

11. BACK TO THE BEACH

In the summer of 1988, The Beach Boys had risen from the ashes yet again. Against all odds, they found themselves climbing to the top of the Billboard singles chart with a maddeningly catchy song called 'Kokomo'. While this surprise hit dominated MTV and vaulted The Beach Boys back into the spotlight, David Marks spent his summer working as an usher at Los Angeles Dodgers Stadium. Beach Boys historian Domenic Priore, who was already a Dodgers usher, got David the job. Among his co-workers was the infamous Rodney King, whose treatment by LA police would result in a massive wave of rioting several years down the line. In 1988, David was happy to spend his summer as an employee of the national pastime. 'I grew up loving baseball, and that was a really a fun job for me,' says David. He drove his tiny Honda Civic to the park every day from his mother's home in Burbank. He often took the daily elevator ride from the ground-level employee parking lot to the upper stadium level in the company of legendary Dodgers announcer Vin Scully.

David also regularly mingled with Dodgers baseball legends such as the late greats Don Drysdale and Roy Campanella. Part of his job was to escort current star players, like Fernando Valenzuela, as they moved about the stadium. While he mingled among thousands of Southern California baseball fans on a daily basis, no one, aside from Priore, seemed to be aware of David's Beach Boys past. In his uniform of Dodger blue blazer and straw hat, David the usher was virtually anonymous. Finally, on one hot summer afternoon in the middle of a game, a lone fan suddenly rose from the masses and yelled towards David, 'Hey, aren't you the guy who got fucked over by The Beach Boys?' Dave just smiled, waved, and kept on ushering.

With the bright LA sunshine, the Dodgers, and 'Kokomo' all celebrating a great summer, the only thing needed to complete the Southern California postcard was a curling Malibu wave and Mickey Mouse. But David paid no mind to the irony of it all. 'You just don't think of yourself as having been a Beach Boy at times like that until someone reminds you,' says David. 'Then you remember, Oh yeah, they're performing in stadiums and I'm working in one as an usher.' During that memorable baseball season, David was present for the legendary Kirk Gibson home run in game one of the 1988 World Series. With Oakland Athletics ace reliever Dennis Eckersley one pitch away from closing out the game, the terminally banged-up Gibson limped to the plate on two bad legs and somehow homered to win the game for the Dodgers. It is still considered one of the most dramatic moments in baseball history, and the miracle win spurred the Dodgers towards a World Series Championship. The very day of the famous 'Gibson game', David was assigned to the players' parking lot. His job was to provide any assistance that team members might need as they arrived at the stadium. When he saw the limping Gibson arriving a bit tardy, David jokingly yelled to him, 'Hey, Kirk, you're late!' Gibson showed no reaction. But as he hobbled past David, he lowered his shoulder into him, nailing him in the chest with a playful but firm football-style block, which promptly knocked David over. Gibson chortled as he limped away. Dave recalls the moment: 'I'm laying there on the blacktop in my straw hat and my blue blazer thinking, Gosh, I just got knocked down by Kirk Gibson, and I yelled back at him, "I hope you're not a Beach Boys fan!" He just grunted and kept going.'

Despite the enjoyment he experienced and the responsibilities he handled during his stint working for the Dodgers, David was still in a very bad way with the bottle. After his friend Mark Groseclose had died so tragically, David drank even more for a while. That is, until one morning in 1988, when he woke up writhing in pain and pleading for God to help him. Jo Ann called the offices of the American Federation of Television and Radio Artists and found a rehabilitation programme that was covered under David's insurance plan. David had to guzzle down a beer to stop his shaking long enough to make it to the hospital. Once he was admitted, the doctors had to put him under heavy sedation to the point that he was unconscious, just so he could detox without dying. His motivation to survive purely came down to his love for Jennifer. 'When Jennifer was six, I finally checked into a rehab centre,' says David. 'After about a month, I came out, about thirty pounds lighter and really pissed off. There was something about the toxins going to my brain that made me angry. So I bought some guns and went to the firing range every day, until the novelty wore off.' For the next eight years, David remained completely free of booze and hard drugs.

It seemed that no matter how effectively David disappeared into the cultural woodwork, the echoes of his Beach Boys past kept tracking him down at the most unexpected times. An incident that occurred in 1990 is a perfect example. 'I was living with my mom and my seven-year-old daughter in Burbank,' says David. 'One day while my daughter was at school and my mom was at work, I was just getting ready to take a nap. I'm laying on my futon, watching my six-inch colour television, and I was smoking a joint, which was my only vice at the time. Suddenly the phone rings, and I answer. There's a very loud and excited voice on the other end. "Hi, David, guess who this is, and guess where I'm at?" I said, "I don't know. Who are you?" By the sound of the guy's voice I thought maybe I'd won a contest or something. And then the guy on the phone yells, "I'm Gene Landy, and I'm calling you from a yacht in the South Pacific!" I was kind of stoned and sleepy and I thought it was a joke. I just said, "Huh?" I was a little stunned.' Dr Eugene Landy was Brian's infamous psychiatrist-turned-career-Svengali who controlled his every move. David's first encounter with him came out of nowhere. 'He just kept talking: "I'm Brian Wilson's executive producer, and we're recording his new project in LA. How would you like to come to a session and record with Brian again?" I practically fell off the futon. It was so bizarre, I still wasn't sure if it was one of my friends playing a joke on me or not. And Landy gives me the day and time of the session and tells me where they'll be recording. I'm scrambling around trying to find a pencil and notebook to write this shit down on. He keeps going on about their plans for Brian's record and he mentions his lawyer, his agent, and some other confusing shit. I'm just beginning to get up to speed with the conversation, and then he was gone. But just before he hung up, he yells, "And don't forget your guitar!" And I sat there wondering if I even had a guitar at that point.'

Under Landy's care, or perhaps despite it, Brian had already released a critically acclaimed solo CD in 1988. He was now in the process of recording the Landy-produced follow-up, to be called *Sweet Insanity*. Ultimately the CD was rejected by Brian's record label at the time, Sire Records, and most blame Landy's meddling for that. Today, bootleg copies of the CD maintain a healthy rotation among collectors. The doomed project is thought of as the beginning of the end in Brian's decade-long relationship with the Dr Landy. For David, *Sweet Insanity* represents a very strange moment in time.

'I was curious to see how Brian was doing so I went to the session,' says David. 'It was at a really nice studio in West LA. I walk in and I see Brian in the studio playing the piano. Brian seemed really happy, and as usual, he asked, "Hey, Dave, how's your mom?" And I told him she was doing fine. Then he said, "Hey, listen to this!" And he played me something on the piano. Then Brian tells me, "Why don't you get your guitar and play something like you used to?" And he starts singing to me like he wants me to play, like doo doo doo doo. So I'm sitting on the console holding my guitar with my feet on a chair. And Brian's sitting in front of me, going, "Remember like we used to play? Remember how that felt? I want to get that old feeling back." And the engineer didn't even bother putting any effects or juice on my guitar. My Stratocaster was just going dry through the system and it sounded really bad. And the engineer says, "You didn't bring any pedals?" And I'm thinking, What kind of fucking studio is this? There's all this state-of-the-art equipment and outboard gear, and they can't find the tone they want for my guitar? It was pathetic.' David played, as best he could, through a few uncomfortable takes. Then he waited for more instructions from Brian. 'I turn around and I notice that Brian has disappeared. When I finally find him, he's devouring a huge vegetable salad outside of the control room. He went into a trance and started eating his salad. It looked like they'd been starving him and they finally let him eat. There was lettuce and croutons flying everywhere! He wouldn't even look up from his salad when I tried talking to him. The situation was really bizarre, and I figured it was time to leave. So I packed up my guitar and tried to say goodbye to Brian. He barely acknowledged me and just kept munching away on his salad. Landy handed me a Polaroid he'd taken of us and ushered me out.'

With a boost from his newfound sobriety, David settled into the simple wonders of fatherhood. 'I walked Jennifer to school and back every day,' says David. 'I always took her to the doctor when she needed to go. It was just the everyday normal stuff that parents do. I tried to focus on the basic stuff. I think she had a semi-normal childhood. She had consistency and she had a home. My mom was a big help. I couldn't have done it without her. But I did my part, too, and luckily she is a great kid. I used to tell her, "Do what you want, but don't break the law, and don't get me in trouble." She was my pal.'

Jennifer agrees that David somehow had an instinct for effective parenting: 'He always made sure he exposed me to good things and he let me do the things I really wanted to do. And he trusted me, which made me behave,' says Jennifer. 'He wanted me to know that he thought I was capable of taking care of myself. And that made me want to do it.'

As he watched Jennifer grow, David also began regularly playing his guitar again and nudged himself towards making some new music. For a time he played keyboards in a speed metal band known as The Grinding Machine which featured a blazing guitar shredder named Vince Lauria, who literally wrote the book – several of them, actually – on heavy metal guitar method. A quick listen to The Grinding Machine's music would make any listener understand how appropriate their name was. The fact that someone with the classically trained, Beach Boys-bred, jazz-loving history of David Marks could find himself in a constantly wheedling, hairspray- and spandex-festooned, Gazzarris-parking-lot-hanging, Mega- deth-soundalike band like this is hard to understand. But if you know David, then you'll know he likes to try different things.

Before long, David had also recorded sixteen original country-rock songs with a talented guitarist named Greg Beck under the project title Cowboy Jack Louise. Nothing got released. In 1992, David became enamoured with MIDI technology (Musical Instrument Digital Interface), and pro- grammed a slew of new basic tracks. Along with Buzz Clifford, Danny Moore and a sax player named Jerry Peter- son, Dave recorded a dozen top-notch songs, like Danny Moore's killer original called 'Hollywood Joe'. David and Buzz also pitched in some great original songs like 'Bamboo Shack' and 'Fool's Guarantee'. Coupled with updated covers of classic rockers like Chuck Berry's 'I Wanna Be Your Driver', the material was polished and the performances were tight. David's lead vocals on these sessions were some of the best of his career. But the project, known as 'The Work Tapes', found no release after Danny's label-shopping efforts came up dry. Some of the material was performed live when David started gigging with Buzz and his two sons as The Marks-Clifford Band. Dave's flirtation with MIDI ultimately brought him one minor payday when he landed an original track in a feature film called *Rap: The Movie*. The track, titled 'Women with the Blues', was credited to Dave and the Marksmen.

Around this time, David received bad news about yet another of his old friends. 'I got a phone call from Greg Jones's sister that he had gone to the hospital and died in the waiting room,' remembers David. 'They never found out what killed him. I went down to the funeral with Louie. Everybody left but I just sat there staring at the coffin . . . his father had to drag me away. He had three kids: little Casey was in elementary school, his son was in middle school, and his oldest daughter was just starting high school. I went back to the house after the funeral and his little girl was in his room holding his shirt. It was tragic. It was so unexpected. Greg could do anything. He was good at all sports. If he wanted to play an instrument, he could just pick up a guitar and play. He was good with people. He knew the psychology of how to deal with people. And he was funnier than shit – just like Mark Groseclose and Gary Montgomery, he always made me laugh. He was bad, too. We used to steal candy together from the Lindner's Little Store when we were kids. Like with Carl, Dennis, Mark and the Hand brothers, he was really like a brother to me. He did things for me that only a brother would do.'

That year, Brian Wilson was awarded a massive settlement due to years of proceeds lost after his former publishing company, Sea of Tunes, had been sold from under him. The lawsuit stemmed from Brian's forced decision to sign over his publishing rights to Murry in 1969. Murry had subsequently sold the entire publishing catalogue outright, for a reported $700,000. By the early nineties, the same catalogue had an estimated value of $25 million. When the suit came to court, it was found that the contract Brian had signed was not valid because of his well-documented mental problems. It was also suggested that Murry might have forged his son's name on the original transfer document. Following the awarding of Brian's $10 million settlement, Mike Love launched a lawsuit against

Brian, claiming that he had made significant writing contributions to many Beach Boys songs that had gone uncredited. Love ended up winning the case, partly due to Brian's admission that Mike's assertions were correct. Brian stated that Murry had badgered him into leaving Mike's name off the songwriting credits of nearly 30 songs. As a result of the case, Mike's name was retrospectively added to the writing credits on all subsequent releases of those songs.

David himself had witnessed Mike writing the lyrics for many of the early Beach Boys songs, including some that he had not been credited for. He offered to help Mike in court. 'I testified that Mike had actually helped write some of those songs,' says David. 'I was present on some of the occasions when he was in the car whipping those words out. It's ironic that I spent my last ten dollars to pay for parking so I could go testify for him to win five million. But I was glad to do it, because people should know the truth. Mike is not an insignificant part of The Beach Boys thing. He was a big part of it. It was really Murry's doing in the first place. Murry screwed a lot of people out of their rightful credit. Rumour has it that Brian wanted to settle with Mike anyway instead of dragging it into court, but his lawyers wouldn't let him.' A federal jury ruled in Mike's favour on 12 December 1994. Eight days later, Brian and Mike agreed on a $5 million settlement and a percentage of future royalties on 35 Beach Boys songs was awarded to Mike.

During this period, David returned to school to prepare for his high school equivalency exam. Never having stood a chance to make it through high school as a teenager due to his hectic touring schedule with The Beach Boys and the Marksmen, David had come to realise that life without a high school diploma had significant drawbacks. 'I didn't want my daughter to think I was a total idiot, so I went back to get my GED. I went to the city college and took the courses I needed to pass the test. I also took a music class and while I was sitting there, in a sea of Fender Rhodes pianos, I looked across the room and there was my old friend Mark Volman from The Turtles, who was also taking a piano class. And he said, "Is that you,

Dave?" We hadn't seen each other in twenty years. We ended up standing next to each other while singing in the school choir for the Christmas show.'

David continued to regularly play the LA club circuit with The Marks-Clifford Band, his guitar and vocal chops re-invigorated by sobriety. In 1994, David was invited by The Beach Boys to appear with them at a 'private' San Diego area concert. He enjoyed the experience of reconnecting with Carl, Mike and Al, and he played guitar for part of their set. Then came more offers from Mike to sit in with The Beach Boys, most of which David declined. In October 1995, David did appear with The Beach Boys again, this time at a concert recorded for an episode of TV's popular *Baywatch* series. Slowly but surely, it seemed The Beach Boys were drawing David back in, and though he was very hesitant about going back full-time, he enjoyed the fact that they kept calling him.

In September 1996, David flew to Las Vegas at Mike Love's request and stayed with The Beach Boys entourage at the Rio Hotel Casino. 'Mike called me and said, "We're gonna be playing in Vegas – why don't you come out and hang out with us?"' remembers Dave. 'When I got there, Carl asked me to play part of the show with them, but I didn't want to, and instead I just watched the concert.' Still, the fanfare, the excitement, the buzz of being around The Beach Boys scene was an emotionally intoxicating experience for David – and unfortunately, after more than eight years of sobriety, this would be the day that David's fundamental weakness took advantage of him again and off the wagon he crashed. While sitting at the Rio bar with Desi Arnaz Jr after the concert, David started his fall with one beer. 'I was just sitting there talking with Desi, and for some reason I decided to have a beer, then I had some more,' remembers David. 'Then I got up the next day to come back to LA and I had a couple more at the airport, and a couple on the flight to LA. Then I had another one at the LA airport. Then I got on the shuttle and I had to piss really badly. I talked the shuttle driver into letting me off on Venice Boulevard. I found myself walking up to Hollywood, and once there I treated myself to an elaborate dinner at a restaurant on Hollywood Boulevard. Then I proceeded to drink some more. I finally got home late that night. From there, I was pretty much back to my old ways.'

As David slid back into the alcoholic lifestyle, The Beach Boys were undergoing internal political struggles. In a major power play, Mike decided to take on the business of producing Beach Boys concerts himself, and Carl didn't object. But it was a move that Al Jardine resisted. 'Who knew that he would want to produce all of The Beach Boys dates?' says Al. 'Who knew that he would really consider himself The Beach Boys? Who knew that he could pull it off? That, to me, is the most amazing event of all time.' In the process of the upheaval, Al became marginalised and estranged from both Mike and Carl. Reportedly, Mike felt betrayed by Al, and from that point on, Al's days in the group were numbered. Ironically, Al has pointed out in a recent interview that Mike was originally interested in eliminating Bruce from The Beach Boys. However, since he couldn't make do without both of them, Bruce survived the upheaval. Wherever the truth lies, it is known that Carl Wilson had virtually given Mike free rein to make the changes he felt were best for The Beach Boys as a business. And apparently, one of Mike's wishes was to bring David Marks back to The Beach Boys on a full-time basis. Most fans assumed that the idea of bringing David back was only considered when Carl Wilson was diagnosed with lung cancer and secondary tumours in his brain in April 1997 but the process Mike initiated of welcoming David to participate in occasional Beach Boys concerts and media appearances had already begun years before. The fact that Carl was sick and beginning chemotherapy, coupled with David drinking himself into big trouble again, temporarily shuffled Mike's plan.

Several months before Carl's illness was announced to the public, Dave was involved in yet another major traffic accident. Intoxicated and driving a vehicle full of friends, he rolled his car. David was charged with drunk-driving and endangering passengers. 'After we were at rest in the ditch upside down, one of my passengers crawled out and scratched her cheek on the broken glass and that constituted an injury, which made the arrest a felony,' explains David. He was given a sentence of 30 days in prison, which he served in ten consecutive three-day weekend stints, and attended mandatory Alcoholics Anonymous and other group therapy meetings in between his weekends in jail.

While David was concentrating on the trial, his sentence and its aftermath, Mike was readying a place in The Beach Boys for him. 'During this time, Mike Love was desperately trying to get a hold of me, and my mother wasn't giving me any of his messages,' says David. 'I had no idea that he was calling.' Mike had been attempting to contact Dave through mutual friends like Steve Brigati and Eddie Haddad. But when intercepted by Jo Ann, these calls reached a dead end. 'I think she was trying to protect me since I was going through the legal mess of court, weekend jail and court-ordered AA,' says David. 'Chances are I wouldn't have been able to go back then because of all that.' After two months of trying, Mike was finally successful in contacting David and asked him to consider rejoining The Beach Boys on a full-time basis. 'I told him I'd try it out until it wasn't fun any more,' says David. 'I was totally oblivious to the political and business conspiracy that I was involved in as a pawn. I'd just gotten out of jail, and I really needed a job.'

In August 1997, Carl Wilson played what turned out to be his last show with The Beach Boys. Ironically, David was finally sold on the idea of rejoining The Beach Boys when he was told that Carl would be coming back to play with him soon. 'Everybody assumed Carl was going to get better, and that's one of the biggest reasons I wanted to come back,' says David. 'I completely expected to be sharing a stage with Carl again.' It was not to be. David played one warm-up gig with Mike's Endless Summer Band in San Bernadino, with Jan and Dean and The Surfaris sharing the bill. Within a few days, he was on a plane to Florida for his first official show of his second tour of duty with The Beach Boys. It almost didn't happen when the airline threatened to bar David from boarding the plane because he was so drunk. 'Mike immediately took me aside,' says David, 'and he told me, "You will *not* be like Dennis!" Mike explained to me how the universe took Dennis out and that he didn't want to see the same thing happen to me. That was Mike's way of showing genuine concern. Unfortunately, I didn't listen very seriously.' On 25 September 1997, in Miami, Florida, David took the stage as an official Beach Boy again, after a 34-year absence.

On 11 October, the *Los Angeles Times* ran a feature story on David's return. In the article, Mike Love was asked about David's return, and said, 'It was very natural and made sense to me. He's a very talented guy, and very intelligent and fun.' According to Carl's ex-wife, Annie Wilson-Karges, when the Southern California media first announced that David was a Beach Boy again, Carl Wilson was as surprised as anyone. The same morning the *LA Times* article appeared, Annie happened to run into Carl at Audree's home. Though Carl was ill and receiving medical treatment for his cancer, he was an out-patient at the time. Audree was very ill too, and The Beach Boys were the furthest thing from both of their minds that morning. Annie asked Carl if he'd seen the morning paper, which he hadn't. She showed him the piece on David's return. 'I could tell he had absolutely no idea this was happening,' said Annie. 'Did Mike tell you about this?' said Annie. 'No,' said Carl. 'But I'm really happy for David.' Then he put the paper down and turned his attention back to his mother.

It was at one of his first gigs back with The Beach Boys that David first met his future wife, 24-year-old Carrie Haight. After a Las Vegas concert, David sat at the Orleans Casino bar enjoying a cocktail when Bruce Johnston sent the future his way. 'I already knew Bruce, and he was there having a drink too,' says Carrie Marks. 'Bruce told me, "Hey, I want you to meet somebody. That guy over there is David Marks. We want him to stay in the band, but he's not sure if he wants to. Please flirt with him so he thinks he's going to get girls and maybe he'll want to stay in the band." So I went up to David and put my arm around him and said, "I'm supposed to pretend to flirt with you so you think you're gonna get me." And he said, "Oh, OK." And he bought me a drink and we stayed there talking for four hours. He told me the guy I was with wasn't right for me because there's no way he should have left me alone talking to another guy for that long.' It wouldn't be until the following spring that David and Carrie finally became a full-time couple.

When David first rejoined The Beach Boys, the regular line-up included Mike Love, Al Jardine, Bruce Johnston and sidemen Mike Kowalski, Mike Meros, Phil Bardowell, Chris Farmer, Richie Cannata and Al's son Matt Jardine. The Beach Boys of that period also featured a well-known guest percussionist, actor John Stamos. Phil Bardowell recalls David's addition to the Beach Boys of 1997 as a very positive development. 'I immediately discovered that David is not only a gifted guitarist, but also an incredibly loving spirit who possesses great passion, introspection and wit,' says Bardowell. 'Meeting and playing music with David Marks was surely a highlight in my Beach Boy experience.' At this point, Carl Wilson was still expected to return once he'd recovered from his illness. 'When [Dave] first went back to The Beach Boys, Carl was alive but too sick to tour, and Al was still in the band,' remembers Carrie Marks. 'After the first couple of shows Dave played, it became obvious that he was back in the band and not just sitting in for a gig or two like he had in the past.' When this became apparent to Al Jardine, he took David aside and asked him, point-blank, 'Why are you back? What's going on?' David was not privy to the political moves that had already been brewing for over a year. 'By the way Al asked me that question, I sensed he was real concerned,' says David. 'Al probably knew exactly what was happening behind the scenes, but I didn't. I told him I was simply there to play with the band as long as it worked out for everybody.' Al wasn't pleased by David's reply and answered very tersely, 'Well, I guess that's it, this whole thing is over!' Then he stomped off in a huff.

Al has made it very clear since then that he understands David wasn't a knowing party to the situation within The Beach Boys' political hierarchy. Al acknowledges that David honestly thought he was coming back to play guitar with Carl, saying, 'David was heartbroken that he never got to play with

Carl again.' In the meantime, Carl sent a message to David through Beach Boys soundman Jeff Peters, saying that he was pleased that David was back with The Beach Boys and playing his guitar on stage with them again. 'That made me feel great, because I'd never really been forgiven by Carl for quitting and acting like an immature idiot as a fifteen-year-old,' says David. 'I never was really sure deep down if Carl still resented me for that.' That December, as David toured with The Beach Boys, and Carl fought for his life, Audree Wilson passed away aged 79.

On 25 January 1998, David, Mike, Bruce, John Stamos and Glen Campbell performed during the pre-game show of Super Bowl XXXII, billed as 'America's Band'. Reportedly, the first Al knew about it was when he saw it on TV. Within months, Al was officially gone from The Beach Boys. Ironically, Dave and Al played musical chairs in The Beach Boys much the same way they had in 1963, with overlap and confusion. 'I was there for a purpose, a political move,' says David. 'I was unaware of that at the time, of course, and I'm not complaining, because it did me a world of good. But I regret having inadvertently been the cause of Al's demise. But I think that was inevitable anyway.'

On 6 February 1998, after a gruelling battle with his disease, Carl Wilson died of cancer. 'It was 6 a.m., and Mike awakened me with a phone call saying Cousin Carl had died,' remembers David. 'Mike was in tears, which I thought was very natural but then he said, "Pardon the emotion," which I thought was strange. It's as if, even under those circumstances, Mike still was guarding his emotions. While he was fighting his tears I said, "It's OK, Mike, I understand," and that was it. Few words were spoken. He hung up the phone and I lay there alone knowing that Carl was gone.'

David found himself in a very odd position in all of this. The circumstances of David's last arrest and conviction continued to weigh heavily on him. Though he'd completed his jail sentence before he rejoined The Beach Boys, David was still left with three years of probation to cope with. This meant every time David travelled outside of California, he had to clear his tour itinerary with his probation officer. And when The Beach Boys toured out of the United States, a written request had to be approved by a judge. While David was juggling the pressure of probation, feeling the tension of political infighting within the group, and emotionally coping with the loss of Carl, many Beach Boys fans figured he was just greedily grabbing at the straws of his past glory. Some perceived him as dancing on Carl's grave by returning to the band. Some saw the legitimacy of The Beach Boys as a thing of the past once Carl was gone. Al Jardine stated publicly he wished that the name 'Beach Boys' had been retired the very moment Carl passed away, and more than a few long-time fans agreed. But David Marks was only a very fallible human being, living with a disease called alcoholism, and desperately trying to stay afloat.

The last thing David wanted was to show any disrespect towards Carl or his memory. David was there with Carl when they found their connection to rock and roll as two young boys. The essence of that discovery was and will be carried by both of their spirits for ever. Because of that childhood bond, David is never far from Carl. 'There was so much more to Carl than most people know. He held a tremendous amount of stress inside of him,' says David about his friend. 'There was a constant struggle of trying to keep the peace between warring parties all around him from the time he was a little kid. Plus the baggage he held from being the porky. That will fuck a kid up, when your best friend and your brother leave you in a dark ditch. It all created a huge amount of stress and sadness, but Carl overcame all of that with his music. It broke his heart when he couldn't physically make it onto the stage any more. For a while after he got really sick, he'd sit on a stool through most of the set. He probably shouldn't have even been up there, but he wanted to. All he ever wanted to do was be on stage in front of The Beach Boys' fans. He had a real connection with the fans, and he was always thankful that they cared about him.'

12. LOST . . . AND FOUND

The Beach Boys were basically three people by mid-1998. That point was underlined when a dodgy-looking CD, entitled *Mike Love, Bruce Johnston and David Marks of The Beach Boys Salute NASCAR*, was offered at Union 76 gas stations. The disc featured predictable oldie remakes and did nothing to enhance David's reputation among those who felt the current Beach Boys were trashing the band's legacy. Touring through this period established David's first real connection to Bruce, who is best known for the work he did with The Beach Boys after David had left the first time around, in the sixties. Although David and Bruce are very different personality types, David grew to respect Bruce's contributions and his work ethic. 'I think he was nice to me because Mike told him to be nice to me,' says David. 'But actually, Bruce is a very talented musician. He was much more together on those tours than I was. I usually drank too much and I'm sure I was hell to deal with.'

That year David toured Australia and New Zealand with The Beach Boys, where the band played to audiences as large as 100,000. On the tour, John Stamos began calling Dave 'Uncle Marv', a nickname that Phil Bardowell had come up with – and one that stuck. 'We were travelling on a bus out in the outback in the middle of nowhere and I had some Jack Daniel's on the bus, so I got pretty drunk,' remembers David. 'Suddenly the bus breaks down, it's past sundown and pitch black, and the bus driver tells us we're in the area where the deadliest spider in the world lives. So they call a fleet of cabs to come get the band piece by piece.' The first cab was supposed to be for Mike, John and Uncle Marv, but Bruce snuck past David, jumped in, and the cab took off without him. Cab number one's passengers left with more than enough room to accommodate David – had they really wanted to include him. With that in mind, David became so pissed off at Bruce that he sprinted after the cab on foot, thrusting his Jack Daniel's bottle in the air and swearing loudly. He actually caught up just long enough to solidly kick the door where a smiling Bruce was sitting behind the rolled-up window. 'I just got a big royalty cheque for *Greatest Hits Volume One*, you bastards!' David screamed through the glass. 'I don't need this touring shit any more, you assholes!' Within minutes, a second cab arrived, and Dave calmed down.

On 19 September 1998, David was a guest at the wedding of John Stamos and model/actress Rebecca Romijn. The event took place at the posh Beverly Hills Hotel and proved to be among the most talked-about celebrity bashes of the year. Romijn was her usual stunningly statuesque self in a traditional square-necked wedding dress designed by Badgley Mischka with a cathedral-length Chantilly lace veil and a crystal and pearl tiara. Many wondered how Stamos, a former teen heartthrob on the downslide, had managed to land one of the world's most beautiful and successful women. The star-studded guest list included models Tyra Banks and Heidi Klum, as well as actresses Mary-Kate and Ashley Olsen, and comedians David Spade and Rob Schneider. Mike Love, Bruce Johnston, Brian Wilson, Billy Hinsche and Jeff Foskett all attended as well. David took his sixteen-year-old daughter Jennifer as his date. 'It was very strange making eye contact with the Olsen twins,' remembers Jennifer. 'The thing that stood out the most was meeting Brian Wilson for the first time, and John Stamos was so sweet, he was so nice. It was very cool.' After a relatively solid five-year marriage, Stamos and Romijn filed for divorce in August 2004.

During his second tenure with the group, David participated in many memorable Beach Boys shows. The highlight came when David and The Beach Boys performed at outdoor festivals in Vienna, Austria and Hamburg, Germany, where they played to audiences in excess of 150,000. But for the most part, David was unhealthy and drunk, and at times he looked nearly embalmed as he plodded through the nightly routine of playing Carl's old guitar solos in note-for-note fashion. Ironically, the very solos Murry insisted only be played by Carl all those decades earlier became David's nightly function in The Beach Boys of the late nineties. Not only could David play them as well as Carl, he also played them distinctly like Carl because they had learned the basic technique from the same teacher, John Maus. However, for someone who had evolved into a fluid virtuosic improviser like David, having to play guitar by numbers night after night was a living hell. No room for any variation from the script was allowed in Mike's travelling circus of the nineties. 'During one of my first shows back in '97, I was really excited about playing in front of big crowds again,' remembers David. 'My enthusiasm got the best of me and during the slow part of "Wouldn't It Be Nice", I started to shred.' As Matt Jardine cheered, Mike turned around and said, 'What's he doing?' Another time David played 'Surfer Girl' with a slight twist in his guitar part. The Beach Boys musical director yelled at him, 'Play it like the record!' Dave snapped back, 'I am the record.' David used to chide Carl for never having grown as a guitarist, but after Carl was gone, David realised his late friend was only giving the people what they expected from him – the tried and true sounds that the fans paid to hear. David gained a first-hand perspective on the corner that Carl had been painted into as an artist.

But there were also many heartwarming moments during David's comeback. Like the fans who unfurled 'Welcome Back David' signs at several concerts, and all the fans who came up to him to say that their long-time wish of seeing *all* the original Beach Boys perform had finally been satisfied. One fan even flew all the way from Japan to an Atlanta show just to see David play with The Beach Boys. While some of the group's fans saw David's addition to the line-up as somehow illegitimate, an equal amount saw it as an appropriate closure of The Beach Boys family circle.

During his nineties tenure with The Beach Boys, David also gained a totally new perspective on Brian Wilson's unique musical gift. 'I didn't have a true appreciation of Brian until I got back together with Mike in the late nineties,' admits David. 'I didn't really understand that he was a genius. I'd been avoiding Beach Boys music after I left the band and had never thought much about it. I knew Brian was special, but I didn't really get how special he was until I rejoined the band. At that point I was forced to sit down with all the music and relearn what I played on, and learn for the first time all the stuff that came after. I was stunned. "Wouldn't it Be Nice" ... what a masterpiece, and so many others. It finally hit me in a real way what Brian had put together. His progressions and melodies were amazing. Even things I originally played on like "Surfer Girl" and "In My Room" stood out in a new way to me.' Between the monotony of performing the dancing bear routine with Carl's nightly solos and the admiration and pride he felt in reproducing Brian's incredible arrangements, there was good and bad in every concert. If you think about it, that was always the way it was with David concerning The Beach Boys: it cut both ways.

As it turned out, Dave's second time around with The Beach Boys didn't last much longer than his first. With his alcoholism affecting his job, Mike Love and Beach Boys manager Elliott Lott suggested that David find a way to sober up, or else. In pure David style, he wasn't fired, and he didn't really quit, but one day he simply stopped showing up for work. On 4 July 1999, David played his last show with The Beach Boys in Kelseyville, California. His last show held one significantly poignant moment when David and Carl's boyhood hero, 'King of the Surf Guitar' Dick Dale, shared the stage with The Beach Boys. Afterwards, Dale walked up to David, holding a vintage copy of the *Surfin' USA* LP, one that already had the signatures of Mike, Brian, Carl and Dennis on it. He held out the old LP cover to David and said, 'This is for my son, and you're the only one I don't have.' As Dave took the cover into his hands, he flashed on the fact that the great Dick Dale had specifically brought the LP to the concert because he knew Dave would be there. He added his signature, completing the original five names who'd recorded the LP 36 years before. That was closure enough for David.

Upon leaving The Beach Boys, David immediately went into a 30-day alcohol rehabilitation programme in California. But when he completed the programme and flew east to be with Carrie, she rushed to Kennedy International airport to pick him up and found a drunken David waiting for her. 'I was so disappointed that we'd spent that whole month apart, which was really hard on us, all for nothing,' she recalls. 'After that month, he decided he wasn't going back on the road so he figured he didn't need to be sober. He just didn't want The Beach Boys bad enough to quit drinking.' And in his alcoholic state, the road was wearing him down beyond repair. 'I had a hard time travelling,' says David. 'I got tired easily, I was getting infections, I had more coughs and colds, and I got more ill than usual when I drank. My liver wasn't processing alcohol as well as it normally did. I decided to take some time off and get on with my life.'

On 2 December 1999, David and Carrie were married in a small ceremony at the Burbank Community Church. The same day David married Carrie, he went to the hospital with what he'd thought was an inflamed liver. Instead, the excruciating pain in his right side was emanating from a rib injury. Though the injury wasn't serious, there was other bad news forthcoming. David was diagnosed with hepatitis C, a viral disease of the liver, and was given six months or less to live if he continued drinking. The virus was more than likely contracted back in the early seventies when David was using needles and it's a miracle his liver wasn't completely destroyed. 'I had one of the first strains, which is the granddaddy of the virus,' says David. 'It's the hardest one to cure.' Reality finally had him cornered.

The first thing David did upon learning he had hep C was to quit drinking for good. He then began a regimen of natural and herbal remedies to attempt to regain his depleted physical strength. Then, thanks to a series of events that included luck and focused determination by Carrie, an experimental treatment became available at the perfect time. David was treated by Dr Robert Brown at the Columbia Presbyterian Medical Center, and was put on a schedule of one weekly injection of Pegasys, a pegylated interferon, and six daily pills of Copegus, a form of ribavirin. The treatment lasted for over a year. David was told that the treatment had been successful on about half of those patients given it. However, there is evidence that, even for those it does not completely cure, the regime can significantly reduce long-term complications and liver damage. During his treatment, David experienced a myriad of side effects, including severe depression and uncontrollable emotional behaviour. One positive side effect was a huge burst of creative energy. Dave wrote and recorded over twenty new songs during his battle with hep C, some of which rank among the best of his career. After staying positive through the darkest days, and meticulously adhering to his medical routine, David was pronounced completely clear of the hepatitis C virus in November 2004.

At the same time David was successfully battling the virus, he threw his weight behind the cause of educating the public about the disease and helping others gain funding to battle it. Dave and Carrie founded a website called Artists Against Hepatitis, and were invited to Washington DC to meet with members of the House of Representatives, the Senate, and the Department of Health and Human Services to lobby on behalf of the hep C cause. At the same time, *Newsweek* magazine ran a major article on hepatitis C that prominently featured David. In 2004, David was named the official spokesman for the American Gastroenterological Association's 'Be Hep C S.M.A.R.T.' programme. David participated in a string of radio and print interviews along with leading hepatologists Dr Michael Fried and Dr Mitchell Shiffman in New York City and Washington DC. Their satellite media tour was covered by countless local and national television news programmes.

David continued to inform the public by travelling to LA, Dallas and Atlanta for more media coverage. He reached the eyes and ears of millions upon millions of viewers and listeners through his extended campaign. In 2005, David became the spokesman for the 'FaCe It Campaign' for the British National Health Services and travelled to the UK for more radio, print and TV appearances. While in the UK, acclaimed London-based photographer Michelle Martinoli photographed twelve people with hep C, including David, and exhibited the 'Faces Of Hepatitis C' photos in an outdoor exhibition featuring huge three-metre-high prints. The exhibit toured the British Isles, stopping in a different major city each month. In the summer of 2005, David returned to Washington DC to continue lobbying, and his commitment to the campaign remains a major focus of his life.

Since leaving The Beach Boys in 1999, David has continued to perform music all around the United States. He has often appeared jointly or with the backing of various classic Beach Boys sidemen, including Jeff Foskett, Mike Meros, Billy Hinsche, Ed Carter, Philip Bardowell, Matt Jardine, Richie Cannata and others. David has also performed in recent years alongside old friends like Mike Love, Al Jardine, Bruce Johnston, Dean Torrence, Buzz Clifford, John Maus, Eddie Bertrand, Bill Trenkle of the Marksmen, and Eddie Medora of The Sunrays. A solo CD entitled *Something Funny Goin' On*, filled with David Marks originals, was released in 2003.

In 2004, David made his first-ever concert appearance in the UK as part of the USA Legends band, which featured Foskett and Hinsche, as well as Scott Bennett of Brian Wilson's band, and Dennis Diken of The Smithereens. When word began to circulate among the always-faithful UK Beach Boys fans, there was an air of disbelief that they might finally see the mysterious David Marks – truly a missing piece of The Beach Boys puzzle for the British. The prospect of seeing the fellow who pointed to the waves on the very first Beach Boys LP cover and then was gone for what most people thought was for ever seemed a bit surreal.

When David took to the Towerlands stage in Braintree, the applause and appreciation that had been stored up for so long was unleashed, and as he looked out at the audience he could see the beaming smiles that greeted his searching eyes were even wider than his own – perhaps even wider than his own as a Pendleton-clad boy in 1962, holding a board, following Dennis Wilson into the Malibu surf. Jeff Foskett introduced David as the '*only* Legend on stage this evening'.

In the audience that night was record producer Steve Levine, a man who'd reached the pinnacle of success with acts like Culture Club, Quarterflash, The Creatures and The Clash, and had even produced the *Beach Boys* 1985 LP and its great hit single 'Getcha Back'. Steve had arrived at the very last minute, rushing to his seat after a busy day at his London studio producing a young singer discovered by Jeff Foskett, a velvet-voiced sixteen-year-old named Charlotte Cooper. Young Charlotte was due to perform 'Don't Worry Baby' with the Legends that night, and Levine was specifically there to watch his new artist. But what also caught Levine's eyes and ears was the reaction David was getting. As a result, he invited David to perform on Charlotte's LP, which already included an impressive list of guest performers including Kiki Dee, known for her string of smashes with Elton John and on her own, Gerry Beckley of America, harmony ace Chris Rainbow, who had sung memorably with The Alan Parsons Project and, of course, Jeff Foskett, who in recent years has served so ably as Brian Wilson's right-hand man. All were contributing backing vocals to Charlotte's CD, adding their vocal gifts to Charlotte's covers of their own material. David was given the same opportunity and contributed a great song he'd composed with Buzz Clifford, called 'Over My Head'. By

2005, when the USA Legends returned to the UK due to popular demand, adding multi-instrumentalist Hank Linderman and Chicago's Robert Lamm to the mix, David's four-decade UK absence was officially ancient history.

Today, David is preparing to release a new solo project titled *I Think About You Often*, featuring a title track that darkly reflects on the loss of the many close friends who have passed away during his bumpy lifetime. The new CD will also include some of the great songs he wrote and recorded during his hepatitis C treatment and recovery, like the magical 'Like 1969', which is perhaps the best David Marks original song ever. David also recently collaborated on new material with Beach Boys and Brian Wilson lyricist Stephen Kalinich, who says, 'I love working with David, it reminds me so much of writing with Dennis and Brian . . . I know that's because they were all like brothers growing up. David has a beautiful spirit and he's always on the edge of discovery.' In a flurry of collaboration, David is also engaged in a new project with his former Moon bandmates, Matt Moore, Larry Brown and David Jackson. Dave has also found a creative outlet in Connecticut at the studio of his friend and recording engineer Emil Halas. There he's spent the last two years working on solo tracks using backing musicians from, of all places, the Berklee School of Music.

Dave's mum Jo Ann is still living in California, and though she's in her mid-seventies, she retains the brightness of a young woman. One of her true joys in life is her lovely granddaughter Jennifer, now twenty-four, who has blossomed into a beautiful and enthusiastic adult. Jennifer studied in Wales for a time, and has a double bachelor's degree in English and Anthropology from San Francisco State University. She's currently on her way to becoming an archaeologist. When asked about her dad today, she says without hesitation, 'He's my favourite person in the world!' And Jennifer underlines the fact that, despite his limitations, David was an engaged and thoughtful presence in her development. 'I adopted my life and spiritual philosophy from him,' she says. 'He sat me down when I was five and gave me the basics of every religion he knew about. He tried to tell me about the good and bad in everything. He's always been so eclectically intelligent about everything. He was my first teacher, and I just want the world to know how smart he is.'

Most importantly, David plays his guitar every day. Through all of his ups and downs, David never completely lost touch with his six-string companion, his longest and truest friend, and today he is a better guitarist than ever. But even the guitar can't claim to be David's *best* friend. That designation would have to go to his constant reality check: his wife Carrie. No one knows better than Carrie how far he's come. Neither of them were in the best of shape when they met – they experienced a very volatile courtship – but they recognised great things in each other. Things that had nothing to do with wealth, fame or status. In David, Carrie saw a deeply bruised talent with a noble heart, but someone who struggled every day to live with himself. In Carrie, David found the ultimate advocate, a sharp, strong, bright presence entirely committed to him – and one who firmly insists that he believe in himself. And somehow it worked. After seven years of marriage, and sobriety, David is on very solid ground. He's clean, healthy, fit and productive, and best of all he's finally comfortable in his own skin. Today Carrie and David live in a small home that sits in a beautiful, quiet country setting in upstate New York, with Carrie's eleven-year-old son, Ryan, and their cat, Lincoln. While the other Beach Boys are all beyond wealthy, David and Carrie are not. But they are certainly rich in other ways, and David continues to heal.

Part of the healing process is reconnecting with his past. That's always been a troubling prospect for someone with a past like David Marks. But in recent years, he's made significant progress in doing so. In 2001, David played guitar at the Carl Wilson Foundation benefit concert at the El Rey Theater in LA. Perhaps this permanently put to rest any trace of resentment that had lingered between the spirits of Carl and David. While honouring Carl, he saw many old friends from the Wilson sphere, and he joined Brian Wilson, Brian's daughters Carnie and Wendy, and their extended musical family on stage for the show's encore song, 'Love and Mercy'.

Similarly, in 2003, Dave and Carrie attended the Dennis Wilson Bash at Chez Jay's in Santa Monica. It was a day to remember Dennis in a casual inclusive atmosphere near the sea, at the very place where some say Dennis's ghost resides. David shared his stories about Dennis, he shed a tear for him, and he happily reconnected with Diane and Marilyn Rovell (now Marilyn Wilson-Rutherford), and Ginger Blake. This may have finally chased away the memory of a painful drunken nightmare – the awful night David was turned away at the Rovell home back in the early seventies. 'When I see David these days, it is always a warm and close feeling we share,' says Marilyn. 'We were young together and there is a bond that does not even have to be spoken about. He has gone through much in his life, and I admire his courage. He is very special to me.' And the healing continues.

Finally, it seems that David has come to terms with his place in history as an original member of The Beach Boys. 'David is starting to see beyond his own hang-ups and see the value that he originally brought to the band,' says Carrie Marks. And in seeing his own value within The Beach Boys story, David is finally able to enjoy a little bit of the legacy of America's Band. Instead of forever denying, minimising, downplaying, fleeing, ignoring and remaining disconnected from The Beach Boys saga, today David has begun to nurture a growing sense of pride that he was part of something great and lasting. No matter what else he does or where he goes, David Marks will always be a Beach Boy and that's a good thing.

On 20 May 2005, The Beach Boys were honoured with an official California State historical landmark at the former site of the Wilson home in Hawthorne. Beach Boys fan Harry Jarnagan initiated a grassroots effort and, with the help of original neighbourhood resident Paula Bondi-Springer, turned an ambitious idea into a lasting symbol at the very epicentre of Beach Boys history. The monument was designed by Carol Barnes and Timothy Lefler and built by Scott Wilson Construction, a company owned by Dennis Wilson's son. At the insistence of the Wilson family, David was included on the plaque and monument along with Mike, Brian, Dennis, Carl and Al. With Dennis and Carl gone for ever, and Mike choosing not to attend the ceremony, David, Brian and Al gathered to unveil the monument in front of a crowd of adoring Beach Boys fans and family. While standing in the California sunshine on the very ground that gave birth to their relationships and dreams, Brian, David and Al smiled and reminisced while soaking in the poignant moment together. During the ceremony David performed Dennis Wilson's beautiful song 'You And I', backed by Billy Hinsche on keyboards and Dennis's grandson Matt on guitar. Being acknowledged and included that day by the Wilsons' extended family, by The Beach Boys family and fans, and by the state he grew up in, was a very enriching experience for David.

The only bittersweet element of the landmark dedication was remembering the close friends who'd already died and wouldn't be there to help David celebrate. Although it was unfortunate that Murry and Elmer both passed away as fairly young men, the real tragedies were the losses of friends David grew up with whose lives had ended much too soon. And the list was long. Dennis drowned in 1983; Mark Groseclose succumbed to alcoholism in 1988; Greg Jones died suddenly in 1992; Carl died of cancer in 1998; Warren Zevon also died of cancer in 2003; Terry Hand and Louie Marotta died of heart failure in 2004; Gary Montgomery also died of heart failure in 2005. As a simple tribute to those he'd lost along the way, David had a specially inscribed brick placed among the monument's many dedications, displaying the initials DW, MG, GJ, CW, WZ, TH and LM.

Unfortunately, Gary Montgomery died shortly after the memorial brick had been designated, and his initials couldn't be included. Death has a habit of showing up at inappropriate moments. Like with Louie, the neighbourhood anchor. He knew The Beach Boys landmark was going to be built and was absolutely thrilled at the prospect. Sadly, Louie passed away less than six months before the day of the dedication ceremony. 'I think Louie, Mark, Dennis and Carl's spirits are all there, hanging out at the landmark,' says David. 'It's a good place for spirits, family and fans to gather and to remember the laughter and fun we all shared, and to celebrate the music that reflects those times.'

As the landmark dedication ceremony ended, Brian and David stood together away from the crowd. They embraced and both shed tears. Brian and David, two of the last living witnesses to the birth of a culture-changing phenomenon. Perhaps they were thinking of Dennis and Carl, and the memory of simpler times. Few words were spoken, but those few were meaningful and heartfelt.

'I always loved you,' Brian told David.

'I always loved you too, Brian,' said David. 'Thank you for ... everything.'

Then David thought about the very beginning of all of this. He remembered silently standing in the doorway of the Wilsons' music room all those years ago, secretly watching Brian learn his harmonies. For a moment, David was a ten-year-old boy and Brian was the local football hero again. David decided the time was right to confess.

'Brian, I used to hide in the shadows and watch you in the old music room, when you were learning those harmonies from your Four Freshmen records. I snuck in, and I tried to be really still so you wouldn't hear me. But I was just so fascinated by what you were doing that I just hid there and I watched you learn.'

Brian looked David straight in the eye and revealed something David never knew. 'I always knew you were watching me,' said Brian with a little smirk.

'You knew that?' said David. 'You knew I was hiding there and you let me stay?'

And Brian looked at David with all the pain and hope and love that still lives within him and he gently smiled and told him, 'Yeah ... I knew. It was OK.'

And at that very moment, David Marks finally came home.

AFTERWORD

On 13 June 2006 the five surviving Beach Boys – Brian Wilson, Mike Love, Alan Jardine, Bruce Johnston and David Marks – reunited on the rooftop of the Capitol Records Tower in Hollywood. Each of them, including David, was presented with an RIAA Platinum Record Award commemorating two million sales of The Beach Boys compilation CD *Sounds of Summer*.

LIST OF INTERVIEWEES AND CONTRIBUTORS

We would like to thank the following people for their generous contributions of time and materials to this project. Without their support this book would not be the same.

Chris Allen
Dan Addington
Philip Bardowell
David Beard
Paula Bondi-Springer
Alan Boyd
Felix Brenner
Nadia Brenner
Andrea Carlo-Simon
Brian Chidester
Buzz Clifford
Betty Collignon
Phil Cooper

Brian Davies
Dan Derusha
Dennis Diken
Andrew G. Doe
Carole Ann Dreier
Howie Edelson
Jeff Foskett
Paula Friedman
Kathy Groseclose-Michael
Skip Hand
Bob Hanes
Steve Heller
Billy Hinsche

Alan Jardine
Neville Johnson
Paul Johnson
Bruce Johnston
Cyril Jordan
Stephen Kalinich
Mark London
Mike Love
Carrie Marks
David Marks
Jennifer Marks
Jo Ann Marks
Lois Marotta-Bencangey
Emma Mckay
Eddy Medora
Mike Megaffin
Mike Meros
Daniel Moore
Matthew Moore

Don Podolor
Domenic Priore
Peter Reum
Phil Rotella
Ian Rusten
Darian Sahanaja
Malcolm C. Searles
Craig Slowinski
Steve Stanley
Ron Swallow
Tom Tourville
Treasure Isle Recorders
Bill Trenkle
Fred Vail
John Maus Walker
Mary Williams
Carole Wilson-Bloom
Annie Wilson-Karges
Marilyn Wilson-Rutherford

BIBLIOGRAPHY

BOOKS

Badman, Keith, *The Beach Boys: The Definitive Diary of America's Greatest Band on Stage and in the Studio*. San Francisco: Backbeat, 2004.

Carlin, Peter Ames, *Catch a Wave: The Rise, Fall & Redemption of The Beach Boys' Brian Wilson*. Rodale, 2006.

Chidester, Brian and Priore, Domenic, *Dumb Angel Gazette No. 4: All Summer Long*. Neptune's Kingdom Press, 2005.

Clark, Alan, *The Beach Boys: The Early Years*. The National Rock and Roll Archives, 1993.

Doe, Andrew, and John Tobler, *The Complete Guide to the Music of The Beach Boys*. London: Omnibus, 1997.

Elliott Brad, *Surf's Up, The Beach Boys on Record 1961–1981*, Ann Arbor: Popular Culture, Ink, 1991.

Gaines, Steven, *Heroes and Villains: The True Story of The Beach Boys*. New York: New American Library, 1986.

Leaf, David, *The Beach Boys and the California Myth*. New York: Grosset, 1978.

McParland, Stephen J., *Smile, Sun, Sand & Pet Sounds*. California Music, 1999.

Whitburn, Joel, *The Billboard Book of Top 40 Albums*. New York: Billboard, 1991.

Whitburn, Joel, *The Billboard Book of Top 40 Singles*, 6th Ed. New York: Billboard, 1996.

White, Timothy, *The Nearest Faraway Place: Brian Wilson, The Beach Boys, and the Southern California Experience*. New York: Holt, 1994.

ARTICLES

Barton, David, '40 Years Ago Today, Sacramento Became Surf City.' *Sacramento Bee*, 24 May 2003.

Beard, David, Various. *Endless Summer Quarterly*, 2000–2005.

Crowe, Jerry, 'Back to the Beach.' *Los Angeles Times*, 11 October 1997.

Davies, Brian, 'David Marks Lands on the Moon.' *20/20*, Issue #1, 2003.

Davies, Brian, 'David Marks in the UK.' *20/20*, Issue #9, 2005.

Doe, Andrew, 'In The Beginning . . .' Beach Boys Britain website, 2002.

DuPree, Robert, 'A Beach Boy Looks Back: Good, Clean Boyish Fun.' *Trouser Press*, 1981.

Hinsche, Billy, 'Al Jardine: Rock and Roll Music.' *Guitar One*, November 2001.

Hinsche, Billy, 'Carl Wilson: The Lost Interview.' *Guitar One*, November 2001.

Hopkins, Fred, 'Surf's Up with David Marks.' *Psychotronic Video Magazine*, No. 28, 1998.

Isadore, Jim, 'Beach Boys – Rocket to Stardom on Surfboard Safari.' *Centinela Sunday Press*, 2 September 1962.

Kaples, Serena, 'Where Are They Now? The Next Chapter. After battling Hepatitis C, former Beach Boy David Marks is happy, healthy and ready to rock.' www.people.com., 12 August 2003.

Little, William, 'The Day the Music Died.' *The Times*, 16 March 2005.

Palmiero, Andrea, 'David Marks – This Beach Boy's Life.' *Hepatitis Magazine*, May/June 2001.

Roeser, Steve, 'Warren Zevon, Left Jabs and Roundhouse Rights.' *Goldmine*, 18 August 1995.

Sharp, Ken, 'Alan Jardine: A Beach Boy Still Riding the Waves.' *Goldmine*, 28 July 2000.

Unknown author, 'Original Beach Boy David Marks Alive, Entertainment: Jack's Music.' Unknown publication, 1985.

Unknown author, 'Beach Boys Here Aug. 29.' *La Crosse Tribune*, Saturday 24 August 1963.

OTHER

David Marks's personal diaries, courtesy David and Carrie Marks.

Marks family archives, courtesy of Jo Ann Marks.

Elmer Marks's Beach Boys tour journals, 1963.

Dave and the Marksmen Fan Bulletin, Vol. 1, 30 June 1964.

Mark Groseclose archives, courtesy of Kathy Groseclose-Michael.

Mark Groseclose, 1986 and 1987 interview, unknown source.

30th Annual Y-Day in Hollywood programme, 1962.

INDEX

DM denotes David Marks.